AN AMERICAN IN ROME

AN AMERICAN IN ROME

by *Michael Stern*

Foreword by Robert Ruark

Published by
BERNARD GEIS ASSOCIATES

Distributed by RANDOM HOUSE

*To my friend, Ben Bodne,
whose venerable Hotel Algonquin
is my home away from Rome*

AMERICAN IN ROME

Foreword   ix

Part I: Arrival

Part II: The City Reborn

Part III: And Ever After

Foreword

MIKE STERN IS A MYTH. He never really existed outside a
scriptwriter's imagination. He dug up and lived with the most
famous outlaw of our time when ten thousand Italian police
couldn't locate Salvatore Giuliano. He wrote the definitive pieces
on such unlikely people as Lucky Luciano, Virginia Hill,
Dorothy DiFrasso, George Dawson, Freddie McEvoy, Roberto
Rossellini, Vincenzo Moscatello and Calouste Sarkis Gulbenkian.
He broke and wrapped up the infamous Holohan story, which
involved hammer and sickle with murder and the American
army. He lives today in a fabulous penthouse in Rome; he used
to live in a castle called the Villa Spiga. He is as much a part of
Rome as the Fountain of Trevi or the Spanish Steps. All his life
has been wrapped in cloak and defended by dagger.

The reason a lot of people hate Mike Stern's guts is that he is
a writer of harsh truth. Perhaps he is not the greatest technical
writer in the world, but he is by all odds the toughest reporter I
ever met, one of the most painstakingly accurate, and certainly
he is completely fearless. And he has a talent for painfully pluck-
ing out buried facts, stepping on pampered corns, and putting

it all down in simple raw print that is matchless in our time.

Don't get me wrong. Mike's an operator. He's an arranger, a dealer, and if necessary, a law unto himself. He does not play to lose. If he were a baseball player, he'd dust off his mother to protect his earned run average, and if he were a boxer he would unhesitatingly club you in the neck to win.

Mike Stern has lived among "*la dolce vita*" of Rome and has been uncorrupted by the softness of the city. He knows all the bums, the pimps and pushers, the peculiar producers, the wheelers and charlatans and phonies, but he keeps them in proper perspective. He is himself abstemious in the general sense of the word; alcohol dulls him not, and he goes to bed early. Apart from the scars which fixed his eye into rather a charming leer, he is a handsome young man in his early fifties. His eyes are clear and his complexion rosy, and he used to swing a cane when he walked his acres at the Villa Spiga. He would also hit you in the head with the cane if it was a necessary adjunct to a story. And laugh when he slugged you.

Mike Stern is a complete paradox. Surrounded by lies—and if necessary, able to improve on prima facie evidence to his own advantage—he has a faculty for seeing the truth absolutely clearly in his reportage. To Stern a bum is a bum, no matter how lofty his reputation reads. And you will not find Stern on the wrong end of any libel suits. When he catches the crook with his hand in the till, he generally nails hand to till until he can drag the evidence into court. If he had to kill the crook in the process I would not put it past him.

Mike doesn't report so much any more, but he has just written a book about his undisputed domination of the seamy Roman scene since 1944. There is dirt and sordidness and sex and high adventure and low machinations in it, but there is always truth in it. And there is certainly a fascinating second look at the people and events which made an earlier book, *No Innocence Abroad,* the best-thumbed reference volume in my library.

As I said, I like and admire Mike Stern. But I have seen people stop by his table in a Roman caffè and say: "You son of a bitch, I'll kill you for what you wrote about me." Mike doesn't even bother to scowl. So many people have been threatening to kill him for years that one more is only a bore.

This is a tough boy, and he writes tough prose. I wish to Christ we had more like him in a soppy, soggy world of cotton-wooled halftruths.

ROBERT RUARK

Part I
ARRIVAL

Chapter 1

Rome, 1944

Fʀᴏᴍ the upper terrace of my apartment on the north bank of the Tiber I look across the roofs of Rome, dominated by the dome of St. Peter's, toward the *castelli romani,* the line of hills in the blue haze to the south. It is Spring. The sky is a limpid blue and there is an air of peace and timeless tranquility. Below, the swollen waters of the Tiber flow swiftly through the graceful arches of Ponte Milvio, a brown stone bridge built by Aemelius Scaurus one hundred years before the birth of Christ. I watch the traffic glide silently across it and empty into the broad piazza.

In 312 ᴀ.ᴅ., on the knoll on which my house stands, Maxentius held his cavalry in reserve as his foot soldiers engaged the forces of Constantine the Great coming down Via Cassia. It was in the battle for this bridge that Constantine won the uncontested rule of Rome. It was here that he stood when he saw the flaming cross in the sky and was swayed from paganism to Christianity.

Beyond the roofs of the city in the plains to the south winds Via Casilina, the ancient Roman road used by the military two centuries before Christ. It was along the embankments of this road that Pompey raised the crucifixes bearing the six thousand bodies of prisoners taken in the battle against Spartacus. And it was along this road that I traveled in another, more recent war.

The haze of two decades has not dimmed the image I have of myself on that far-off day: bearded, haggard from lack of sleep, wearing dirty OD's, a green scarf knotted around my throat and an uncomfortable helmet on my head. Men about me were being killed, and although I had a normal concern about sharing their fate, a deep-seated fatalism made me seem less fearful than I was. I was brash and bold to cover my own uncertainty, a groping idealist wearing an iron mask of cynicism. And beneath the mask was a provincial New Yorker, thirsting for an intimate knowledge of the outside world.

Now, as I look out over the rooftops, the whole fabric of history stretches out before me, and I feel that somehow I am woven into it. I am an American in Rome, but I am not a stranger.

I belong.

It was a day of destiny for a weary war correspondent traveling northward on the road to Rome. But destiny sometimes wears so commonplace a guise that years may pass before it is recognized. I had no way of knowing that this strange city, which I was now about to enter for the first time, was to be my home forever.

A glaring sun burned in a blue Mediterranean sky. The thick, choking, eye-searing dust churned up by a confused movement of men and vehicles of war lay over the countryside. I tried to beat its discomfort by wearing goggles set in heavy foam rubber on the upper half of my face and a handkerchief, Jesse James fashion, over my nose and mouth. Sweat fogged the inside of the goggles while dust and the sickening, sour-sweet smell of human dead left too long in the hot sun seeped under the open sides of my kerchief.

The command car in which I rode was part of a long line of slow-moving American military vehicles crawling in for the capture of Rome. The railway tracks paralleling the road were bent into long spirals that looped toward the horizon. Bomb-shattered buildings dotted the landscape, their twisted guts indecently exposed. The shoulders of the road were littered with charred tanks, halftracks, troop carriers, overturned Volkswagens and jeeps, all indiscriminately brushed aside by bulldozers to clear the way for the advancing 5th Army. White tapes fluttering from sticks indicated where the shoulders had been deloused of mines.

It was early June, but there was not a leaf on the trees. Shellfire had broken branches and left gaunt carcasses standing. There were dead stretched out in the dusty weeds. They looked like tired soldiers who had just lain down to sleep. One body was covered with a canvas upon which some compassionate person had thrown a handful of field flowers. A German soldier hit in the face by shrapnel had his features obliterated. Soldiers moved about gathering bits of dead in shovels.

A command car is a high, ungainly and uncomfortable vehicle that has a tendency to magnify the bumps and ruts in the road. My helmet was loose and it bounced around on the top of my head. Jimmy Kilgallen and Alex Uhl, who were riding with me, got out at a hastily requisitioned villa that was serving as a press camp. It was a dull red sandstone structure surrounded by a picket fence. A bronze plaque on the door bore the name D. Meacci. Continuing on the road to Rome, I was forced to a halt by shellfire at the seven kilometer marker. Since road distances are figured from the golden milestone set in the center of the Roman Forum, this meant I was less than five miles from the heart of the city. Rome had been declared an open city, but this did not prevent elements of the Hermann Goering Division, the 3rd Panzer Grenadiers and the entire 65th Infantry Division from putting up a stiff rear-guard action. Three Piper Cubs hovered low over the German lines, ferreting out the camouflaged enemy and transmitting signals to pin-point our artillery fire.

There was the unmistakable whoosh of an incoming shell. I threw myself out of the car and flat onto the cobblestoned street. My helmet clattered off into the gutter. Several shells burst close by, sending a shower of shrapnel slicing through the air. A second salvo exploded and I saw the treads fly off a Sherman tank about a hundred yards up the road. It caught fire. No one got out. A jeep came tearing toward the rear. In it I recognized Sergeant Fred Rosen, then of *Yank* Magazine, today a prosperous public relations counsel, and Milton Bracker of *The New York Times*, who died in Rome in 1964. Draped across the hood was a soldier who had been hit in the stomach by shrapnel.

The sound of church bells mingled with that of exploding shells. The door of a church opened and a priest in a long black cassock walked out with a wedding party, the groom, a young farmer, looking awkward in his polished shoes and store-bought suit, the bride in a flouncy white wedding gown. The couple walked across the road, squeezing between a jeep and a troop carrier. The groom waved his right hand and shouted: *"Viva gli Americani!"* Then, with his bride clinging to his arm, he set out across fields where an infantry wave was gathering for an assault. The priest stood on the steps and blessed their departure. While he was at it, he blessed the *Americani,* too, and went back into the church.

The shelling that had pinned us down came from a pair of German 88's. A Piper Cub floated down to within fifty yards of the gun position and then glided upward. A salvo of artillery shells exploded long and left of the enemy guns. The Piper Cub corrected the fire and a second salvo exploded too far right. Another correction and a third salvo landed directly on target. I climbed to my feet and retrieved my helmet.

The confusion increased as the afternoon shadows lengthened. Several units had gone off on their own in the hope that to them would fall the honor of being the first to enter Rome. The few enemy strong points holding were enough to keep the American army, along with their British and French allies, at a distance. A photo reconnaissance jeep driven by Sergeant Steve Hall cut over to the Appian Way in the San Giovanni section of the city where it was trapped by a German tank. It came limping back an hour later, peppered with bullet holes, its rear tires cut to ribbons.

"When they write the history of this war, I don't think they'll ever know who was the first one in the city," Sergeant Hall said. "But they'll sure as hell have to write that I got the first flat tire in Rome."

Since there would be at least a two-hour wait before the infantry would advance, and an even longer delay before the outskirts of Rome could be reached, I returned to the press villa. Engineers were busily pulling mines out of toilets and driveway entrances. I went into the fields with Private Bryant Huffman for a belated lunch. With a blow torch he heated a couple of cans of C-rations and a pot of coffee. Fred Rosen came by, and I asked him about the wounded GI I had seen him hauling in from the front. Rosen shook his head sadly. I said it was too bad, and we continued eating.

There was a mass of men and armor in Centocelle. Off to the left, surrounded by umbrella pines, was a Roman watchtower behind which soldiers had crouched centuries before Christ. Soldiers were crouched behind it again, while the artillery opened up to prepare their way. A row of jeeps and self-propelled guns moved into position as part of a special task force whose job it was to race into Rome and guard the bridges that span the Tiber. A major up forward shouted something and it was relayed from man to man. It was a warning to stay away from a mined area.

The command to fix bayonets was given and several squads filtered into the wheat fields. An old Italian came toward them, both arms filled with bottles of wine. One of the soldiers, a blond-haired kid of about twenty, walked off to meet him. He took one of the bottles, raised it to his lips and swallowed. A rifle cracked and he keeled over. A GI ran to his side. A tank lumbered up and a crewman stuck his head out of the turret. "Is he hurt bad?"

"No," the GI replied. "He's dead."

I walked to a first-aid station that had been set up in a tumble-down *trattoria.* The inside smelled of sour wine. There were two bare wooden tables with long, filthy benches. A swarm of flies buzzed around. A jeep ground to a halt in the courtyard, and a hysterical mother climbed out carrying a ten-year-old boy who had been shot in the back. The war's tragedy was clutched tightly to her breast, its anguish and heartbreak etched in her prematurely lined, tear-streaked face. The medics laid the child face down on the table and cut his clothes away with a pair of scissors.

While they worked, four litter bearers, red crosses painted prominently on a white circle on the front and back of their helmets, brought in a pair of infantrymen who had been wounded in the legs. One of them, his tired face clearly showing how long he had been in the lines, gave a cry of pain and tried to struggle to his elbow. A medic pushed him back. "I don't want to lose it," the wounded man moaned.

The medic patted his face. "You won't lose it," he said.

I stepped into a courtyard formed by a lattice of broken vines, took a deep breath and tasted the dust. Seated on the ground in a double row were German prisoners of war, most of them in their teens, who had been deposited just a minute before. A pair of bored infantrymen stood guard with submachine guns cradled in their arms. One blond boy didn't look any more than fifteen.

"How old are you?" I asked.

The prisoner gulped. "Seventeen, sir."

One of the guards laughed. "Hitler's draft board gets them early," he said.

The sun hovered in the northwest over the dome of St. Peter's, and the late afternoon shadows deepened. Some of the German rear guard units and snipers had been wiped out; others were already pulling out and running the gauntlet of partisans and enraged Italians as they fled through the northern exits from the city.

Not since Belisarius in the sixth century had the city been taken from the south. The road to Rome was open.

I entered the city through the San Giovanni section, where a whole row of workers' apartment houses had been sliced in half by bombs that had missed the San Paolo freight yards. Masses of people lined both sides of the street. The air held that kind of excitement that is generated by a once-in-a-lifetime event. There was a profusion of flags, almost as many American as Italian ones. How they got them so quickly was a mystery, since under the German occupation that was ending at this very moment, the mere possession of an enemy flag was a capital crime.

The warmth of the greeting was surprising, because plastered on billboards and the walls of houses was the insidious voice of the enemy. It was a shrewd and powerful voice, directed at people who are in the path of advancing armies. One poster showed a man and child, heads bandaged, faces grim, their busts rising out of a destroyed village. Above their heads were departing B-24 Liberator bombers. The top caption said "The Liberators have passed," and the bottom, "These Italians have met them."

Another one showed a crying peasant woman near her destroyed home. Across the top flew bombers returning from a mission and the words, "The Liberators." A bomb bearing the legend "Made in USA" fell down the right side of the poster, and across the bottom were the words, ". . . And God deliver us from them." Less effective were the old-fashioned atrocity pictures, and even weaker was the *Life* Magazine series supposedly based on an article in the March 22, 1943, issue in which instructions to American saboteurs ran principally to sticking daggers into the backs of young Roman mothers.

One particularly harrowing bit of propaganda that had been backed by a press campaign showed two Italian children with their hands mangled from booby-trapped mechanical pencils that had been dropped by our Liberators. But in this one the poster expert over-reached himself, because it depicted children picking up the pencils from the seat of a trolley car. It was perfectly obvious, except to the artist, that Liberators flying at ten thousand feet would have had difficulty dropping them through a trolley window. The propaganda experts, to cover their embarrassment, pasted streamers across the trolley scene to make it appear that the children had been hit during a bombing raid, but the damage to Italian credulity had already been done.

The broad street led to the Aurelian Wall, massive, forty feet high, completely circling the inner city and turning it into a fortress. It was ancient Rome's Maginot line, built some eighteen centuries before by Marcus Aurelius, an emperor obsessed with the idea of fixed defenses. The ancient Romans learned, as Maginot never did, that such lines are untenable. The Aurelian Wall didn't keep out the barbarians. Instead of trying to force it, they merely cut the aqueduct and let thirst and pestilence reduce the city.

I came through the gateway of San Giovanni in Laterano, past the cathedral, down a short street to the Colosseum (the Italians were already telling the story of the GI who stood open-mouthed before this imposing ruin and said, "Jeez, I didn't know our bombs were so powerful") and into the Boulevard of the Empire with its chiseled marble maps showing how Mussolini had raised Italy to the grandeur of ancient Rome, stopping at Piazza Venezia. Here in the Venetian Palace Mussolini had had his office. From the narrow balcony overlooking the piazza he had harangued himself into and out of an empire. I told the driver to force the gate at the rear of the palace, and as we drove into the inner courtyard we were met by a squad of Italian-African police troops who levelled their carbines at us.

Hoping they had been informed that the fall of Rome was now official, I drew myself up imperiously and saluted as though their guns were meant as a formal welcome. I walked directly toward them, speaking in English, though I was certain not one of them understood me. I continued through the squad, saw that the guns were lowering indecisively. A junior lieutenant followed me and I told him that it was an order that I be taken to Mussolini's office.

I entered the museum-sized room from the side near the desk. It was absolutely bare. Not even a speck of dust. I looked into the Zodiac room, once thickly carpeted, softly lighted and perfumed, where each day during the siesta hour Mussolini was visited by a lovely and willing companion. It, too, was bare and cold. I walked midway through the office to an enormous pair of French doors, swung them inward and stepped onto the historical balcony. In the piazza below an unorganized mob of Italian citizens milled about. Some of them looked up and saw me, a uniformed American with a three-day growth of beard and an oversized helmet obscuring the upper part of his face. In dress I was no different from the tens of thousands of Americans already moving through the square on their way northward in pursuit of the Germans. That I was an American was enough, and in an incredibly short space of time several thousand were jammed in the square.

A speech was in order. *"Popolo di Roma,"* I shouted, and a mighty roar went up. I never got beyond this point. Each time I started to say something, they cheered.

I looked down at them and thought how easy it was to manipulate crowds, whatever the cause, when their emotions have been stirred.

The houses on Via Tasso, a street that runs from Piazza San Giovanni to Piazza Vittorio, have a certain *fin-de-siècle* charm. Most of them were built during the Piedmont occupation of Rome, and today they are inhabited by moderate-income tenants. Only the six-story apartment building at No. 145 is of modern design; yellow marble and new stucco in straight lines. On that day it looked out of place, not only because it was wrong architecturally, but because the windows of the upper floors had been solidly sealed with concrete blocks. The German SS, for whom it had served as headquarters, called it, with a certain amount of perverted, though perhaps unconscious, humor, the "Educational Section of the German Consulate," and it was so listed in the Rome telephone directory.

Long before I entered the Holy City I knew that the Gestapo was using this building for the detention and questioning of their

prisoners and that the manner in which the questioning was conducted left few of those interrogated alive. I pushed through the
agitated crowd in the street and entered the building. The first
two floors had been administrative offices and billets for guards. I
climbed the dirty marble steps to the third floor, where the cells
were of solid concrete. A small S-shaped pipe near the ceiling
furnished the only means of ventilation. The doors were of solid
oak. A cell eight by twelve feet held twelve prisoners. The sole
furnishings were three cots and three blankets. The prisoners had
to sleep in shifts. All paper had been strictly prohibited: no writing paper, no reading matter, not even toilet paper. The single
toilet on the floor could be used only between 10 A.M. and 5 P.M.
Since most of the prisoners suffered from diarrhea from the rancid
food, their only alternative was to use their lunch pails.

As I was examining one of the cells with a flashlight, I heard
footsteps. Walking back into the corridor I saw the battered
frame of what once had been a man being led up the stairs by an
attractive young woman and a middle-aged *signora*. The man
shook so violently that it was apparent he had lost control of his
nervous system. His wide, staring eyes did not see me until he
was five feet away, and then he drew back sharply, the features
of his face assuming a look of absolute terror. Sensing the reason,
I held out my hand and said, "No, no—*sono Americano.*"

Almost a minute passed before the words were absorbed; then
he threw himself forward, wrapped his arms about my neck, and
kissed me on the cheeks. The tears rolled down his face. His
daughter broke down and cried. His wife was sobbing as she
tried to take him off my neck.

"*Botte, botte,*" she kept saying. She was trying to make me
understand that beatings had reduced him to this condition.

The man's name was Angelo Joppi. He was thirty-six years old,
though he looked fifty. Joppi had been arrested in March, while
taking his sixteen-year-old daughter, Liliana, to the Flaminia
railway station. An Italian spy pointed him out as one of the
carabinieri from the Lazio barracks in the Piazza del Popolo.

Since these *carabinieri* had gone over to the Allied cause, and since some of them were suspects in several bombings, his first days of questioning were particularly difficult. He was strapped to a table and his head held down by his hair. A complicated device operated by a delicately balanced system of weights inflicted excruciating pain on his genital organs. It would be far easier for him if he confessed and told the names of his confederates, an SS captain told him. No? Again the weights were applied. When the refined torture failed, they struck him in the face and body with an iron bar, fracturing his jaw and breaking three of his ribs.

I followed him to the cell in which he had been incarcerated and looked at a box score he had scratched with a rusty nail on the concrete wall. Of seventy-two recorded days, he had been beaten on seventy, and these were plainly marked with the word *botte*. The shortest beating was five minutes; the longest, twenty-four hours.

On the same wall was a name, General Castaldo Martelli, and next to the name the word *morte*. On the opposite wall, neatly scratched into the plaster, was a doomed man's farewell to the world. This was the final message of Lieutenant Arrigo Palladini, whose crime was an admission to the Gestapo that he would remain loyal to his oath of allegiance to his king. With a nail he had etched:

> On this eve of a most beautiful day I take leave of life without regret, and with the certainty of having accomplished my mission as a soldier according to the commands of my conscience, and with the knowledge that I have offered all that I am, or that I possess, to that ideal which for me has been the only rule of life. The thought that the path I followed through this life has been straight, however halting and unsure, enables me to face death with serenity and a high spirit. In these hours I think constantly of this privilege given me: to be able to give my life to a cause for which, heretofore, I have not found a worthy contribution.

To my father who is my guide from the grave. Your son has never deviated from that line which by your sacrifice and example you laid down.

To my mother. I ask forgiveness that, being faithful to myself, I must be faithless to her love. I hope that in her sorrow at losing me she will not forget to be proud for the way in which I have died.

To Rivetta, caretaker of my memory whom I love dearly. I enjoin you strictly to keep alive my ideal and forgive me that I have unwillingly broken your happiness.

To all Italians. I bequeath you my example. To those whom, through necessity, I may have harmed, I ask pardon. I bear no grudges. *Viva l'Italia!*

I knew nothing about the young lieutenant who had written this farewell message, but it stirred me profoundly. Finding it in this sordid cell was as unexpected as finding a prize rose growing from a dungheap.

Angelo Joppi was alive only by chance. At 11 P.M., less than twenty-four hours ago Joppi and twenty-five other prisoners were taken out of their cells and brought down to the main floor corridor. Their hands were bound behind their backs, each prisoner linked to the next. Five SS guards armed with submachine guns were their escorts. They stood near the front door for five hours, waiting for the truck that was to take them to the place of execution. But the truck, as it drove through the blacked-out streets of Rome, had been destroyed by partisan gunfire. An SS official raced up on a motorcycle to report this fact and say that they must await the arrival of another vehicle. The prisoners were led back to their cells while the guards set about burning case-loads of documents in the furnace room and rear garden.

By this time several American units had entered the city. Shortly after dawn, relatives and friends of the prisoners began to filter into Via Tasso. They took courage from the vacuum created by the retreat of the Germans to shout up to the prisoners that there were only a handful of guards left. "Throw them out!" they screamed. At 7 A.M. one of the prisoners said, "We're sentenced to die, anyway. Let's die fighting." The others took up the cry and began to batter at the cell doors. By the time they were broken down, the SS guards had fled.

Joppi showed me the lovely gardens in the rear of the prison, led me up a graveled path to the adjoining garden of a large villa in which lived Captain Schultz and Captain Pripket, the SS officers who had direct charge of this "Educational Section of the German Consulate." The villa was furnished with second-rate copies of early Italian masters, and over a fireplace mantel hung an enormous painting which, appropriately enough, showed the devil teaching his disciples the art of evil.

"Pripket and Schultz were beasts," Joppi said, "but their superiors were even worse. They were Colonel Herbert Kappler and Colonel Eugene Dollmann of the SS."

I try not to let my emotions sway me, even in situations as moving as this one, but right now as I pushed my way through the disorderly crowd in Via Tasso toward my PRO motor pool jeep, I had, in the void between things seen and things thought, a definite reaction that defied any attempt at objectivity.

I hated Gestapo Colonels Eugene Dollmann and Herbert Kappler.

A jeep attracted a good deal of attention on that first day. The Italians watched in awe the sloppy manner in which gasoline was sloshed into the seat tank and the cavalier approach of the GI to the tens of thousands of five gallon cans.

After having seen the Germans use horses in an effort to preserve the precious fluid, they were sure that ours was a nation of unlimited resources and for the first time were convinced that we would win the war. Around my car were the plainly curious, friends and relatives of the newly-freed prisoners, some light-fingered delinquents eyeing the tires and extra gas cans (for which there was a booming black market) and some lightmoraled *signorinas* wearing cork-wedged shoes and rumpled suits with padded shoulders who wondered if I didn't want to drive them home and pass a most pleasant afternoon. A few urchins were asking for "chewngum, Joe," and others wondered if I couldn't let them have a cigarette, an item priced in local currency at fifty dollars a carton.

Through this crowd pushed a young priest in a long black cassock. He wanted me to know that he was English, and that he had waited a long time for this moment. "When you landed at Anzio nine months ago, you caught the Germans by surprise and they fled from Rome in great disorder. You should have come in right then. But when you didn't, they came back. It gave them time to set up their defenses. You would have saved us untold heartache if you had done the right thing." He spoke as though I were personally responsible for the delay.

Had we come in time the greatest tragedy of all, an event that plunged all Rome into mourning, would have been avoided. In the name of justice I could do no less than visit the site of this atrocity. He would be only too glad to show me the way and then, if I wished to pursue the matter further, he would have me meet the only eyewitness to the slaughter. I said that the matter did, indeed, interest me, and he climbed into the jeep beside me. As we drove off, he told me the story.

At 3:10 P.M. on March 23, 1944, a smart, goose-stepping formation of the Bozen Battalion of the SS came marching up the sharp incline of Via Rasella, a narrow, cobblestoned street scarcely wider than an alleyway. A communist partisan, dressed in the faded blue denims and blue cap of a street cleaner, stood in front of his metal trash cart. As the battalion approached, he touched off a one-minute fuse attached to seventy pounds of dynamite, then hurried to the street corner where a woman partisan waited with his trenchcoat under her arm.

There was an enormous explosion just as the column drew abreast. Twenty-six SS men were killed outright and another twenty were wounded. Those who survived leveled their machine guns and fired blindly on everything that moved. Of the SS wounded, six died during the night, making the total dead thirty-two. The number was important, because Hitler personally ordered an immediate reprisal; ten Italians were to be put to death for every German killed.

There is a visual record of what took place. It so happened that a German army major had his Leica focused on the marchers just as the bomb went off. He kept snapping until his roll of film was exhausted. It is a remarkable document showing the actual explosion with the bodies of the SS men flying in the air. It also shows the bodies of children who had been playing in the street and innocent passers-by who were literally cut to ribbons by the surviving SS. It shows the block-long line of Italians, hands on their heads, in the round-up that followed. These photos came to me through an Italian who was eager to become a secret agent and thought that this could be accomplished through me. As proof of his great friendship for the Allied cause, he handed me a sheaf of rejections to his applications for admission to Columbia and New York Universities. He had carefully preserved these credentials through the years.

The English priest and I drove through the Aurelian Wall at the turreted gateway of San Sebastiano. Peter had walked here, his feet treading the very stones my jeep was now bumping over, as he fled a Roman pogrom some two thousand years ago. He had reached a point on the Appia Antica about a mile from the gate when Jesus appeared before him and asked, *"Domini, Quo vadis?"* Ashamed at having deserted his faithful followers, Peter turned back to martyrdom and sainthood.

At the church of Domini Quo Vadis, erected on the spot where the Roman soldiers had seized St. Peter, I turned right onto Via Ardeatina and pulled to a halt in front of a series of caves that had been dug into the sheer side of a hill by a sand and gravel company. There were five chambers, each leading back roughly fifty yards. The entrances had been sealed off by exploding mines.

I clambered up to the top of the weed-grown hill. The earth in the center had collapsed from the force of the explosion and there, hovering around the opening, was a swarm of giant flies. Inside were mangled bodies. The sights and smells turned my stomach and I was ill. When I came down I found that the English priest had brought Father Bruno Brunori from the Church of the Catacombs of San Callisto across the road.

The day after the explosion on Via Rasella, Father Brunori told me, the SS arrived on motorcycles to seal off Via Ardeatina. In the early evening trucks joined these motorcycle detachments and they kept their motors revving loudly from seven in the evening until far into the night. Their headlights were focused on the five entrances to the caves. During this time trucks delivered the victims, who were linked together in batches of ten and forced to march toward the rear of the caves. As they started walking, the machine guns opened fire.

When the thirty-second batch had been killed, the SS commander found that, through an error in bookkeeping, he still had five people left. Because it was too much trouble to send them back, he prodded them, too, into the caves to their deaths.

A guard was maintained on the Ardeatina caves for three days. The moment it left, Father Brunori, who had appointed himself a one-man investigating agency, began the difficult task of identifying the victims so that he could inform their families. Word of this spread by devious channels throughout Rome and the good priest was beseiged by anxious relatives and friends of prisoners. It was only natural that the SS should learn of this, too, and an agent came to the priest's office to warn him that his activities were arousing Colonel Dollmann's displeasure. Father Brunori told me that he obeyed the orders of the SS chief, not because of personal fear, but because he had thirty Italian partisans hidden in the catacombs and did not wish to jeopardize their safety. On April 1st, the SS returned, planted mines in all the entrances and detonated them.

I could never quite figure out the SS mentality. These blasts were intended to cover the traces of a foul mass murder. Did they think that by this act they could erase the anguish from the hearts of wives, mothers, fathers, brothers and sisters left behind? Did they feel that just covering the bodies with tons of earth would hide their crime or wipe out their guilt?

Until I had first set foot in Rome early this same morning, I had never heard of Colonel Eugene Dollmann. Now I had an urgent desire to know all about him, and somehow, somewhere, to catch up with him. It took a long time, but I finally did.

Behind the Venetian Palace, in the cramped space between the Teatro Marcellus, the Octavian Gate and the Tiber, is the ghetto, a collection of narrow alleys and ancient tenements clustered around an imposing pale yellow, square-domed synagogue. This ghetto is probably the oldest on the face of the earth, since Jews first began living there in pagan times, when the archway dedicated to Octavius, sister of Augustus, was built. This once-splendid structure had been designed by the Greek slaves Batrax and Sauro. Slaves were not permitted to sign their work, but the pair managed to evade the Roman directive, and still stay within the limit of legality, by sculpting a lizard (*batrax*) and a frog (*sauro*) on one of the columns. A large part of the marble of the original gateway was removed by Pope Stefan I in 755 and used to erect the Church of Sant' Angelo in Pescheria, where the Jews were forced to assist at the prayers of the Dominican fathers, an order to which they submitted after pouring wax into their ears.

As in all lands they occupied, the Gestapo had decimated the local Israelite community. Under Mussolini's regime, despite the racial laws passed by the Grand Council, enforcement was so lax as to be almost nonexistent. This was because anti-Semitism has always been foreign to the nature of the Italian people.

I drove slowly through the crowded alleys and stopped in front of the synagogue. Jews swarmed over my vehicle, not quite certain how to act in their new-found freedom or how to thank their liberators. Many wore *mazuze* on strings around their necks and they shoved them at Frank Conniff, Hearst editor, who evidently looked like a *landsman* to them.

A young, aesthetic-looking man of about thirty, his face showing lines of suffering, told me how his father, an uncle and two brothers had been taken off by the SS and killed. Would I— please, would I come to his home for dinner, so that what remained of the family could celebrate their liberation? I took his address, gave him a handful of C-ration cans that were in the car (these were the days when the cat population of Rome had almost been entirely wiped out by hungry civilians) and moved on to the synagogue.

Standing in one of the doorways was Angelo Zolli, chief rabbi of Rome, who had just come from the Vatican, where Pope Pius XII had personally given him sanctuary. He was trembling with excitement. He kissed my hand, tears in his eyes, and gave thanks that his people had again been delivered from evil. "The truth about the tragedy of my people must be made known," he said with deep feeling. As long as the Italians maintained physical control of their own country, he went on, all went comparatively well for his co-religionists. So well, in fact, that the local SS leaders complained bitterly to Adolf Eichmann, head of Bureau IV 4B for Jewish affairs, that their confederates in the Axis were impeding efforts to get rid of these undesirables. So important was this matter considered that Joachim von Ribbentrop made a personal visit to Mussolini in Rome and extracted a promise from the Italian dictator that henceforth all Jews would be shipped to labor camps in Germany.

After the German Foreign Minister left, happy that he had succeeded in his mission, Count Ciano showed *il Duce* documentation on what "labor" camps signified. Mussolini, personally horrified and appalled at the possible political consequences, issued precise orders: a "publicity campaign affirming my solidarity with Hitler on the Jewish question but undercover sabotage of their efforts to ship out Jews."

This state of affairs existed until September 8, 1943, when an armistice was signed between the Allied forces and the King of Italy. The German army moved on Rome and took physical possession of the capitol. Now the SS was free from all restraint. On the night of September 26, an Italian police officer presented himself at the homes of Signori Foà and Almasi, highly regarded members of the Jewish community, and told them to appear the following morning at the office of Ambassador von Mackensen at the palatial German Embassy in Villa Wolkonski.

At the designated hour Foà and Almasi made their appearance. In the Ambassador's office were the leaders of the SS. Dispensing with the social niceties, they came directly to the point. The Jews of Rome were doubly guilty, Colonel Dollmann informed them: first, as Italians who were betraying the Axis; second, as a religious group traditionally opposed to Germany. In spite of this treachery, Hitler was disposed to be magnanimous. If the community would pay one hundred and ten pounds of gold to the SS, it would be spared. They had until 11 A.M. on September 28 to pay the ransom. Should they be one minute late, two hundred hostages would be rounded up and shipped to concentration camps in Germany.

The conversation was reported to the Chief Rabbi, who immediately called on the Jews to gather in the synagogue. The discussion was brief. A vote was taken and it was unanimously decided to pay the ransom. Throughout the day collections were made. Pope Pius XII also contributed. Early the following morning Foà and Almasi drove to Via Tasso, headquarters of the SS, and lugged five cardboard cases filled with gold into the office of Captain Schultz. The gold was weighed, placed in a safe and the Jews unceremoniously ejected.

At dawn the next day two columns of uniformed SS troops marched into the ghetto through the gateway of Octavius. An old woman with the descriptive nickname "Popeye" saw them first and cried out, *"Arrivano i Mammoni!"* There was a general flight of terror-stricken inhabitants in their nightclothes. The SS took possession of the synagogue, carried away the register of membership, took the two million lire worth of gold that had been over-subscribed and destroyed those sacred relics that had not yet been hidden.

The first raid was merely a test. They came back on October 11 and loaded two requisitioned trolley cars with paintings, furniture, silver and jewels. They came again on October 16 in force. Three hundred SS troops in full battle gear moved before dawn into positions that sealed off all exits from the ghetto. Then the trucks rolled in and the round-up began. Popeye had no time to cry the alarm that Mammon, the Syrian god whose name is synonymous with avarice, had arrived.

Only in the confusion of the first fifteen minutes did some of the more daring manage to escape over roof-tops into safe areas. One of those who escaped was the Chief Rabbi. Women, children, and men of all ages were awakened from their sleep and, still dressed in their nightclothes, were hustled into trucks. The first stop for these Roman Jews was a concentration camp in Fossoli; the last stop, the gas chambers of Auschwitz and the furnaces of Dachau.

Now that the SS had finally shown its true design, the Jews who had eluded the roundup scattered for safe-keeping into monasteries, convents, hospitals and Christian homes. As Israeli prosecutor Hausner said at the trial of Adolf Eichmann, "Amongst the Italian people there began a contest of generosity and brotherly love that the Jews of the whole world will never forget."

I was still speaking with Rabbi Zolli when the lay head of the Jewish community came up to me. "This man deserted his people in the time of need," he said. "He is no longer our rabbi."

Rabbi Zolli looked pleadingly at me. "He knows that my name was on the top of the Gestapo list of Jews to be liquidated. Dead, what good would I have been to my people?"

"No matter what might have happened to him, his place was here," came the stubborn reply.

A new rabbi was named, but Zolli refused to leave the synagogue, and there were many, though in the minority, who supported him. It was the beginning of a bitter fight between the pro- and anti-Zolli elements that did not end until Zolli, in one of Judaism's great scandals, converted to Catholicism.

I bathed, shaved and dressed in a clean uniform. Instead of the flopping helmet, I wore a smartly cocked overseas cap. Tonight I was going to dinner at the home of the man I had met in the ghetto. At best it is a disagreeable chore to visit with people one doesn't know, but it was the least I could do to show my sympathy for the sufferings of the Jewish people on this historic eve of their liberation. It was a sort of pilgrimage.

I packed a musette bag with sugar, coffee and canned goods that came from a friendly sergeant attached to the correspondents' mess and set off for my appointment. The buildings were blacked out and the streets, because of a sundown curfew, were deserted.

There were about a dozen members of the family crowded into a small living room lighted by a single twenty-five watt bulb and spluttering candles. The blinds were drawn and black cloth draped over the windows. In the adjoining kitchen I could see women working over a pair of open charcoal burners, one of them vigorously fanning with a bunch of tied-together chicken feathers. The family had numbered thirty-three, counting aunts, uncles and cousins, before the SS began its deportations. I found it odd that none of them spoke Yiddish. This language has only lately been brought to the Roman ghetto by the few survivors of the concentration camps who had picked it up from the eastern European Jews.

My presence was an important event in their lives. I was seated beside an uncle of the young man who had invited me earlier in the day. From the deference paid him by the others, I took him to be the head of the family. Without preamble, he draped a confidential arm over my shoulder and began to talk of the fortune to be made in woolens, a business he knew very well. Rome was starved for cloth, and it was available in Milan. With

the liberation of Rome, the occupying forces had arbitrarily re-
valued the lira from twenty to one hundred to the dollar. Up
north, however, the lira still maintained its old value. Did I
follow him? This meant that he could buy the cloth for one-fifth
of its value. And having a virtual monopoly, since with my help he
would be the first importer, there was no limit to the profit he—
or rather, we—could make. The problem was to get the cloth
down from the north. He could take care of bringing the goods
past the German forces, but if he had me, an Allied officer, as his
partner, why there would be no problem at all in transporting or
disposing of the cloth.

I took my leave the minute the difficult meal was over. It was
the first and last time I ever saw this family. Five years went by
before I set foot in the ghetto again.

In the shock and horror at Hitler's murderous madness, it is
easy to forget that not all his victims were noble people. Amongst
them were sinners as well as saints, the courageous as well as the
cowardly, the weak as well as the strong. But to Hitler, they did
not exist as individual humans; he destroyed them indiscriminately, for power and for profit.

Once I had set out on Dollmann's trail, it was not too difficult
to build up a fund of information about him. He was born in 1900
in Regensburg, Germany, studied at the University of Munich,
and here met and became friendly with Adolf Hitler. After the
rise to power of the Nazi dictator, Dollmann came to Italy in the
guise of a literary scholar. At the outbreak of the war he donned
his SS colonel's uniform and worked in the open. He was stocky in
build and ruddy-cheeked, with the right side of his face marked
by a livid, horizontal scar. He had a fine nose and heavy lips set in
a large, fleshy face. He was extremely fond of good wines, good
food, perfume and flowers. He had an imperious manner. When
he wasn't satisfied with a person's actions, he would trot out the
familiar threat of Via Tasso. The colonel would periodically send
roving squads of SS men through the city to make mass arrests.

Most of those picked up, quite obviously, were innocent. These persons could gain their release by paying off Mario, his chauffeur and confidante, who was, in the parlance of the New York fixer, the "bag man" for the SS mob of Rome. The colonel was, by his own twisted code, a most honest person—he would not allow the guilty ones to buy their freedom.

The trail led me to his Roman lodgings in the Pensione Trinità dei Monti on Salita San Sebastianello, a short, sharp incline that winds from Piazza di Spagna to the Pincio in Villa Borghese. I examined the name plates in the lobby, but Colonel Dollmann's name was not there. An Italian came through the corridor and I asked him if he knew on which floor the colonel had lived. He not only knew but was most eager to show me. He led me to the top floor and knocked loudly on the door. A maid answered, and the Italian, his chest puffed out importantly, announced that the American secret police had arrived to look into the matter of the SS chief's residence. The maid hurried off and in a moment the mistress of the establishment appeared. She was a faded blonde of about forty-five with birdlike features. I told her that I had come to question her about Dollmann.

"He fled yesterday," the woman said.

"Where is the Italian chauffeur who worked for him?"

"He fled with the colonel."

"And the blonde mistress?" The question was a stab in the dark. I figured that if I erred, the error couldn't be any worse than the color of her hair.

"Blonde mistress?" she echoed in surprise. "I don't understand what you mean."

"You know very well what I mean," I said sharply.

"Oh no," she replied quickly. "That is quite impossible. Let me show you." I was led into what had been the colonel's bedroom. She patted one side of the large-sized double bed. "Here slept the colonel," she said firmly. "And here," she patted the other side of the bed, "slept the chauffeur."

It was on the whim of this homosexual that the lives of hundreds of thousands had depended. It was he who had sent entire families, hero generals and university students, laborers and artisans, an eighty-year-old man and a fourteen-year-old boy, Via Tasso prisoners and men picked up off the streets at random, to their death.

The German Reich's propaganda machine had first invented a "Jewish Problem" and then had created creatures like Dollmann to "solve" it. What was real and terrifying was the "Dollmann Problem," for he and his kind are the moral lepers who can infect our society with a loathsome disease. What had happened to this monster? And more important, what would happen to him as the world returned slowly to sanity? As I stood there I realized that not until we solved the "Dollmann Problem" would we be truly safe.

I slid behind the wheel of the jeep, drove up the short, steep Salita San Sebastianello to Villa Borghese, Rome's equivalent of New York's Central Park. In the distance the sun was an enormous orange ball descending, like a huge stage backdrop, behind the dome of St. Peter's. I was on my way to the press billets at the Hotel de la Ville, at that time called Albergo della Città because French names were unpopular. On the Trinità dei Monti, the short stretch of road between the Salita and the hotel, stands the twelfth-century palace where Galileo was held for inquisition because of his heretical notion that the world moved around the sun. I couldn't help but wonder what kind of a tribunal could try, and what kind of punishment could fit, the crimes of a Dollmann, a Himmler and a Hitler.

I had seen much blood spilled, much pain visited on the ordinary people of the world, much of human wealth and human endeavor directed toward killing and destroying. It couldn't be a senseless waste. I had to believe that it was the price we were paying for a newer and a finer world dedicated to higher moral principles. It was unthinkable that tens of millions of lives should have been sacrificed for less. I tried to fix the awful events of the past few years into an understandable pattern, but somehow I couldn't. The happenings about me could move me to pity or to anger, to love or to hate, but not to find reason in this mad imbroglio. As for the future, I was just as confused.

Chapter 2

Life in the Fallen City

SHORTLY AFTER the triumphant entry into Rome, I spent an entire day walking and driving along the Tiber, exploring the streets that run off it. The muddy stream snakes through the center of the city, each loop forming a distinctive quarter. There is Trastevere on the left bank, each winding street little more than an alley so narrow there is no space for sidewalks, the houses built so many centuries ago that one can imagine the marks of chariots on the uneven streets. Along Passeggiata di Ripetta in Campo Marzio and Via Giulia in Ponte the houses are a blend of yellow, warm brown, and faded terra cotta, a distinctive hue produced by centuries of hot Roman sunshine. Unexpectedly, through the massive, sculptured doorways, glimpses of beautiful gardens appear.

Almost all the streets of Rome begin and end in a piazza, and these are of every conceivable size and shape. There is the circular Piazza Esedra, with its colonnaded buildings, the ruins of Emperor Diocletian's bathhouse and, for a centerpiece, an imposing circular fountain where young lovers cluster on hot summer evenings. Not far away is the Piazza del Popolo, with its narrow twin churches and muted brown-yellow buildings, the gray-brown Flaminia gateway through the Aurelian Wall, the lush green of the Pincio rising above and the dramatic Egyptian obelisk in the center, its spire making the piazza the world's tallest sundial. Farther along is the bustling Piazza Colonna, with its centuries-old column on which are depicted, in a continuous spiral, the heroic military exploits of Emperor Marcus Aurelius. Here are gathered the House of Parliament, the Foreign Office and the black-market money brokers. Many other piazzas dot the city, each with its own history and each with its own distinctive beauty.

On all sides of me the centuries rolled away as I viewed the pre-Christian arches and columns. There was a feeling of permanence. The people who now live in Rome are descendants of the ancient inhabitants. The Ruspolis, Borgheses and Colonnas have lived here for centuries. Each person, no matter how insignificant, is part of the fabric of history. He has roots, and they appear everlasting.

Each individual member of a family, if only for reasons of real estate, is woven into his environment. The effect on me was profound. I was born in New York in a house that was torn down to make room for another one that, in its turn, was torn down to make room for still another. On that street not a single structure has survived the inexorable march of economic progress. Of the families that lived there when I did, not one remained. I returned once to find myself a complete stranger on an unfamiliar street.

Walking these ageless streets, I realized that it has always been part of Rome's genius to make those who feel like transients in their own lands feel at home within its ancient walls. Prince Ranieri San Faustino once told me, "Our city has been occupied by almost every race on the face of the earth. There were the Gauls, the Goths, the Arabs, the Byzantines and the French. They are all gone. Lately we have had the Germans. They are gone. Now you Americans. Soon you, too, will be gone with the others. But we Romans, we will always be here." Simply, what he meant was that Rome could be captured but not conquered, because she always absorbed her victors.

Almost from the moment I entered Rome, I felt its appeal. When one falls in love with a woman, it is impossible to select a single feature and say that it was responsible for the grand passion. One falls in love with the entire woman, with her virtues and faults. So it was with Rome, though at the start I didn't bother to analyze my feelings. I only knew that there was a daily delight in the discovery of the Holy City's wonderful sights and people.

Germaine de Staël, visiting Rome, found words for the city's special magic. Rome was more than a matter of real estate; it was a kind of musical, picturesque, poetic, aerial way of life that opened a new sphere of ideas and sensations through its monuments, memories and beautiful sky, all works of art that reinvigorate the despondent soul. The Italians are witty and gay, all of them amorous and adorers of women—a little too much for their own dignity but not too much for rendering a woman's life agreeable thought Mme. de Staël. All of it creates a feeling so young and sweet that nowhere else is it possible to live in quiet and obscurity as happily as here. There is a strong empathy between nature and man that no other city quite matches, and there is a uniquely noble and calm image of death in the ageless tombs and traces of great men.

Many times that day and later I found myself thinking what a wonderful place this would be in which to live and work. I knew that it was day-dreaming, at best, because there were still so many uncertainties: the war, survival, the aftermath of world conflict, the shape of the world that would emerge from all this brutality and hate. And even if all else went well, could I uproot my family and transplant it in an alien land, an immense ocean separating my wife and children from friends, relatives and the familiar things that are America? Having been brought up in a tradition that accepts diaper service, daily pasteurized milk delivery and central heating as necessities of life, they might easily fail to appreciate the romance of a frigid Renaissance palace.

Thoughts of a future in Rome seemed little more than happy fantasies, and in my letters to my family I never even mentioned it. But the seed was planted.

In the early dusk I found myself in the center of the city. Convoys of infantrymen, troop carriers and all the paraphernalia of war were heading northward toward Via Cassia and Via Aurelia. The Italians were beginning to hurry off the streets to beat the curfew. I drove up Via del Tritone and stopped for a moment to inspect the wedge-shaped, six-story home of *Il Messaggero,* the morning paper that had been, until the day before, the most widely sold apologist for the fascist regime. Now *Stars and Stripes* had taken over the building to house its Mediterranean edition. The location can be compared to that of the old Times Tower at Broadway and 43rd Street in New York City. From a narrow alley behind the plant spilled scores of excited Allied soldiers being held in a semblance of a line by military police. I pulled to the curb to ask a GI what was going on.

"It's a whorehouse," he explained. Then, noting the so-what look on my face, he said, "Man, it's only a hundred lire. That's less than a pack of cigarettes."

I moved on to the Via Veneto, a broad avenue that starts at the Pincio gateway of the Aurelian Wall and winds in a slow, right-hand curve downhill for five blocks to Piazza Barberini. In ancient times the street was part of the gardens of Emperor Claudius' villa. Here Empress Messalina, his wife, wrote new meaning into the phrase "sexual misconduct." Here, too, is the famous chapel that houses more than four thousand skulls of Capucine monks. In peacetime it is a tree-lined promenade flanked by sidewalk cafés and expensive hotels, the gathering place for tourists from all over the world.

That day, weary from traveling the streets of Rome, I dined at the brightest jewel on the street, the world-famous Hotel Excel-

sior, to become again after the war an authentic crossroad of the
world famed for collecting the richest men, the most beautiful
women and the most interesting people under a single roof. Now
the hotel had been requisitioned by the military and was a
transient camp for 5th Army officers. This was the lushest paradise that a fighting soldier had thus far encountered, and lieu-
tenants, just off the line with a three-day pass, were living it
up. (One of them, in a fit of pique, had tossed a girl out of a third
floor window.) The large dining room was rowdy and gay and
the tables were crowded with girls, all wearing the current style
of padded shoulder, tight, short skirts, wedge-heel shoes and
large handbags. There were streetwalkers and countesses, mar-
cheses and mistresses mixed indiscriminately. Although the Excelsior chefs are among the best in the world, they were having
tough going with the powdered eggs, Spam, C-rations and dehydrated vegetables.

At the end of the meal the female diners passed through a
small exit where two Italian plainclothesmen from the *Buon
Costume,* as the local vice squad is called, stood alongside the
MP's and watched each woman open her capacious bag. It was a
leveling experience for the lady of quality, who found herself
treated like her untitled sister in sin. On the floor alongside the
policemen was a small mountain of silverware, crockery, table
linens and food.

The entry into Rome had been the biggest story of the day.
Everything we correspondents had to say was eagerly devoured
back home. Then, suddenly, we were pushed off the front pages
as American editors sent out orders to hold down the amount of
copy. By far the most important reason for this reversal in interest
was the invasion of the continent at Normandy. Besides, after the
fall of Rome any territorial conquests in Italy were anti-climactic.
The American forces were weakened by the withdrawal of several
divisions to be used for the amphibious landing on the southern

coast of France. British forces also were taken out of the line and sent to Greece, a move personally ordered by Winston Churchill. It had no military purpose, since the Germans had already withdrawn, and I recall the loud yelps of complaint emitted by General Mark Clark and his staff. Just how right Churchill was will be seen later. This single act saved Greece from being swallowed by the communists.

The abbreviated army moved painfully northward, slowed down before the Arno River, finally crossed it and soon spluttered to a halt, bogged down in the mud of the Apennine Mountains.

It was during this breathing spell that I grew more familiar with Rome, an acquaintanceship that passed quickly through affectionate friendship and developed into an enduring love affair. Since I would be spending an indefinite number of weeks in the city, I set about making myself comfortable. Finding an apartment was comparatively simple. Many fascists had fled to the north with their families, and it was merely a matter of locating one of their flats and moving in. The one I took over evidently belonged to a third-rate fascist, judging from the many photographs he left behind. Most of them dealt with visits to factories and party meetings. The owner must have been the black-shirted figure wearing heavy, horn-rimmed glasses whose face appeared in all of them, but he was always at least three rows removed from Mussolini and two rows from Count Galeazzi Ciano. He made an appearance in the front row only at meetings with provincial party hacks.

The apartment was on the fifth floor of a large building on Corso Trieste, in a middle-class section of the city. The furniture was of a style deprecatingly called Mussolini modern and compared unfavorably with our Grand Rapids product. The floors were of cold marble; the elevator didn't run; gas was rationed to one hour a day, and then just enough for a tiny flame in a single burner; electricity, when it was finally turned on, was for a three-hour period. But it was like heaven after the way I had been living.

The next morning I visited the real estate section of Allied
Military Government and obtained a requisition form making
me the proud tenant of the flat. Acquiring a car was just as easy.
I found a Fiat 1100 sedan that lacked tires, had four jeep tires
mounted on it, and went for another requisition order from
AMG. An unemployed truck driver—practically all Italians were
unemployed at this time—named Nello came to work for me. He
was of medium build, sallow, horse-faced, with a calculating
laugh that showed a mouthful of gold and a face full of larceny.
Trying to keep him honest in black-market-ridden Rome was as
simple as holding back the dawn. In black-market terms his
monthly salary was two cartons of Chesterfields. A spare tire in
usable condition would net him six months' salary.

The *portiere* found a maid for me, a squat peasant of thirty-
five who looked as though she was on the dark side of fifty. Her
name was Maria, and she lived in a shantytown about two miles
away with two daughters and a worthless husband whom she
supported. Her monthly salary was fifteen hundred lire, officially
valued at fifteen dollars. Unofficially it came to five pounds of
sugar or a pound of coffee or three dollars in U.S. currency.
Maria considered herself fortunate, so fortunate that she wouldn't
trade places with a professor or a lawyer. She ate regularly and
there was enough left over to feed her family. In time she moved
in both daughters, one as assistant cook, the other as maid. I
never knew, in those days, that she walked the two miles back
and forth from her shanty to the apartment. She never mentioned
it because she never dreamed that it was anything but natural
that she do so.

So my ménage grew to include Maria, with her stolid, plodding
resignation; the seventeen-year-old daughter, who had six toes
and a propensity for acquiring a new *fidanzato* daily (or so it
seemed) and who looked strangely out of place with the poorly
applied, hard-to-get lipstick that was four shades off for her hair
color; her fifteen-year-old sister, Italia, as stolid as her mother
and highly religious; and Nello, as merry a rogue as ever siphoned

a gallon of gasoline out of his boss's car. While I was at the front, he would rent the vehicle to those Italians who could still afford to pay. The one time I caught him, he had a perfect explanation. The man's wife was dying, and it was clearly necessary to take him back and forth to the hospital and also to deliver the doctor back and forth. Since the necessary drugs were available only on the Neopolitan black market, he had to take the poor man down there, too.

It was these humble people, with all their faults and virtues, who brought warmth to the cold flat and turned it into a home.

An office was available in the modern insurance building on Via Bissolati, which had become headquarters for the advanced section of the public relations office of the Allied forces. I moved in, complete with a set of dictaphones (I had the dubious distinction of being the only war correspondent who dictated his articles) and a young, attractive blonde secretary built along generous lines that became, in a sweater, altogether stupendous. I acquired her and the dictaphones through the help of a friend in the counterintelligence corps. Her presence among the males of the press had a most upsetting effect, and after Herbert Matthews, mild-mannered, dignified correspondent for *The New York Times*, complained that he couldn't keep his eyes on his typewriter, I had to banish her to a private room.

There came a time, after about a month in my service, when I had to let her go. It was not because of her attributes, which were admirable (she was an excellent interpreter and could take shorthand in German, French, English and Italian), but because I was leaving for Bari on the first step of a most unusual assignment in which I was supposed to parachute behind the German lines in Yugoslavia and join Tito's forces. I had promised the girl that when I left Rome, as a bonus for good service, I would see to it that she secured other employment. I introduced her to Colonel Charles Poletti, the ex-governor of New York State who was now the Military Governor for Rome. In no time at all she was his receptionist, screening visitors who streamed by the hun-

dreds into his palace-sized waiting room. All might have gone
well except that a friend of mine, a British major who commanded the rocket guns in Algiers, had come to visit me in Rome
and taken a fancy to the girl. When he put in an official request
to marry her, a routine check by British intelligence revealed the
girl to be the daughter of a general in the German SS. The embarrassment ran all the way from Poletti, who immediately retired her, to Stern.

Later, I ran across my friend in the counterintelligence corps.
"How could you send me a girl like that?" I asked sharply.

"Calm down," he said. "How was I to know you wanted her for
work?"

For the first Americans in Rome the black market spelled the
difference between a gray, canned diet and delightful culinary
experiences. For most Italians it spelled the difference between
life and death. Everyone was fashionably slim, but it was considered tactless to comment on it.

The Germans had carted away all the food they could lay their
hands on, and with lines of communications disrupted, supplies
were only trickling in. For some there were the soup kitchens of
the Pontifical Aid and other charities or the leftovers that came
out of service doors of Allied requisitioned hotels.

In a city packed with women whose men were away and who
had considered it *déclassé* to be seen with Germans (an attitude
that put severe restraint on their sexual exuberance), the arrival
of the open-handed Americans was heaven, and earthy nature
took its course. From the lowliest private to the highest commanding general, each took unto himself a maiden and with her
a feeling of responsibility for the maiden's family. The class
distinction that still exists in Italy meant that the private went to
bed with a *figlia del popolo,* the commanding general with a
contessa or *marchesa.* This very normal, human process—and our
admirals and generals were so human that I can remember few

who didn't have at least one title attached to their beds—opened wider the doors to the supply depots.

It was this food of love, added to the small amounts of fresh meat, olive oil, cheese, flour and vegetables that managed to find their way into Rome and were on sale on the *bancherelle* in innumerable market places, that kept Romans alive. The sale of food without ration cards was highly illegal and the local police made a few, desultory attempts to halt the traffic. There would be a raid on Piazza Vittorio, and in the round-up the cops would seize thirty pounds of meat, eight pounds of cheese, and a few gallons of olive oil. A short time later the pushcarts would re-appear and business would resume as usual, with a single difference: the prices would have gone up to cover the losses caused by the previous raid.

The Roman black market was child's play compared to the one in Naples, where gangs of operators corrupted members of the port battalion and drove off with thousands of truckloads of clothing, food and automotive products. They went so far as to steal the entire cargo of a Liberty ship. Even the kids were experts. When a jeep slowed down at an intersection, *scugnizzi* would heave a rock through the windshield. The surprised GI would jump out of the vehicle and take off after the vandal. When he returned, empty-handed, he would find his gas tank siphoned dry and all the tires gone.

The Neapolitans had their timing down to an art. An indiscreet soldier who let himself be lured off the main road would sud-denly find himself surrounded by a populace that apparently regarded him as a hero. The soldier would be hoisted aloft in a triumphant march, at the end of which he would find his pockets picked and his shoes, an extremely valuable piece of merchandise, missing. There was even a brisk trade in urine of diabetics. It was sold in small bottles and was expensive, because it guaranteed that the user could fool the medical inspectors and get a diabetic rating on his ration card.

The Italian is a highly adaptable person. If that was the way things were, then that was the way he would live. He even brought a semblance of normalcy to his zany, war-torn life. The theater re-opened with a musical comedy starring Anna Magnani, in which she sang the famous couplet, "We ask for spaghetti, but you send us Poletti." I went to Villa Glori to watch the trotters and saw the newly rich black marketeers and their cousins in trade, the American supply officers, lining up at the 1,000-lire windows.

Money was easy and the get-rich-quick schemes so simple that it was difficult not to make money. It was a matter of simple arithmetic and a U.S. Army uniform. An American soldier spends two dollars for four cartons of cigarettes, sells them on the black market for two hundred dollars in inflated lire, then takes the lire to the Army post office and buys a money order for two hundred dollars. At the illegal but flourishing money market in Piazza Colonna, the money order brings him one thousand dollars in lire. He uses the lire at the Italian post office to buy new stamp issues and mails these back to the United States, where collectors pay over mint value, bringing the price to above one thousand dollars, which is not bad for a two-dollar investment. One American general sent back thirty-five thousand dollars in money orders.

Rome had become an enormous Luna Park in which soldiers on a holiday from death grabbed for as many brass rings as a two-day pass would permit. In the midst of the carnival were the hungry people. A few simple statistics tell the story. Ration cards furnished 11 per cent of a person's minimum nutriment. The remaining 89 per cent could only be found on the black market and the prices, naturally, reflected the strong demand.

The middle-class Italian may have been hungry, but he couldn't resist the snob appeal of an American cigarette. He would puff on it as though it were a Corona-Corona, then he would carefully extinguish the butt and put it in his pocket.

I went hunting with Field Marshal Badoglio in the private pre-
serves of Italy's munitions czar in the Maremma. The game was
pavoncelli, a rather small, pathetic-looking sparrow. The field
marshal, also Duke of Addis Ababa because of his victory in
Ethiopia, sat on a shooting stick while a gun bearer spun a globe
covered with tiny squares of mirror. The refracted light brought
pavoncelli swarming around the seated hero and he emptied
load after double-barreled load of his shotgun at them until the
falling birds practically rained down on us.

At the hunt was the head of the Allied Commission's rubber
section. To further the war effort, he had requisitioned a factory
complete with machinery, stocked it with rubber recovered in
large amounts on the battlefields and handed it to the munitions
czar, along with a contract for the production of tires for the
civilian economy. Car tires sold for four hundred dollars each on
the open market and price controls were almost nonexistent, so
the enormous net of this brilliant commercial arrangement can
be imagined.

Politically, we were beginning a long series of errors that was
to cost us the peace. I saw it happen; I recognized some of the
errors at the time they took place, but my protesting voice was
like a whisper in the wilderness. Most of the important fascists
had fled northward with the Germans. To precipitate the down-
fall of those who remained, our military government issued an
order limiting all public offices, all jobs on newspapers and in
labor unions—in fact, all positions of any importance—to anti-
fascists. Into the political void created by this edict moved the
Communist Party. And it received two unpardonable assists from
the immature directors of our military government. The first was
an order recognizing a Communist Party card as proof of anti-
fascism, a move that single-handedly ran an almost nonexistent
organization into one with millions of card-carrying adherents.
The second was bringing Palmiro Togliatti, head of the Italian

Communist Party, from Moscow to Italy. Traveling under the alias of Ercole Ercoli, he made the last leg of the trip aboard an American destroyer, and it is difficult to understand how our diplomatic and military leaders could have failed to see that they were depositing in the port of Naples a contagious pest worse than a carrier of bubonic plague.

Togliatti made no bones about what he intended to do. He openly published this directive for the members of his party: "America's and England's war has changed character. We must no longer say that it is an imperialist war, because in that case the working class of these countries would be asked to oppose it and this would damage the U.S.S.R.'s chance for victory. It is the victory of the Soviet forces on which hinges the future of communism. The Communist Party must unite around it all the progressive forces to fight for the destruction of Hitlerism and fascism so that the power of the Soviets will be augmented and so that the influence of Anglo-Saxon imperialism will be limited."

The fascists who remained in Rome had a rough time, and many of them secured a Communist Party card as a way out. Others were served by the "proletarian union," part of a supposedly patriotic formation headed by Giuseppe Albano, *il gobbo del Quarticciolo*. This hunchback was a shrewd swindler who issued certificates heavy with signatures and stamps that gave a political clean bill of health to rich fascists. For those who had been notorious in their activities, the document showed in an unequivocal manner that their fascist acts had been performed on the direct orders of this partisan band. The toughest cases called for a day and night guard to prevent other partisan forces from performing summary justice on the client. Benjamino Gigli, the great tenor, used the hunchback's protection.

It was a hot summer morning. I stepped into my Fiat, and Nello, with the protection of an Allied uniform behind him, sped perilously through the city, crossed the Vittorio Bridge and screeched to a halt before the massive Palazzo di Giustizia, an

ornate structure built at the end of the Napoleonic era in French
polyglot style. I pushed my way up the stairs through a crowd of
civilians, entered the marble hall and fought through the angry
audience in the courtroom.

I was covering the trial of Pietro Caruso, Rome's chief of
police, a man with an ugly reputation for brutality. He had remained in Rome to the bitter end; only when the first American
tanks began rumbling through the streets did he flee. Negotiating
a difficult curve on the northern outskirts of the city, his car had
overturned and both of his legs had been broken. He had regained
consciousness in a hospital that had already been seized by the
partisans.

The principal accusation against Caruso was that he had furnished the SS with many of the victims for the Ardeatina massacre. Understandably, the trial was of enormous interest to the
Romans, since the massacre had been so recent and the sufferings
of the families of the victims so great. Less understandably, there
was a lack of interest amongst Americans, for the trial was supposed to illustrate how the anti-fascist Italians were able to clean
their own house.

I stood in the courtroom alongside Colonel John Pollack, British
head of the military police. "I hope we don't have any trouble
here," he said.

"You should have brought more men," I commented.

"It's not my show. This is an Italian trial all the way. Their own
judges, prosecutor and, I suspect, hangman."

"Where is the prisoner?"

"He was brought in at 3 A.M. and hidden somewhere in the
building. They've taken this measure for his security."

The few *carabinieri* in the corridor were having their troubles.
A crowd had broken through the police block at the Via Ulpiano
gate, had surged up the stairway to the courtroom and had
broken down the door. There were not enough *carabinieri* to
push them out.

"A *morte Caruso!*" they cried. "Give him to us!"

The voice of a clerk of the court was heard over the uproar. "You are only impeding the progress of the trial. *Calma, calma, vi prego.*"

But the crowd pushed forward, overturning benches and chairs, breaking down the railing that separated the public from the official section. They swarmed around the eleven prosecution witnesses sitting calmly on a bench just inside the broken railing, surged over the judge's bench and rapped on the bars of the vacant prisoner's cage, yelling, "We want Caruso!"

Colonel Pollack, who spoke only English, managed to make his voice heard. "It is impossible to hold a trial in this atmosphere," he shouted. "I want each of you to return to your home with my personal assurance that justice will be done." The words were translated by an assistant, but they had no appreciable effect.

I had just turned to ask the colonel a question when I heard the shrill voice of a hysterical woman. "It's the jailer! He sent my son to his death!" she screamed. She pointed to one of the prosecution witnesses, a short, stocky, inoffensive-looking man of about forty-five dressed in a double-breasted gray suit. She threw herself at him, tearing his hair and clawing at his face.

He was Donato Carretta, the man who had been, until the fall of Rome, the director of *Regina Coeli*, the Queen of Heaven, prison. Earlier, he had testified before the investigating magistrate that the order to turn over fifty prisoners to the SS had been given to him personally by Caruso over the telephone. Caruso had told him only that these people were to be transferred to the north, not that they were to be shot in the Ardeatina caves.

"To show that I acted in good faith, I even ordered that their personal belongings and money be returned to them," Carretta had testified.

"Was the order given only by telephone?" the investigating magistrate asked.

"No. It was followed by a written order."

Most of the crowd didn't even know Carretta's identity, but they hurled themselves at him in fury, covering him with blows. The *carabinieri* fought through the crowd, reached him and separated him from his tormentors. With difficulty, part of the crowd was pushed into the hallway, where it splintered into small bands that went hunting for Caruso in the immense edifice.

"I am doing my best to punish the fascist crimes," the Italian prosecutor shouted over the hubbub. "I understand the spirit that moves you, and if I do not say more it is because I do not wish to compromise the work I must do. But I solemnly promise you that full justice will be done here. What I deplore is that people like you, moved by a spirit of justice, are damaging the cause of justice by your behavior."

The words had no effect on the crowd.

The presiding judge then announced that the case was postponed and that the public would be informed of the new trial date.

I was walking down the long, wide stone steps toward my parked vehicle when I heard a cry. Part of the mob was racing into the Palazzo di Giustizia again. They had caught sight of Carretta. The ex-prison director saw them coming and locked himself in a room, but the door was broken down and he was dragged out by his heels, his head banging on each marble step as they hauled him toward the Tiber. Once again the *carabinieri* came to his defense, and after an almost superhuman struggle, managed to liberate him and put him into one of their military vehicles. The driver quickly stepped on the starter, but the engine remained silent. Again and again, and still the motor did not catch. He jumped out to start the motor by hand and was literally buried by the crowd. They tore the steel crank from his hands and struck Carretta over the head with it. Carretta's hair was literally torn from his scalp, blood rendering his face unrecognizable as he was hurled to the pavement. A tram had just halted at the near corner and the victim was placed on the tracks in front of it. The con-

ductor was ordered to ride over him. Horrified, the conductor
jumped out of the trolley and fled.

"To the Tiber, to the Tiber!" the crowd cried. The inert Carretta was dragged to the Umberto Bridge, lifted and thrown over
the side. The water brought Carretta back to his senses and he
started swimming toward shore. A few youngsters, red handker-
chiefs about their throats, jumped into a rowboat and pulled
toward him. They battered him over the skull with their oars, then
towed the half-conscious victim to shore. Others in the crowd,
grabbing his ankles, dragged him for more than a mile to the
Queen of Heaven prison, with the crowd behind them growing in
size and fury. Someone offered a cord, and the victim was hanged
by the feet from the entrance to the prison he had recently directed. His wife and young son, still occupying an apartment on
the premises, witnessed the scene. Their cries of anguish were lost
in the louder cries of hate.

But the mob wasn't through yet. As the body swung like a
pendulum, they heaved rocks at it. A paddy wagon, bringing
three common thieves and an SS spy, edged toward the prison
entrance. Thinking that Caruso was inside the wagon, the crowd
overpowered the driver and guard and opened the van. The four
prisoners, overjoyed at their unexpected liberation, lost themselves in the confused mass.

Shortly before 1 P.M. American MP's arrived in force. They
quickly established order, the crowd departed and the body was
cut down and turned over to the Italian authorities.

Caruso was kept hidden in the Palazzo di Giustizia until 2 A.M.
Then, under extremely heavy guard, he was returned to his Queen
of Heaven cell. His later trial was anticlimactic. The fascist radio
of the north applied pressure. "So-called judges are at the point of
trying an honest fascist, a man of good faith who was ready for
any sacrifice. We want it known that he has good friends who are
ready to help him, today and tomorrow," it announced meaningfully.

The threat fell short of the mark. Caruso was sentenced to a dishonorable death and taken to a military camp on the outskirts of Rome. There he limped on crutches to a wooden chair, where he was seated with his back to the firing squad. Italian soldiers fired a single volley.

Chapter 3

The Big Decision

SUNDAY in a Rome at war was still Sunday. The streets had a holiday air. Bells chimed. Churches filled and emptied. The glaring sun, which would become unbearable after midday, shone down from a cloudless, cerulean sky. Nello was off with the Fiat, supposedly making necessary repairs. I couldn't complain too much, because he kept the car in fine shape. When it broke down, his divining-rod nose led him straight to a rear-end transmission system, or piston rings, or brake linings, which he got by trading a spare tire or a few gallons of gas. On this Sunday I borrowed a motor pool jeep and drove down to the sharp bend in the Tiber, which reaches like a pair of arms around *Ponte*, the old (as distinguished from ancient) quarter of the city.

I parked the jeep across Ponte Umberto from the *Palazzo di Giustizia*, carefully removing the distributor and padlocking the steering wheel. I strolled down Via del Orso, five centuries ago the gay, mundane center of Rome. Osteria del Orso, the deep brown brick structure of Renaissance architecture, had been an inn in which Dante had lived during the Jubilee of 1300. Petrarch and Rabelais had also patronized it, the latter only for a short time because he found his bed infested with bugs. Montaigne, another guest, described a papal parade that passed under his window on January 3, 1581. Now, in the summer of 1944, it was serving the British forces as an officers' club, but it would soon again become Italy's most expensive restaurant. Close by was Hotel del Leone, once owned by Vanozza dei Catanei, mother of Lucretia and Cesare Borgia. The famous courtesans of the day rode along this narrow street in the litters and carriages of their gallants. The cobbled streets echoed their names—Grechette di Campo dei Fiori, Laura La Bona, Antea and Pina di Monserrato. Here lived La Fornarina, mistress of Raphael, who immortalized her with his brush. Farther up the street, in a small and lovely piazza, was a Renaissance palace where once the lovely mistress of Cesare Borgia lived. She was Fiammetta, "the little flame," the most beautiful girl in the Rome of her time. The piazza is named after her.

At the corner of Via della Scrofa and Via dei Portoghesi stands a modest stone structure that now serves as an apartment building. A niche has been cut in an angle of the building and in it, protected from inclement weather by a small cupola, is a painting of the Madonna, looking heavenward, dressed in a flowing Renaissance robe. It was placed there four hundred years ago to commemorate a miracle.

The family that lived there at that time returned home one afternoon to find that their pet monkey, which was kept on a chain, had broken loose and had lifted a crying infant out of its cradle. The animal was sitting in a corner of the room with the baby in its arms. The family let out a cry and the monkey, frightened, clambered up to a beam on the high ceiling, still holding fast to the child. The parents fell to their knees in prayer. Reassured by the silence below, and perhaps moved by the power of prayer, the monkey descended and deposited the baby safely in its cradle.

I walked along Via dei Banchi Nuovi where the arrogant

genius Benvenuto Cellini had his workshop. The elegance of that day has faded, but the brick and travertine marble structures still give off an aura of the past. There is history in every step of the cobblestoned street, and I was beginning to feel it as though it were part of my own heritage.

I paid a visit to the grave of another foreigner who had felt at home in Italy, the English poet, Shelley. His ashes lie in the cemetery of Testaccio, near the towering pyramid of Caio Cestio, a Roman consul under Julius Caesar. An inscription at the base of the 120-foot structure proclaims that it was built in 12 B.C. and that it required only 333 days to complete. That would be a record today.

Shelley was drowned when his boat capsized during a storm in the Tyrrhenean Sea. His body was recovered and later cremated on the beach at Viareggio. This was done in accordance with the law promulgated by Queen Maria Luisa of the Spanish Bourbons, who ruled this narrow strip of coast line, then a penal colony. Lord Byron and Trelawney, great friends of the poet, saw to it that the ashes and the unburnt heart, which Trelawney had snatched from the funeral pyre, were transported to Rome. Byron selected the burial place. He hired a sculptor to do the tombstone, selecting as an epitaph three lines from the immortal "Ariel":

Percy Bysshe Shelley

❀

Cor Cordium

❀

Natus IV AUG. MDCCCXCII
Obiit VIII JUL. MDCCCXXII

❀

Nothing of him that doth fade
But doth suffer a sea change
Into something rich and strange

The heat of day caused me little discomfort as I wandered through the city. At dusk I drove slowly homeward, conscious of a deep stirring within me. It had been, somehow, something more than a sightseeing expedition. The things I had just seen I had also felt. To this day I cannot say with precision just what it was that had moved me, what it was that was different from the hundreds of other occasions when, as a tourist, I viewed other lovely, one-dimensional vistas.

It might have been the sharp contrast between the war-blasted, suffering cities I had come through and this architecturally delightful and almost untouched city. It might have been the sympathetic understanding I had already begun to feel for the Roman people, the sort of understanding that kept their defects from becoming irritating. It might have been that my unconscious desire to set down roots somewhere felt a vague stirring that this might be the place. It might have been all of these reasons and many more that I have been unable to define. Certainly it was the time, the place and the feeling.

From my car I watched the enormous orange ball of sun go down behind the dome of St. Peter's, and I felt more at home than if I had seen it go down behind the tower of the Empire State Building.

Despite these sentiments, I never once said, or consciously thought, that I intended to make Rome my home. That would have been far too daring for this somewhat insular journalist, scraping along on a modest income. The decision to live in Rome came later, as the end of a long sequence of incidents that were set into motion by the invasion of southern France.

This is the way it happened. The three military services were shopping around for correspondents to cover their particular phases of the invasion. I made a deal with the public relations officer attached to the Mediterranean fleet to go in with the navy. At the conclusion of this assignment I was to report on the shipment of a battle-wounded naval veteran to a stateside hospital. It was to be a human interest story to tug at the heartstrings—a

seaman who would have his mother at his bedside short hours
after having been wounded in a foreign land. The important part,
from my point of view, was that I would have to accompany this
man on his trip to the U.S. in order to get the full value out of
the story. So if I survived the invasion, I would get an unexpected
and most welcome trip home.

Although it was an open secret that we were going to invade
the southern coast of France, such details as time and place were
tightly held military secrets not shared with war correspondents.
We needn't have been too upset about this lack of faith, though,
because it was possible for us to learn all about it from the broadcasts of Axis Sally, an American girl of Italian extraction whose
broadcasts were designed to weaken the morale of the American
fighting man. She was a remarkably accurate reporter, at least as
far as this operation was concerned. As time went on she named
the units that would make the invasion, the beaches they would
land on and the date the landings would take place. It was all
very disconcerting.

Almost at the last moment I took sick. I came down with a
virulent case of GI's, or Neapolitan tourist trots, combined with
an uncontrollable fit of vomiting that had me running between
my room on the top floor of the Terminus Hotel and the hallway
bathroom. Sometime during the early morning hours, I collapsed
in the hallway. Someone found me and had me carted off to the
military hospital. I have often wondered whether this illness, if it
had lasted one day longer, might not have broken the chain of
events and thus prevented the course of my life from taking the
decisive turn it did.

In any event, four days later, barely cured and hardly able to
stand, I rode in an ambulance to the shore and boarded the
U.S.S. Tulagi, a midget aircraft carrier, an hour before the ship
raised anchor. She turned out to be a wonderfully comfortable
ship, and I felt as though I were on a Mediterranean pleasure
cruise. A good feature of this kind of vessel (or bad, depending on
one's point of view), is the fact that one would feel no discomfort

even if the ship were hit—being loaded with aviation gas and gunpowder, it would erupt like Vesuvius.

The ease with which the invasion was carried off, combined with our successes in northern France, looked like a sure sign that the war would come to a quick end, probably by Christmas. We had steamed eastward to Malta, taken on bombs, and in the darkness, sailed westward to the French Riviera. The feint didn't fool the Germans. They knew exactly on which part of the beach at St. Tropez the landing would be made, but they were too weak to do anything except withdraw.

Except for a quick assignment that involved my flying a mission with a medium bomber group from a base on the island of Corsica—they made me work for my passage as bombardier—I was now ready to cover the story that would bring me home.

I flew to the navy base hospital in Oran to pick up the wounded sailor I was to accompany to the States. The hospital was filled with pneumonia and venereal cases, jeep accident casualties, and similar war ailments, but of war wounded there was only one.

I sat in the office of the navy captain who was the commanding officer. "What is the rank of your wounded man?" I asked.

"An ordinary seaman."

"Where is he from?"

"Newark, New Jersey."

"What's the matter with him?"

"He has a broken vertebra and is in a cast from his head down to his knees."

"How did it happen?"

"The damnedest thing imaginable. He was on a PT boat going to Marseilles when it hit a mine. The explosion looped him into the sea. He wasn't wearing his inflatable life vest, and he would have drowned if a Free French fishing boat hadn't been in the vicinity. The first thing the captain did after hauling him aboard was to fit one of those old-fashioned cork life jackets on him. Damned if five minutes later this boat didn't hit a mine. The poor fellow blew straight up in the air and landed flat on his back on the deck. It was the cork life jacket that broke his spine."

I got permission to talk with the wounded man. After the usual sterile formalities, I asked, "How would you like to go home?"

He looked up at me but didn't answer. "Say in twenty-four hours," I continued.

"Are you kidding me?"

"If you say the word you'll be on a navy hospital plane that will have you home tomorrow." I explained that the ride itself was not dangerous but that if any trouble developed, such as storms en route or bad landings, the bouncing about might have serious consequences.

"Look, mister, if you mean it, get me on that plane," he said. "I don't care if it kills me."

Twenty-four hours after take-off, our DC-4 landed at Floyd Bennett airport. An ambulance took the wounded seaman off to a navy hospital near his home. A Red Cross driver volunteered to take me home.

As we drove toward my house in Lido, Long Island, the ugly stucco bungalows and wooden shacks along the treeless stretches of beach filled me with distaste. The city of Long Beach bustled with peacetime activity. The hardware store was crowded. Young fry were lined up in front of the local movie house, where a Bob Hope picture was showing. A mailman ambled along his route. Scores of filling stations were doing good business. The war was five thousand miles away in distance, and even farther in spirit.

As we reached my neighborhood I was painfully aware of the forest of telephone poles that overshadowed the spindly young trees and manicured lawns. I had looked forward to these familiar landmarks of home, but now I saw them through eyes still attuned to the ageless beauty and dignity of Rome.

The Red Cross vehicle dropped me at my door. I saw my wife playing with our two children on the lawn. My arrival had come as a complete surprise, since the press censor had not allowed me

View of Rome from the terrace of Mike Stern's apartment. To the left is the Milvio Bridge across the Tiber, and in the background the dome of St. Peter's rises above the city. (Below) The author stands in Villa Borghese at the Trinità dei Monte after the liberation of Rome. The car is a Fiat 1100 liberated by him.

The Stern children, Michael, Jr. and Margaret
on their arrival in Rome at the close of the war.
The cross and helmet mark the grave of a German soldier buried near Villa Spiga.

Posters on the walls of Rome. (Above) Election poster in which child
threatens, "If Papa and Mama don't go out and vote, we will peepee
bed." (Below) The author's wife and children stand before posters advert-
ing Stern's story on Giuliano.

The author chats with Pastor Martin Niemöller, shortly after his rescue from the SS.

the liberation of Dachau. (Right)
e body of one of the two SS
rds who were pulled from the
hor's jeep and beaten to death
prisoners. (Below) The infamous
th train, where prisoners were
fined until they died of starva-
n. Note Star of David at one side
car.

The author, wearing the "war correspondent" shoulder emblem, pauses between hops during the hectic closing days of the war.

The bodies of Mussolini and his girl friend hanging by their feet in Piazza Loreto.

uring the investigation of the famous Holohan murder, the author is shown
bove) on the shore of Lake Orta at the spot where the Major's body was loaded
to the rowboat, and (below) with Giorgio Migliari, a key figure in the case.

The communist newspaper story attacking the author as a spy and reproducing the letter addressed to Stern from the bandit Giuliano. The author chats with Giuliano (below) and the bandit chief's father on a hillside near Palermo.

In more recent years, the author and his luxurious Villa Spiga have become a mecca for travelers. In these pictures he is chatting with Cornel Wilde and Sinclair Lewis (above left), Helmut Dantine (right), Sofia Loren and Vittorio de Sica (below).

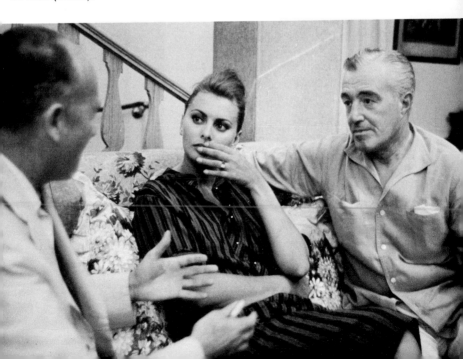

Mike Stern at home on the terrace of his penthouse above the city he knows so well.

to tell them of my movements. (Think how important this information could have been to Hitler!)

As I embraced my wife, my three-year-old daughter tugged at the shirt of her five-year-old brother. "Is he our Daddy?" she asked.

I put my hand on her head. "Honey," I said, "the day this war is over, you're all coming to live with Daddy in Rome."

The words were spoken without thought. It was a reflex action triggered by the frightening realization that my daughter hadn't recognized her father. But having spoken them and faced the enormity of such a decision, I found myself rationalizing. During the week I spent at home, the idea of living in Rome went from a mere possibility to an absolute certainty.

There would be many difficulties to face, such as the matter of employment. At the conclusion of hostilities I would become an ex-war correspondent. The magazine I wrote for had no need of a foreign correspondent, and it expected me to return and resume my local reporting. Because of the insular interests of the magazine-buying public, the foreign field had always been a slim one for magazine writers. However, I was sure that the war would bring us a consciousness of international affairs that would endure at least for the first two post-war years, by which time I hoped that Rome would become a center of mundane and artistic interest, much as Paris had become in the Hemingway-Gertrude Stein post-World War I era.

Although my wife had always dreamed of visiting Rome, the prospect of moving there permanently—I had told her to get ready for a two-year stay, and that had seemed permanent enough —was frightening. She felt like the wife of a pioneer who had just begun the dangerous westward trek in a covered wagon, and nothing could convince her that our eastward one would be any less hazardous than the one undertaken by our hardy forebears a century ago. No argument of mine could remove her fear of this trip, nor could the arguments of others dissuade her from making it.

A week later I was back in Italy, dividing my time between the static front lines and the Corso Trieste apartment. Now that I knew I was going to bring my family over, I viewed my surroundings in another light. The five long flights of marble stairs no longer had a romantic appeal, now that I pictured children struggling up them. The few schools that were operating were in appalling condition, and the young scholars that I saw, bundled to the ears in tattered woolens in the frigid classrooms, were a pathetic sight. Milk was not pasteurized, and the food merchants hardly practiced what an American housewife would regard as elementary hygiene. The countryside, the beaches and even the cities were strewn with mines planted by the Germans, so that simply moving about presented a certain menace. I kept reminding myself of the perils faced by frontier women, but the reminders were not entirely reassuring.

The war didn't end by Christmas. A winter lull set in and dragged on into spring, when the final offensives were launched.

I lay in a foxhole on a hilltop near the Apennine village of Pianora. Around me was an infantry company of the 91st Division. During the night every cannon, mortar and rocket thrower lobbed tens of thousands of tons of steel and explosives over our heads. The earth rumbled and the sky was bright with perpetual fireworks. At dawn we took off along Highway 65. Resistance was spotty. Where the enemy held out in entrenched positions in the rugged mountain peaks on each side of the road, the low-flying planes eliminated them with napalm bombs. It was a liquid fire that ran into crevices. There was no hiding from it. Not a single German plane appeared in the sky to oppose the Allied bombers. By afternoon we were in Bologna. The last of the nazi defenses was smashed and their only hope of temporary salvation was to retreat through the flat Po Valley to the Alps as fast as possible. The total liberation of Italy was a matter of days.

In the midst of chaos, as the Italian and German armed forces were pressed to the breaking point, I found myself thinking of the kind of Italy my family would be coming to in a few short months. Would it be a monarchy ruled by the House of Savoy, with the sort of pomp and ceremony such a rule would entail, or a democracy on American lines, or a parliamentary form of government along British lines? Or would the communists, who had taken control of the partisan armed forces and who were the only truly trained professionals in the field, take over?

And what would happen to Benito Mussolini? Would he be tried by his own people? Would it be a fair trial, or would his people turn on him as they had on the hapless keeper of the Queen of Heaven prison, not so much from hatred as from a desire to destroy the symbol of their own guilt? For blood does wipe out guilt, although the new guilt it creates is often as bad as the one that cried for blood. In the case of many Italians it was the guilt of those who had believed and followed a leader on a road they knew to be wrong.

Somehow the path that Italy would take in the future, the Italy my family would live in, would be affected by what happened to the Italian dictator. The battle for control of the country by the communists was already joined in the Mussolini question. Public morality, justice, desire for revenge and political opportunism would all play their part in the struggle. I would know the outcome soon enough, for just on the other side of the enemy lines, to the north of the Po River, the Italian dictator was strutting across the stage in the last act of a drama he had created, but whose end he could not foresee.

Soon enough I would be taking a front seat at this tragedy, and would be involved in its aftermath.

Chapter 4

Mussolini: The Murder and the Mystery

THE ITALIAN DICTATOR was in Milan. With the Allied armies
closing in rapidly from all directions, he was ready to admit for
the first time that surrender might be the only way out. Cardinal
Schuster had arranged a meeting between him and the Committee of National Liberation, the governing body of the revolutionary partisans. It was held in the cardinal's somber study. The
partisans offered Mussolini two possibilities. Either he could
retire immediately to the Alps north of Lake Como and there
await the arrival of the American forces to whom he could safely
surrender, or he and his cabinet could remain at the cardinal's
residence with the cardinal personally guaranteeing their safety.

Field Marshal Graziani said: "*Duce,* we took up arms in order
to defend our treaty obligations with our German allies and I, as
Minister of War and Supreme Commander of the Armed Forces,
ask that they be informed of our dealings before any decision is
taken."

The partisan leader said, "Perhaps you are not aware that for
the past week we have been discussing surrender terms with the
Germans."

"What!" Mussolini exclaimed in surprise. Cardinal Schuster nodded in confirmation. "The Germans always treated us like servants and now they have betrayed us," the dictator said bitterly. "I declare that from this moment I resume my independence of action. I shall take the matter up with my Grand Council immediately and give you a reply tonight."

As he left the cardinal's residence, he turned to the men about him. "The Italian people have need of me. I shall return to them." It was the twilight speech of a god incapable of accepting the awful truth that his domain no longer existed.

At his temporary office in the prefecture a heated argument took place. Black-shirted hotheads wanted to fight to the last man, but *il Duce* had lost his taste for bloodshed. He was very weary and had no more stomach for running. He said that he found Cardinal Schuster's offer of asylum a fair one and favored accepting it. A messenger reported that his son was at the airport with a plane that would fly him to safety in Spain, but that he would have to hurry because it was uncertain whether they could hold the airport through the night. Mussolini refused to desert his last-ditch followers.

Before a vote could be taken on the partisan proposals, Prefect Tiengo, a regional governor, came rushing into the room to announce that the cardinal's proposal was part of a plot to turn Mussolini over to the people, a terrifying possibility that brought up visions of Carretta's fate. There was no truth to the statement, but Mussolini, easily suspicious, allowed it to change his mind.

"We leave immediately for Como," he announced.

During the hectic hours of the early night the national treasury was loaded onto trucks. The entire cabinet, undersecretaries and other government officials carried with them all the portable wealth of their ministries, families, mistresses and even servants. For example, Rose Mittag Romano, wife of the Minister of Agriculture, carried with her one hundred thousand dollars in lire, sixty thousand dollars in American cash, nine hundred gold pieces worth about fifty thousand dollars, three thousand dollars in French francs, several thousand dollars in Spanish currency, a loaded jewel case and all her furs, gowns and monogrammed bed linen.

Mussolini was more concerned about his state papers than he was about his money, for he pinned his hope of winning an acquittal in an American trial on his secret correspondence with Roosevelt, Churchill and Stalin.

The caravan of fleeing fascists ran a partisan gauntlet of small arms fire as they fled through blacked-out Milan. They traveled slowly along the *autostrada* for thirty miles to the famous vacation resort of Como, arriving at midnight. Here bad news awaited *il Duce*. Not a single one of the ten thousand *fedelissimi* black shirts was on hand to meet him. They had insured their own safety by surrendering *en masse*. A light truck containing many of Mussolini's documents, developing motor trouble, was pushed over to the side of the road for repairs, where it was sacked by the local peasantry.

Word was brought to him that Claretta Petacci had put in an appearance and wanted to be received. Mussolini made a tired gesture of his hand, indicating that he did not want to be bothered. The news of her arrival was an added complication in his life. At one time this young brunette with the full bosom and flashing Latin eyes had been his favorite, and that, coming from a man who had been serviced in his Zodiac room in Palazzo Venezia by various women almost every working day of his life, was an unusual compliment. But lately her jealous scenes no longer gave him the feeling of youth; they merely annoyed him. Like the old roué who turns to religion for solace when the end is near, Mussolini turned to his wife. He did not know that only a few hours of life remained, but he sensed it.

He reached for a sheet of paper and wrote a hasty note:

. Dear Rachele,
Here I am at the last phase of my life, the last page of my book. Perhaps we shall never see each other again. I ask your pardon if I have involuntarily caused you pain, but you

know that you are the only woman that I have truly loved.
I swear it to you before God and before our dead son,
Bruno.

He sent the note off by messenger to the villa in Cernobbia
where his wife had taken refuge.

At 3 A.M. a disconsolate Mussolini changed his mind again.
This time he was determined to make a dash through a nearby
mountain pass to neutral Switzerland. It still lacked three hours
to dawn when he gave the order to move north. He climbed into
the front seat of an *autoblindo*, a lightly armored troop carrier
with mounted 20mm machine gun. The column wound along the
twisting, two-lane macadam road that skirts the western shore
of Lake Como, finally reaching the village of Menaggio, eight
miles away. From here a road runs through the valley to Lugano,
Switzerland, less than a half-hour drive to the northeast. As a
precaution two cars were sent to reconnoiter the road. Although
there were fewer than twenty partisans in that section, the first
car had the misfortune to run into a few of them and its occupants docilely surrendered. The second car sped back to the
dictator, its occupants reporting breathlessly that the road was
blocked by a regiment of partisan forces armed with tanks.

The report was the sort of exaggeration that could be expected
from frightened people who need an excuse for their lack of courage. I traveled along this road a few weeks later and saw how
close Mussolini had been to salvation. If he had made a run for it
in his armored car, he would easily have reached the Swiss border
in safety. It was on this scene, where I arrived from the German
front soon afterward, that I was able to piece together the chain
of events that follows.

Mussolini believed the report of his frightened followers and
changed plans again. He decided to remain in Menaggio and await
the arrival of the Ettore Muti Legion, one of his crack divisions,
which had departed Milan at dawn and was heading northward.
With this body of troops he would force a passage to the Swiss

border. But the Muti Legion never made it, for when the troops
reached Cernobbio, a short distance away on the shore of Lake
Como, someone in the village fired a shot in the air. It was the
only gun in town, but it was enough to frighten the well-armed
legionnaires, who promptly surrendered. Many of them insured
their immediate freedom by signing up with the Communist
Party, to whom they consigned three million dollars in legion
funds.

When a long line of German military vehicles carrying Luftwaffe and SS troops in full retreat came through Menaggio the
following dawn, heading toward the Swiss-German border on the
longer lake road, Mussolini changed his mind once more. He attached his convoy of thirty-nine vehicles, all that remained of his
empire, to their rear. It was a cold, rainy morning. Claretta, who
had joined her reluctant lover, wore mechanic's blue overalls over
her dress, an aviator's leather helmet on her head and heavy
goggles on her face. She rode in a car with her brother, Marcello.

The column had moved only eight miles when it came to a
sudden and unexpected halt midway between the tiny towns of
Musso and Dongo. Mussolini's *autoblindo* rested on the Passo
bridge, about a mile back from the head of the line.

Some trees had been felled across the road during the night by
angry villagers who were protesting the brutal murder of four
of their townspeople by local fascists. As a matter of fact, there
were under five hundred armed partisans in the entire region
bordering the forty-seven-mile lake front, and these were so
widely scattered as to be ineffective against the well-armed
column. But the commander of the German forces thought that
he had run into a trap, and his uneasiness led him to discuss his
predicament with some of the villagers, one of whom was the
notoriously partisan local padre. This priest frightened the convoy leader by saying, confidentially, that there were thousands of
heavily-armed partisans waiting for a signal to attack. While the
discussion continued, the leader of the partisan 52nd Garibaldi
Brigade, which at full organizational strength was under fifty

combatants, put in an appearance with a handful of his fighters. The brigade commander was Count Pier Bellini delle Stelle, a bearded, dashing young aristocrat who, unlike other partisans, had no political axe to grind. His uniform owed allegiance to several armies, but the Alpine hat, worn at a cocky angle, was all his. Draped carelessly over his left shoulder was a machine pistol.

Count Bellini informed the German commanding officer that his men were swarming in the hills and that the bridges ahead were mined and ready to blow should the column try to run for it. The curious conference lasted from 7:30 A.M. to 1:30 P.M. before an agreement was reached. The count would permit the Germans to leave unmolested, their vehicles to take off one at a time and at half-mile distances. The Italians were to remain behind as prisoners. During the lengthy palaver, the count's men did actually mine some of the bridges and set up roadblocks to the north. At the first one, the German vehicles, arriving singly, were easily disarmed. At subsequent roadblocks, unable to defend themselves any longer, they fell easy prey to a peasantry whose patriotism ran as deep as their pockets.

Word of the agreement reached the Italians in the rear of the column, and they bitterly pointed to it as the final sell-out by their German allies. Several ministers argued with Mussolini that it was better for all of them to make a run for it; better to die fighting than to submit meekly to a partisan firing squad. "I want to avoid bloodshed," was Mussolini's answer. "There is nothing to do but surrender."

Claretta jumped out of her car, secured a German military overcoat and a helmet and thrust them at *il Duce.* "You must save yourself," she insisted. "The Italian people are lost without you." She helped him into the coat, corrected him when he placed the helmet backwards on his head, then assisted him into a German troop carrier and started to climb in after him. A German lieutenant roughly pushed her back and she fell to the pavement.

Mussolini's confidential secretary took the dictator's knapsack full of gold coins and currency and his black leather briefcase and placed them in Marcello Pettaci's car. This seemed like the safest thing to do, because Marcello was carrying forged papers passing him off as a Spanish diplomat.

Rose Mittag Romano also had no intention of giving herself up. With the aid of a white uniform and a pillow she disguised herself as a pregnant Red Cross girl and pleaded earnestly with a German ambulance driver to allow her to get in. Although at this moment the only pleas that touched the Germans were those consonant with their own safety, the pregnancy act moved him. Even the mountain of luggage that her husband's functionary stowed in the ambulance did not entirely erase the driver's noble sentiment.

It was about as easy to disguise Mussolini as it would have been to hide the Colosseum. His well-known jaw jutted out of billboards, newspapers and newsreels everywhere. It jutted just as recognizably from under the German helmet. Who it was that first spotted him is not clear—some say that it was the priest, others that it was two peasant boys who stuck their heads into the truck, still others that it was the German commander. In any event, the count and his chief of staff walked directly to the German car in which the dictator had taken refuge, asked him to get out and marched him to the city hall in Dongo.

Giuseppe Rubini, the white-haired anti-fascist patriarch of Dongo, had been elected mayor by acclamation as soon as the fascist administration had taken off for the hills. He met the dictator in the doorway of city hall and told him to have no fear, that as long as he was mayor, law and order would prevail. He placed the prisoner in a small, ill-furnished room on the ground floor and served him coffee. Up to this time no one had thought of disarming Mussolini, so the dictator unhooked his revolver and handed it to a guard.

Partisans, motivated by curiosity rather than hate, crowded into the room during the afternoon. The dictator carried on lengthy conversations with them. If there was any feeling of rancor over the fact that he, a man who had made half the world tremble, now found himself helpless in the hands of a badly-armed, sloppily-dressed group of guerrillas, he made no sign of it. He was affable, friendly and apparently at ease.

Even after he was transferred, late in the afternoon, to the military *caserma* in the tiny hamlet of Germasino, hidden in a narrow valley that runs laterally off the lake, he remained imperturbable. He acted as though he were seated in a café, carrying on a political conversation with old friends. He spoke with all comers, chatting about England, the United States and Russia, insisting that Stalin was the greatest political figure to emerge from the war since he was the only winner. He kept up the conversation until midnight, when he was closed in a cell for the night.

At Dongo, a wave of gold fever swept the town. Forty million dollars lay in the cars, trucks and military vehicles vacated by Mussolini's ministers, and partisans methodically stripped each car and carted part of the wealth to the city hall. Toward the tail end of the motor column, out of sight of the partisans, peasants, like a swarm of locusts, stripped cars bare and took off for the hills. But the greater part of the treasure was taken into custody by Count Bellini and kept in a high-ceilinged room on the second floor of the city hall.

In addition to the money taken from the ministers and their families, from Mussolini and from the state treasury, the partisans hit an unexpected bonanza in the German column. Two officers, suspecting what was about to happen, made a deal with Alois Hoffman, a Swiss living on Lake Como, to take over five million dollars worth of lire and hide it for them, with Hoffman to receive one-half of it as a reward. Hoffman turned the money over to the partisan leader. More wealth came in when a fisherman saw some Germans dump a sack into the Mera River. He dragged it out, found that it contained seventy pounds of gold ingots.

Rose Mittag Romano made it to the Swiss border in the ambulance only to be stopped by a Swiss customs guard. He took one look into her capacious purse, which bulged with jewels and money, and turned her over to the partisans. Her half-million dollars joined the count's hoard. All during the afternoon, suitcases bulging with cash and valuables were tossed into the treasure room. A typist tried to make a list of what the room contained, but it was impossible to record everything that piled up in fabulous mountains of gold around her machine.

Count Bellini's immediate problem was Mussolini, and on this score he needed orders from the Committee of National Liberation, under whose authority he operated. Since there was no means of direct contact with them, he had to wait until they got a messenger to him. In the meantime he felt it wiser to move the dictator to still another place of concealment, just in case a last-ditch fascist outfit or even another partisan commander decided to take justice into his own hands. The best person to do this was Captain Neri, his chief of staff, a man who knew the surrounding countryside and who was highly regarded by the local residents.

Captain Neri was in his mid-twenties, a college graduate fired by the ideal of a liberated Italy governed by a democratically elected communist congress. He didn't realize until it was too late that this is a contradiction in terms, like "honest crook" or "virtuous whore." He had been born Luigi Canali, had served with distinction as a lieutenant in the Italian army and had joined the partisan movement in 1943. During the final winter campaign, as he was about to take off for Switzerland on a mission, he was arrested. With him at the time, and also taken into custody, was Gianna, the sloe-eyed, attractive partisan message bearer who was his mistress. For weeks they underwent indescribable tortures. Once Gianna was stripped naked and locked in a telephone booth with a huge rat for an entire night; another time lighted cigarettes were pressed against the nipples of her breasts and other delicate parts of her anatomy.

Neither of them cracked. Captain Neri escaped the night before his scheduled execution. The fury of the fascist jailers was vented on Gianna, and this time she broke down, giving the names and locations of partisan forces. For this a communist committee sentenced both of them to death. Captain Neri, already under sentence of death by the fascists, found himself the worst life-insurance risk on record. It took two months for him to get the facts across to his own unit and be rehabilitated. Shortly before, Gianna had been returned in an exchange of prisoners.

It was Neri who selected Mussolini's escort. There were Count Bellini, Gianna and three gunmen called Pietro, Lino and "Sandrino Me Ne Frego" (roughly translated: "Sandrino I don't give a damn"). In the car with Gianna was Claretta Petacci, who had begged on her knees to be taken to her lover. The Italians being a cavalier people, and Count Bellini especially romantic, the request had been granted. The escort drove to Germasino, arriving there at 3 A.M. Mussolini was awakened and taken from his cell. His head was swathed in bandages as a means of disguise, and he was driven back through Dongo and southward along the lake to Azzano. Here the car turned into a narrow dirt road, climbed up the base of steep Monte di Tremezzo and stopped just beyond the tiny hamlet of Giulino di Mezzegra.

Neri got out of his car and ran ahead of the party to a crude peasant house owned by a family named De Maria. Claretta, holding Mussolini by the arm, asked the guards several times if they would stop because the dictator didn't feel so well. The old peasant woman who opened the door asked no questions of Captain Neri. She took a quick glance at Mussolini (whom she did not recognize) and his mistress and thought it unusual that so ugly a man could have so pretty a daughter. Captain Neri whispered a few words in her ear, slipped a five thousand lire note into her hand. She awakened her husband and two children and took them off into the night.

The De Maria house consisted of a kitchen and a bedroom. The latter contained a large bed in which the family slept. Over it was a wooden crucifix, a picture of the Madonna and a certificate attesting to the first communion of one of the children. The dictator and his girl were assigned this room.

Count Bellini left Sandrino and Lino behind with orders to keep out all persons who did not have a permit in writing from him, then headed back to Dongo. The guards remained in the kitchen while Mussolini and Claretta undressed and went to bed. At one point Sandrino's curiosity got the better of him and he suddenly thrust open the door and switched on the light. What he saw was testified to under oath at a trial in Italy recently. "They were doing what any couple would be doing when the girl is good-looking and they are in bed together. They stopped and Claretta pulled the sheet over her head while Mussolini swung his feet to the floor, remaining seated on the bed. 'What wrong have we done you that you are so rude?' he asked. I fumbled an apology, closed the door and stayed in the kitchen for the rest of the night." Although no one in that house knew it, this was to be Mussolini's last night on earth.

When word of the dictator's capture reached Milan, a single communist partisan, operating under the cover name of Colonel Valerio, went into action. As an underground fighter this mysterious man had earned a reputation for waging ruthless war against all enemies of his party, whether they were nazis, democrats, liberals or fascists. He was then thirty-five years of age, above medium height, with a receding hairline, intent, piercing eyes and a heavy, drooping mustache that followed the bitter lines of his mouth. Who he was or where he came from was not known until much later.

At 7 A.M., April 28th, while Mussolini was fast asleep in the arms of the lovely Claretta in the peasant hut, Colonel Valerio climbed into a Fiat 1100 and, followed by twelve of his own partisans in a light truck, sped along the *autostrada* toward Como. An hour later he stormed into the prefecture building, now in the hands of the partisans. Incredible confusion reigned. Valerio was suspicious of the new bureaucrats and they, in turn, were suspicious of him. It took two hours of palaver to learn that the capture had been effected in Dongo. He raced into the square in front of the prefecture to find that his escort had disappeared, and that his Fiat had either gone with them or had been stolen. Raging, he re-entered the building to find that his predicament did not excite an iota of sympathy. Finally, he went to Oscar Sforni, local representative of the Committee of National Liberation, and convinced him that he was the bearer of authentic orders from central headquarters in Milan authorizing him to take charge of the fascist prisoners.

Although Valerio's orders appeared to be bona fide, Sforni didn't feel that a mission of such importance should be entrusted to the hands of a single unknown. He offered Valerio a car and a pass through partisan lines in the Como area only if he, Sforni, were permitted to go along. This was an unforeseen hitch in Valerio's plan, but he raised no objection. Just north of Menaggio some partisans in the hills, mistaking the occupants of the speeding vehicle for escaping fascists, let go with a burst of machine gun fire. The car swerved off the road, balanced precariously on two wheels, righted itself again, shot back onto the pavement and outran the hail of bullets.

They pulled up in front of the Dongo city hall at 2:10 in the afternoon. Armed partisans immediately surrounded these unknowns and took them before Count Bellini. Valerio demonstrated his partisan documents and explained that his orders were to take Mussolini to Milan, but that under no circumstances was *il Duce*, alive, to be permitted to fall into the hands of others. At first his story was greeted with skepticism, but he took Captain Neri aside for a private conversation that must have been convincing, for at its conclusion Neri said that he was satisfied with Valerio and would take him to the Mussolini hideout.

As they headed for the square, Oscar Sforni declared that he was going along to make sure that the mission was carried out in strictly legal fashion and in a way that would reflect favorably on the new democratic regime. At this point Valerio had no further need of him and said so bluntly. When Sforni insisted, Valerio dug his machine pistol into Sforni's guts and, helped by Captain Neri, led him to a cell in the basement and locked him in.

Captain Neri and Gianna drove Valerio to Mussolini. It was mid-afternoon when they arrived at the peasant hut. Mussolini was dressed in a simple military uniform without decoration. The white bandage that had been used to disguise him lay in a heap on the kitchen floor. Claretta was fully dressed and had a cloth coat with fur collar draped over her shapely shoulders. The guards had served them a meager meal of black bread, cheese and wine.

Valerio wasted no time on preliminaries. He told the prisoners to start down the incline toward the parked cars.

"Where are we going?" Mussolini asked.

"I am turning you over to the Allied forces," Valerio answered.

As they slithered downhill through the mud, the dictator inquired calmly what disposition the Allies were making for his son, Vittorio, and for his ministers. He was told that no decision had been reached on this score. The couple was crowded into the back seat of the lead car while Valerio, his machine pistol leveled, draped himself over the left fender so that he was facing them. The car had proceeded only about three hundred yards, just far enough to negotiate a single hairpin curve near the entrance to a small villa called Belmonte, when Valerio ordered it to halt.

The prisoners were asked to step out. Valerio swung off the fender and pointed to the footpath leading to the Villa Belmonte. Mussolini and Claretta took a few hesitant steps toward it, and then, because it was all very odd, looked back questioningly at him. Without a word Colonel Valerio, machine pistol at his hip, squeezed on the trigger. Mussolini just had time to raise his right arm as though to defend himself. The arm was shattered as a dozen shots ripped through his body. He fell to his knees, then toppled backward and lay still, his left eye closed, his right staring sightlessly at his executioner. Claretta took the full burst in the midsection and toppled over near her lover. Although death was instantaneous for both, a guard delivered a *coup de grâce*, firing a single shot from a pistol into their heads.

Captain Neri ordered his guards to watch over the bodies until a truck could be sent back for them. His reaction to the shooting made it obvious that it came as no surprise to him.

Wordlessly, Valerio climbed back into the car and sped north along the lake to Dongo. He no longer made any pretense about what his "orders" were. It is quite evident that to the people accompanying him he had told the truth: that his mandate had come from the Communist Party. And, since Captain Neri and Gianna were both loyal party members, they were expected to follow the command blindly.

But at Dongo he told Count Bellini, who was not a communist, that the executions were in furtherance of direct orders from the Committee of National Liberation and that now he would carry out the rest of his orders by immediately executing the sentence of death on the other members of the fascist council. Whatever doubts might have been raised by this sudden shift of position were lost, partly in the general confusion and partly by the full support he received from Captain Neri and Gianna.

It was now 5 P.M. The prisoners were herded into the gold salon and Valerio went amongst them with a list, checking off their names. In some cases he was wrong. For example, he mistook Marcello Petacci, still posing as a Spanish diplomat, for Vittorio Mussolini. In order to humiliate the dictator's favorite son, he ordered that his shoes be taken from him and that he be marched to the place of execution barefoot. Because Marcello's shoes were as heavy as lead, the heels were pried off. They were found to contain gold coins valued at five thousand Swiss francs. Another error concerned a captain of the air force, Pietro Calistri, who pointed out calmly that he was merely an ordinary soldier who found himself in the column by accident.

"You are Mussolini's personal pilot," Valerio said.

"I never flew Mussolini in my life," Captain Calistri replied.

At this point Mayor Rubini, returning to city hall, passed a priest in the waiting room. "Padre, is there anything I can do for you?" he asked.

"No, thank you," said the priest. "I have an appointment here with the colonel, although I don't know why."

As they spoke, Colonel Valerio strode through the room. The old mayor turned to him and, in the courtly Italian manner, said, "Sir, are you the colonel who came to this town a few hours ago and who seems to have taken control here, and whom I, the mayor, have not yet had the pleasure of meeting?"

"You will excuse me," Valerio replied. "I should have presented myself when I first arrived, but time is so short and I have many important things to do, even in other towns."

"If there is anything I can do for you, Colonel, you need only ask."

The priest asked the reason for his summons. Valerio pointed to the gold salon across the hall and said, "The people in there are in need of religious comfort, because they are all going to be backed against a wall."

"How much time do I have?"

Valerio looked at his wrist watch, said drily, "You have exactly three minutes." The padre protested that three minutes was barely time enough to throw a benediction at them from an open window. Valerio snapped that military exigencies did not permit him to do otherwise.

It was by overhearing this conversation that Mayor Rubini, a gentle, peace-loving man, found out about the pending executions. "I forbid you to shoot the people in my town, in the midst of this crowd of women and children," he said sternly. "If you have an order to execute, go to the cemetery."

"These are the orders of my superiors," Valerio said.

"The orders of your superiors only interest me up to a certain point. I obey the orders of my conscience and what I interpret to be the good of my people."

"I suppose the Germans didn't act this way?" Valerio sneered. "My orders are to execute these people in public."

"But we are Italians. We hate nazism and fascism because this is their way. I prohibit you from carrying out the sentence in Dongo."

Valerio brushed past him. A partisan came up to him and said, "Colonel, the man with the Spanish documents wants you to re-examine his papers. He claims that he is not Vittorio Mussolini. He says he is Marcello Petacci, and that he has nothing to do with the others." Valerio waved him off. Mayor Rubini immediately seated himself at his desk and began writing out his resignation as mayor, assigning to public opinion the task of judging the events that were about to take place.

Fifteen condemned fascists, meanwhile, were marched single file out of the building and straight across the square to a low stone wall that skirted the lake. As they passed Valerio, Captain Calistri tried to explain his case, but the latter cut him short. "Very well," the captain said, flipping away his cigarette, "if you want it that way, shoot me, too."

Lined up against the wall, the condemned men were ordered to about face. They executed the maneuver with precision. They faced Lake Como, the executioners at their backs, the sign of a dishonorable death. Valerio gave the orders quickly, as though he was afraid of some last minute interruption. As he did, blind Minister Barracu, holder of the gold medal of valor, Italy's highest military decoration, swung about and shouted, "I have the right to be shot here." He held a hand over his heart just as the guns went off.

Mayor Rubini was still writing when he heard the guns. He looked down at his watch. The time was 5:48 P.M. and he made note of it in his resignation.

Marcello Petacci was walked barefoot to the place of execution, but at the last minute he dived over the wall into Lake Como. Partisan gunfire riddled him in the water.

As underground soldiers went along the line of bodies firing single shots into their heads, guns went off from windows on the square. Mussolini's fascist republic had just gone out in a hail of lead. Captain Neri released Sforni from his cell and apologized for having found it necessary to take such forceful measures.

A truck was backed into the square and the bodies were loaded into it. Then it was driven to Giulino di Mezzegra, where it picked up the bodies of Mussolini and his mistress. It then hurried on to Milan, where the bodies of *il Duce* and his mistress were strung up by the heels as targets for an hysterical mob.

Valerio re-entered the shadows from which, if he had had his way, he would never again have emerged. Amazing as it may seem, not a single person in Dongo had ever seen him or even heard his name before he put in his appearance at two o'clock on that afternoon of April 28th.

And who was the mysterious Colonel Valerio? For years he was able to hide his true identity behind this cover name, but at last the truth came out. He is Walter Audisio, ex-bookkeeper in the Borsalino hat factory at Alessandria, now an honored member of the Senate representing the Communist Party.

Half of the fascist problem, as seen by the Communist Party leaders, had been solved by Valerio's machine pistol. The other half was still being collected and counted in a large room in the city hall. It amounted to a tidy forty million dollars. The partisans now had to decide what to do with it, and Count Bellini, Captain Neri, Gianna, Michele Moretti (the political commissar) and other members of the 52nd Garibaldi Brigade, the overwhelming majority of them members of the Communist Party, held a lengthy and sometimes heated discussion. The majority opinion was that the money should be turned over as a gift to the party. The brigade commander was not a card holder, although he sympathized with the party's aims, for he thought that they, too, were fighting for a free Italy. However, he held that the money should not be given to an individual group, but should go to the treasury of the new Italian state when it came into being. At one point several of the communist partisans, including Captain Neri, Gianna and Moretti, withdrew for a private talk. It was suggested that they pretend to go along with Count Bellini's idea now, but that when the car loaded with the treasures headed southward along the lake, it would be highjacked and those in it killed. In that way the party could take possession of the loot and nobody would be any the wiser, because the whole thing would be written off as an ordinary stickup and murder.

Only Captain Neri and Gianna were against the diabolical project. "The lives of two Garibaldini are worth more than ten times that treasure," Captain Neri said angrily.

An agreement was finally reached. The money would be given over for safe-keeping to the Reds and they, in turn, when the new government was formed, would have the honor of turning it over to the government. This is the exact wording of the resolution: "The high command of the 52nd Brigade, meeting in the persons of Commander Pedro [*nom de guerre* of Count Bellini] Chief of Staff Neri, and with the approval of the War Commissar for Como, feel that the only organization that interested itself in the heroic efforts of the Garibaldini was the Communist Party of Como. Thus interpreting the thoughts of all Garibaldini, and of the population in this area that helped our battle, we have decided to entrust this wealth to Communist Party headquarters in Como for safe-keeping."

A few days later a partisan chauffeur with the descriptive nickname "Carletto il Scassomacchina," which means "Charlie the Autowrecker," accompanied by Gianna and by the War Commissar, took the forty million dollars to Como. There it was delivered to Dante Gorreri, the regional communist boss. The day before Gianna had given Gorreri a large jewel case filled with diamonds and assorted precious stones, insisting that she receive a receipt for this as well as the treasure she was now delivering.

Gorreri was a dictatorial, Moscow-trained roughneck whose single dedicated idea was to build the Communist Party. Mussolini had imprisoned him for ten years, from 1926 to 1936, for subversive activity in his native Parma where he had worked as a plumber. This suffering only strengthened his determination. Anyone who stood between him and his goal, even a loyal comrade, became a hated enemy; anyone who helped, even the most rabid fascist, became a good friend. Gianna's insistence on a receipt made her an enemy. As a good party member she should understand that the resolution of the 52nd Garibaldi Brigade, if carried out literally, would be an act inimical to the interests of communism. It was only after a bitter quarrel, during which the girl stubbornly stood her ground, that Gorreri reluctantly signed the receipt.

Captain Neri followed up the visits of Gianna. He was going to make certain that the communist leader respected the dictates of the 52nd Brigade. At first Gorreri said that it was wiser to hold onto the forty million dollars and wait until they saw how stable the new national government would be. Then, when he ran out of excuses, he said flatly that the party would never give it up and anyone who thought differently could very easily get hurt.

The partisan fighter accused Gorreri of being the iron fist of Russia, instead of an Italian patriot, while Gorreri countered by calling Neri a traitor to the cause and a fascist spy. A clerk in Gorreri's office heard snatches of a violent argument between them. She was later called in by the leader and threatened with instant death if she ever repeated what had taken place.

A few days after this argument, Count Bellini overheard Dionisio Gambaruto, chief of the People's Police in Como, say that he had been ordered to execute Captain Neri, but that he was waiting for instructions from Gorreri in writing before he would do it. These provisional police organizations had been established in towns throughout northern Italy by the communists, and their authority was backed up by the Anglo-American military government in what can only be explained as the sheer political ignorance of our occupying forces.

Late in the afternoon of May 7th, Captain Neri walked into party headquarters in Como. It was dark when he came out and got into a car of the People's Police with Gambaruto and a partisan known as Nado. From that moment Captain Neri disappeared without a trace. Gambaruto and Nado, both under indictment for his murder, have fled behind the iron curtain. The exact whereabouts of the former is unknown, but Nado is working as a mechanic in Warsaw.

It was many days before Gianna learned that her sweetheart was missing, but when she did, she dropped everything and threw herself into the single job of finding him. Gorreri first told her that Captain Neri was off on a secret mission. Another party comrade said that he had evidently tired of her, and had taken off for parts unknown. But friends, and she had many, told her that he was dead, that it had been done for the good of the party, and that if she valued her own safety, she would stop her search at once. Gianna knew that if Neri was indeed dead, he had been put out of the way because of his firm stand on the Dongo treasure; she knew, too, that the same menace also hung over her. But it didn't stop her. She got confirmation of his death from Pietro Verbani, communist leader in Milan. At first Verbani had tried to put her off, but when she created a scene in his office, he shouted that Neri had been executed as a traitor. "And if you don't keep your mouth shut you'll meet the same end he did."

Disillusioned and heartsick, the girl sat down and wrote a letter to Vincenza Coen, a faithful friend who had shared a cell with her in a fascist prison.

Dearest Vincenzina,

I don't know how I will ever finish this letter because I am not fully certain of my mental faculties. First the fascists and now my comrades, the men who guide my party, the party for which I lived, have reduced me to this state. They have stripped me of my honor. They have even taken the person who is most dear to me, a person for whom I would voluntarily give my own life. I don't think that I will be able to bear this much longer. Even when one is very strong, as I was in the past, certain blows struck against our dignity and against our ideals make the burden impossible. To see your own companion die like a vile person, when you know that he has lived for a pure ideal, makes me so depressed I can only look for death. Living I can only suffer, seeing the men who represent our party, men who should be pure in spirit, act, instead, like the fascists—even worse. . . . I have been prohibited from going to Como again at the risk of giving up my own skin.

On June 23rd, six weeks after Captain Neri's disappearance, Gianna was still continuing her own investigation along the lake. Friends told her to visit the commissar of the People's Police at his headquarters in Como for a message of interest to her. She did. Here she was told that if she would meet with him later in the evening, she would be taken to her lover's body. She reported this to her friend, Annamaria Bianchi, a typist at party headquarters, before going off to keep the appointment. That night she climbed onto a red Guzzi motorcycle, a partisan driver in front of her and a second man behind. At Pizzo di Cernobbio, a young married couple named Della Torre were necking in the shadows when they saw the motorcycle stop alongside the stone wall that skirts the lake. Two men and a woman walked down to a small, hidden landing. There was a sudden scream of terror from the woman and the sharp crack of gunfire, followed by the sound of a falling body. The two men returned unhurriedly to their cycle and drove off in the night. *Signor* Della Torre raced down to the landing. All he found was a newspaper covered with blood. There was no sign of the woman.

The matter was referred to the police, but during this era the only police were those of the Communist Party, while in Rome, sitting as head of the Department of Justice in the first free Italian government, was Palmiro Togliatti, secretary general of the Communist Party. The police made no effort to search for the body until more than a year had passed. It has never been found.

The murder of Gianna solved one problem, but it created another one. There was still Annamaria Bianchi, the chubby, man-crazy kid who would sneak off from her job as typist for a swim or a dance or even a late date in a bar, all of which were decadent democratic time-wasters. For this she was often scolded. But her capital offense was that she knew what had happened to Gianna.

She was dispatched with even more ease than her friend. She had bicycled to the office of the People's Police at their invitation, and she was seen leaving after dark with two cops in a *topolino*. Later that night her body, horribly mutilated, the fingertips of both hands rubbed away to the bone, was found on the shore of Lake Como at Acquaseria.

Sometime later a communist official named Dante Cerutti reported what had happened at headquarters: "Gorreri sent Nado and Negri to put her out of the way," he said. "A third person was supposed to go along, too, but something came up and he couldn't. Gorreri was very mad. 'Stupid one,' I remember him saying, 'thank the heavens if one day you don't pay for it.' I was still there when the pair came back and told Gorreri how they made out, adding that they were a bit apprehensive because they didn't hear any splash when they tossed the body into the lake. Gorreri said, 'These things are either done well or not done at all. One shot in the head and another in the stomach. That way water is sucked in and the body goes down fast. Get back there right away.' When the men returned they found that Annamaria Bianchi's body had fallen between two rocks. But before they could do anything about it other people had arrived."

The car in which the victim was taken for her last ride belonged to the assistant chief of the People's Police. The latter complained that the back seat was dirtied with blood and brain tissue and that if the homicide squad couldn't exert a little care, he would never lend them his vehicle again. It was a most unusual period in Italy's history. This particular homicide squad didn't solve a single murder, but the number they committed ran to well over a hundred.

I saw this assistant police chief recently in a courtroom in

Padua, sitting in the dock, his hands bound by heavy chains. He had been sentenced to serve a twenty-four-year prison term for a simple armed robbery, a crime that had nothing to do with his political principles.

By a strange error in timing the bicycle on which Annamaria Bianchi had ridden to police headquarters and her party membership card were returned to her family before her body was found. Annamaria's father, Michele, up to that moment a good communist, knew generally where the responsibility for his daughter's death lay. He strapped a gun to his side and went to Acquaseria along the lake. Standing near her body, he swore an oath of vengeance. "If the dead won't talk then the living will talk for them," he said, tapping his gun meaningfully. Five days later he, too, was killed and his body dumped into the lake.

Gorreri paid for the coffin, sent red hammer-and-sickle banners and a brass band for the funeral parade. He thought of everything; funeral, flowers, music—and the bullet in the head.

In trying to cover the traces of the Dongo treasure the communists had committed many murders, but Count Bellini still lived, and he was now regarded as the gravest menace to their security. Naturally the count was unhappy over the fact that the communists hadn't passed the treasure on to the government. When Gorreri informed him that it had, in fact, been turned over to higher authorities and that regular receipts had been issued, he was momentarily reassured. He later learned, however, that "higher authority" meant central headquarters of the party, not the nation's treasury.

A meeting was called at the Hotel Turismo in Gravedona, exactly one month after Mussolini's execution. To avoid a scandal each participant swore a solemn oath never to reveal what took place. Using this forum, Count Bellini loudly opposed the retention of the funds by the communists. In this he was alone, because the other members of their 52nd Garibaldi Brigade followed the line of their political superiors instead of their military ones. He was taken aside and told by a well-meaning friend that no matter what happened the funds would remain with the party, and he had better accept this if he knew what was good for him.

Walking in the piazza after the meeting, he was surrounded by his ex-pals, who reviled him with the names of fascist spy and traitor. At one point he answered sharply. A partisan whipped out a revolver and aimed it at his heart. Bellini lunged at the man just as he squeezed the trigger, and the bullet spent itself harmlessly in the air.

After he had retired for the night in the Hotel Turismo, someone threw a pebble at his window and called out his name. Being an old hand at guerrilla in-fighting, he climbed quietly out of bed and flattened himself on the floor. Keeping low, he crawled to the window, gingerly raised an arm and tapped quickly on the glass. A burst of machine gun fire sliced across the room.

For months Count Bellini carried on the fight against the communists almost single-handedly. Finally, realizing that he could get no one to listen to him, and in the certitude that the homicide squad of the People's Police would not rest until they had put him out of the way, on October 30, 1945, he wrote a final testament that was supposed to have been opened only after his death. However, he made it public at a later trial at which he was a principal witness. "I have decided only now to write what follows because I have the impression, confirmed by facts, that it is important to seal my lips in order to get rid of a witness who is very dangerous to the Communist Party," he wrote. "Since I had given my word of honor not to reveal what took place that night [at the Hotel Turismo meeting] I am taking this means of insuring that the knowledge of it will get out in the event I am killed." There followed a recital of many of the events that have been set forth here.

After Togliatti ceased to be minister of justice, the new minister and the chief of staff of the army began independent investigations in an effort to trace the Dongo treasure. The finger pointed squarely at Gorreri. The provincial leader, however, had been elected to the lower house of Parliament and thus was immune from arrest. In 1949, when he was not re-elected, he was arrested and imprisoned. He remained behind bars for more than four years awaiting trial. In the elections of June 1953 the communists put Gorreri at the top of their list. This is an electoral nicety in Italy's system of proportional representation that permits a party to elect one of its candidates even if he gets no votes. He was re-elected, regained his parliamentary immunity and was freed.

He was again re-elected in 1958, and his term of office expired with the new national elections of 1963. Once more he was placed high on the list and returned to Parliament. Today he is free, a high-ranking member of Congress and an object lesson on how to attain eminent respectability through murder.

The Communist Party has made three official explanations about the Dongo treasure. The first was that it was a matter of interest only to the partisans and that, therefore, there was no reason to discuss it. The second was that the entire story of the treasure was fiction; it just never existed. And the third, which is their current defense, is that it did exist, but that all of it was distributed to the partisan units as payment for their services.

Chapter 5

A Nightmare Called Dachau

In THE FIRST DAYS of spring, 1944, while the Communist Party made its plans for the final solution of the fascist problem, I took off for the German front. My editors in New York requested permission for the change, which was transmitted to SHAEF in Paris, who in turn transmitted their consent to Rome from whence it was relayed to me on the shifting Italian front, now spilling rapidly over the Po River plains north of Bologna.

As soon as approval arrived, I drove the shell-pocked road to Rome and picked up eleven copies of my newly cut orders. Early the next morning, a duffel bag slung over my shoulder, I was at bombed-out Ciampino airport. I used what charm I possessed to get an operations officer to fit me into the first C-47 flying to Marseilles, then hitched another plane ride from there to Paris. After a half day of red tape, I drove off to Heidelberg, headquarters for the 12th Army group, where, somewhat exhausted but finally ready to go to work, I checked in with the public relations officer.

The two stories on which I intended to concentrate were the liberation of the concentration camp at Dachau and the battle for the southern redoubt in the Bavarian Alps, where die-hard nazis had sworn to hold out to the last man. The winning of this final battle would mean the end of the war in Europe without the necessity of a formal treaty. The situation map showed that the fall of Dachau was imminent, even though our troops were still many miles away.

I sped my jeep over bombed roads, through towns that were completely destroyed and others that were strangely untouched. In the latter white flags fluttered from every window. At Augsburg I caught up with advance headquarters of the 7th Army and again was briefed on the up-to-the-minute situation.

This was a precaution I had learned the hard way, having once whizzed down a surprisingly quiet road that appeared to be well within our own lines and run head-on into a squad of Germans who, as surprised as I was, permitted me to outrun the few desultory bullets that followed my hasty retreat.

I now sped swiftly down the *autobahn*, the super highway that Hitler had built from border to border. It was a modern, concrete, four-lane highway with a wide center strip. On the hills this strip was lush with trees and foliage, but on the flat it was paved in concrete and painted a mottled green. Our intelligence service didn't learn till later that this highway had also served as an ingenious airstrip for German fighter planes.

I made excellent time on good stretches of road, but at several blown-out spans I had to crawl in four-wheel drive along the tortuous trails of the by-pass, down muddy tracks, through swollen streams and up again to rejoin the *autobahn*.

At nightfall I drove off the road at the small hamlet of Furstenfeldbruck, which showed no signs of life even though lightning flashes of artillery fire lit the skies in dozens of points to the south.

The countryside was alive with the rumble and clanging of war machines in movement. The American army poured over the land in organized confusion, like streams of quicksilver that flowed around points of resistance and moved steadily southward. There were no front lines in this relentless thrust; the enemy might take a pot-shot at you thirty miles behind the forward troops.

I parked my jeep in front of a neat chalet and pounded on the door. There was no reply. I lifted the hood of the jeep, pulled out the distributor to prevent the car from being stolen, broke a window in the house and crawled inside. I ate a K-ration dinner and, exhausted by the arduous trip, climbed into an upstairs bed fully clothed. As a precaution I kept a loaded .45 automatic under the pillow and my helmet perched precariously over the door-knob, so that any movement would send it clattering to the floor.

I awoke at dawn to find the hamlet still deserted, though white strips of cloth fluttered from windows in a sign of surrender. I replaced the distributor, closed the hood and spread a road map over it. It was only eight kilometers to the Amper River crossing. From there a good secondary road paralleled the river bed another seven kilometers to the town of Dachau. I put the automatic back into the glove compartment and, munching on a K-ration fruit bar breakfast, set out for the *autobahn*.

Though it was spring, snow still dotted the landscape, and the air was cold and damp. Military traffic moved bumper to bumper. Everything on wheels was moving forward in a tremendous surge. For three days the 7th Army had been held up at the banks of the Danube at Ulm. Then the 44th Infantry and 10th Armored Divisions broke through, and organized resistance virtually came to an end.

I swung off from the main line of traffic and followed the Amper River to Dachau. The well-kept fields, the beautiful forests and the meandering stream made a peaceful scene. At the entrance to the town there was a long row of single dwellings, each with a well-tended lawn. Parallel to it was a railway siding that ended at the concentration camp. On the siding stood a long freight train, but even before I reached it I knew that this was no ordinary train. A dozen bodies, all face down, stretched along the right of way. There were about a score of freight cars, some of steel and some of wood, some boxcars and some flatcars. Some bore the emblem "FS Italia" for the Italian state railways, "DR" for the Deutsche Reichsbahn and "CDF" for the French state railways.

The boxcars were marked with the six-pointed Star of David. The doors had already been opened, and I looked in at the incredibly emaciated, horribly contorted corpses that covered the straw and filth-littered floor. These were prisoners, mainly Polish Jews, who had been transported from the concentration camp at Flosenburg. They had died of hunger. The weaker ones had fallen first, those who had resisted a little longer had fallen on top of them and still a third strata lay on top of the second. They hadn't even been given room to die decently.

Around the doors stood a group of tired infantrymen wearing the red eagle patch of the 45th Division, veteran fighters for whom death and destruction were commonplace. They stood dumbstruck, jaws gaping in horror.

At the end of the siding was the gateway to the camp; over it a sign said "Konzentrationslager Dachau." Inside the gate thousands of prisoners, wearing striped suits and striped berets, were milling about in the yard. They were incredibly gaunt, with eyes so sunken and cheeks so tautly stretched that they looked like walking dead.

One prisoner, better fed and clothed, attached himself to me and served as my interpreter. He told me that before the SS picked him up in Yugoslavia he had been fire chief of Zagreb. "Notice the barracks along the main road," he said. "You won't believe what you will see in there." On the left side the barracks bore even numbers from B2 through B16; on the right were the odd numbers running from A1 through A15. Each building housed 2000 prisoners.

I drove the jeep to the first clapboard and tarpaper barrack, alighted and entered. The bunks were in triple tiers so close together that a person had to climb in from the foot. Many of the beds were still filled with people who were too feeble to move.

Many had typhus and almost all suffered from diarrhea. Hundreds of eyes gleamed in the weak light, registering neither joy nor sorrow but only the blank stare of a people beyond caring. I stayed in the barrack as long as I could, a handkerchief over my nose, until the putrid odor forced me out into the open again.

The reason for my interpreter's well-being, I discovered, was that he was in charge of the important prisoner detail that worked the crematorium. We went down the far end of the road to a low, long, neat one-story brick building with a new red tile roof out of which jutted an enormous chimney. There was an open porch at one end. Attached to hooks driven into the wall were thousands of garments. The sign over the entrance read, simply, "Building 243." Inside, six ovens were going full blast. Over them was a drawing of two headless SS men astride a pair of bloated pigs. Painted over the drawing were the words: *"Reinlichkeit ist hier pflicht deshalb; hände waschen nicht vergessen."* (Cleanliness is an order. Don't forget to wash your hands.)

"Let me show you how it works," my guide said matter-of-factly.

He opened the door at the right end of the furnace room. Inside, more than a thousand bodies were stacked carelessly, like logs in a storeroom. The bodies were so emaciated they seemed no thicker than my arm. It was amazing how little space they occupied. With a pair of heavy tongs, very much like those used by the old-fashioned iceman except that these ended in knobs and not in points, he expertly hooked the back of the head of a corpse and dragged it across the floor. He returned for a second one and then lifted both into a steel cradle, which he pushed into the roaring furnace. This operation consumed less than a minute.

"We work two twelve-hour shifts here and we go right around the clock. It takes fifteen minutes for two bodies to burn completely at one time, and with all six furnaces going, we can only manage to burn about five hundred a day."

The sickening smell of burning human flesh filled the furnace room.

Coming out into the open again, I saw a group of some thirty Deathshead SS guards who had surrendered leaving the administration building. A few soldiers led them to a moat and ordered them to line up. As they stood stiffly at attention, the Americans fired a short burst from their semi-automatics. The force of the impact toppled the guards into the moat where they lay, submerged in the water, for several days before being carted away.

A supply colonel from another sector hurried over to a major and told him that what had been done by the soldiers was contrary to the rules of war. The major, whose haggard face showed how much time he had spent in the line, wearily agreed with him. "I couldn't stop my men," he said.

"Is that all you have to say?" the colonel shouted.

"That's right."

"I'll have you court-martialed for this," the colonel said angrily.

"Colonel, I don't care about your court-martial," the major said in a still weary voice. "Just get out of my sector and stop interfering with my men."

At the pottery factory, where Jewish prisoners had manufactured noble busts of Hitler and sets of crockery that bore family greetings from Heinrich Himmler, I found two SS guards hiding. They wore the coarse, gray-green uniform, the heavily hobnailed jackboots and the distinctive skull and crossbones emblem on their caps.

I ordered them onto the back seat of the jeep, called over Gene Kammerman,* cameraman for *Yank* Magazine, and told the interpreter to seat himself on the hood of the jeep. My idea was to take my two prisoners to the administration building and interrogate them. During the short drive I asked how anyone could treat human beings as these people had been treated, and I pointed to the walking skeletons in the main compound. It took a minute for the meaning of my question to sink in, not because they didn't

---

* As this was written, I noted a news item reporting that Gene Kammerman, European photographer for *The Saturday Evening Post*, was killed in an auto accident in England.

understand the words, but because I had referred to the tragic mass as "people," members of the same human race as they were. Their reaction gave me a glimpse into the inner soul of the Deathshead SS. No large group of people in a civilized land can be compelled to carry out such inhuman tasks. It becomes comprehensible only if they are educated to think of the victims as animals that have been shipped to the slaughterhouse.

As I drove slowly through the crowd, several hundred prisoners formed around the jeep, pointing their fingers at the SS guards and gesticulating wildly. I halted the car. I could gather from their attitude that these were a pair of particularly bad ones. My interpreter said that one of them had playfully pushed a Jew into a concrete mixer, and that the body was now part of a road bed. Both of these guards were particularly sports-minded. Instead of racing cockroaches, they immersed Jews and captured Russian soldiers in ice cold water in the dead of winter and placed bets on who would die last. Because the Jews were weaker, they figured out a handicap system to even up the odds.

By this time, the mob had completely encircled my jeep. It is likely that if I had raised my voice and ordered them to disperse they would have done so, but I looked into their tortured faces and did nothing. I folded my arms and looked away. A few of the more aggressive prisoners began punching the guards. Then a dozen arms reached up and dragged both of them to the ground. One man had the butt end of a broken rifle, which he swung with all his might. It hit one of the guards along the side of the chin with such force that I saw the head go lopsided, like a baseball caught at the moment of impact by a high-speed camera. He was killed instantly. The second guard was beaten mercilessly. Twenty-four hours later I saw him stretched out in the same spot, still twitching. On the second day the body was still.

I have always been sensitive to the pain in others, even in animals. I have witnessed the executions of some of the worst types of humans and felt sorry for them. But at that moment I

was completely dry of emotion. Even now, looking back, I feel
not the slightest remorse.

In the administration building I found a well-fed pair of Jewish
clerks who satisfied the German passion for keeping files orderly.
They showed me the records of the 31,601 prisoners still alive by
yesterday's count.

They were cross-indexed by nationality. There were Poles,
Russians, French, Slovenes, Italians, Czechs, Belgians, Americans,
Hungarians, Dutch, Austrians, Greeks, Spaniards, Luxemburgers,
Iranians, Croats, Norwegians, Serbs, Rumanians, Slovaks, Lithu-
anians, Albanians, Letts, Armenians, Swiss, Arabs, Danes, Iraqi,
Maltese and Finns.

One of the clerks wrote his name out for me, Edmond Palewod-
zinski. He was a Pole who had worked in the records office for
five years. He told me that conditions had not always been this
bad at the concentration camp. There had been a period when
SS Obersturmbannführer Martin Weiss was in command. He had
permitted the prisoners to receive packages, organize their own
entertainment, including a full band, and correspond with the
outside world.

Under the Weiss regime prisoners had also died in awesome
numbers, but the rate had been somewhat slower and the outward signs of brutality were missing. He lasted less than a year.
After him came such bad ones as Oberführer Lauritz, who issued
the order that any SS man who killed a Jew was to be rewarded
with a forty-eight-hour pass and a pack of cigarettes. He ordered
the punishment of twenty-five lashes on the bare back for prisoners caught smoking at work. Also, those who committed minor
infractions not punishable by death were treated to refined bits
of torture. The prisoners had their hands tied behind their backs,
with the backs of the hands together, and were then hauled up
toward the ceiling, just high enough so that the tips of their toes
touched the floor. As the bodies sagged lower, a tuck was taken
in the ropes. It was an unbearable torture that maimed and killed.

The head of the crematorium detail was an Oberscharführer

Pongratz. "We had a French general named Charles Delestraint, who had fought in the underground before he was taken prisoner," the clerk said. "Just a few days ago Pongratz called him and informed him that, since the American forces would be at the camp any day now, he was being freed. Delestraint very happily said goodby to everyone. As he walked in front of the crematorium, Pongratz pulled out a revolver and fired two shots into the general's head. He snapped his fingers and ordered the prisoners on crematorium detail to throw the body into the furnace."

The clerk, as he spoke, pulled out a registration card for me to read: "Charles Delestraint, 103027 SCH Frz, born Biache, March 12, 1899. Brought to Dachau September 6, 1944, from concentration camp at Natzweiler." This was followed by the sign ✠, signifying death, and the date: 19 April 1945.

The clerks said they had been particularly incensed with Sturmbannführer Piorkowski, a loud, obscene East German who was responsible for a nicety in mass execution called the invalid transport. One of them flipped out at random a small card about three-and-a-half by two-and-a-half inches and I read: "Ludwig Adamzewski, born May 19, 1908, prison number 25503 SCH, laborer, home residence Stuttgartstrasse 28, Litzmannstadt, brought to Dachau from Mauthausen, 21 May 1941, and sent out on the invalid transport 28 May 1942."

Adamzewski and the tens of thousands of other "invalids" who were "transported" never traveled further from their barracks than the crematorium, but, because the Germans had to keep precise records, this was registered as the invalid transport. It was Piorkowski, also, who initiated the system whereby ten insane prisoners were put to death each month. Never less, never more. He had no need of a psychiatrist to certify the victims as insane. He could do it with a glance. One of the prisoners who had been a clerk in a tobacco store in Brussels acted as an infirmary attendant and injected victims with a deadly drug. The Deathshead SS guards never needed force to drag the victims to their appointment with death. Although they knew what was about to happen to them, they stood docilely in line awaiting their turn. They took off their jackets without protest and stared ahead unseeingly as the injections were made. Very quietly and without fuss they lay down to die. The concentration camp had so thoroughly dehumanized them that the final act of death was meaningless.

Oberscharführer Bach and Obersturmführer Ruppert condemned men to the lash and to a torture called "the bench" for such offenses as smiling, or for looking too well-fed, while Hauptscharführer Eichberger, who was head of Department III, condemned them to death for even less. In the table of organization of Dachau, Department I was in charge of SS personnel; Department II, political section; Department III, prisoners; Department IV, administration and food; Department V, transport. It was Eichberger who took a group of ninety-seven Russian officers, divided them roughly into five groups, led them to the courtyard in the rear of the crematorium and shot them all. The reason? "We never heard what the reason might have been," the clerk said. "It might have been a report of a Russian victory at the front, or an atrocity story, or a radio speech from Himmler or Goering. Or it might have been for no reason at all."

Dachau was opened for use in 1933 for political prisoners. In 1939 it was closed down, but with the start of the war it was reopened. In the following brief years, 228,000 prisoners passed through it. Of the 30,000 survivors, 9,000 required hospitalization. For many of these, liberation had come too late.

A specific assignment from my editors had been to find Pastor Martin Niemöller and, if possible, to get his exclusive by-lined story. The pastor had been a leading minister of the Evangelical church of Hesse, Germany. He had early seen the menace of Hitler to his own church specifically and to religion and the rest of the world generally, and from his pulpit he had spoken out with an eloquence that fired the imagination of people around the world. He personified, in Germany, the physical struggle against Hitler. I was one of those strongly attracted by the drama, and I remembered watching with a breathless interest his week-to-week defiance of the nazi bullies. Exasperated, the Führer personally gave the order that he be locked up in the concentration camp at Dachau. The year was 1933.

I asked the clerk to pull out the file on Niemöller so that I might see in which barracks he was confined; that is, if he were still alive.

"He's still alive, all right," the clerk told me, "but he was taken out of camp last week."

"Who took him out?"

"Some of the SS officers."

"Do you know why?"

"They collected the most important prisoners when they fled so as to have human hostages in making a deal for their own freedom."

"Do you know where they went?"

"Oh, yes. We keep records as carefully as a bank." He went through a filing cabinet, drew out a carbon copy of an order and handed it to me. On it was written the following:

Konzentrationslager Dachau
Arbeitseinsatz

Dachau, den 25.4.1945

Dem SS-Sonderlager Innsbruck zugewiesen:

Mannlich	Sch-Engl.	140926		KA
Piquet Gabriel	Sch-Frz	103001	24.2.87	KA
Kunkel Karl	Sch-Dr	146200	8.11.13	KA
Tamburini Tullio	Sch-Itl	146201	22.4.92	KA
Apollonio Eugenio	Sch-Itl	146199	13.8.03	KA
Burda Josef	Sch-T	48109	20.12.93	KA
Van Dijk Johannes	Sch-Holl	67182	1.12.21	KA
Ferrero Davide	Sch-Itl	69807	21.10.10	KA
Fuchs Richard	Sch-Dr	28848	9.4.93	KA
Neuhauser Johann	Sch-Dr	26680	27.1.88	KA
Niemöller Martin	Sch-Dr	26679	14.1.92	KA
Popovic Novak	Sch-Serbe	50288	31.10.98	KA
Roscecac-Rys Josef	Sch-T	48111	1.11.01	KA
Tomalewski Dimitrije	Sch-Jug	66436	24.9.91	KA
Zamoyski Alexander	Sch-Pole	28835	19.6.98	KA

Cerini Fritz	Sch-Dr	116473	25.11.95	Potsdam
Joos Josef	Sch-Dr	26800	13.11.78	Winzenheim-Els
Praxmarer Konrad	Sch-Dr	136838	16.9.95	Gottschee
Freuben Leopold	Sch-Dr	116474	27.8.95	Kl. Glienniche
Prince de Bourbon	Sch-Frz	101057	26.5.89	Camaiore
Schmitz Richard Karl	Sch-Dr	928	14.12.85	Wien
Garibaldi Sante	Sch-Itl	99296	16.10.85	Rom

(ist als Kalfakteur Einzusetzen)

Ubergeben: SS Oberscharführer und
              Arbeitseinsatsführer.   Ubernommen:

On April 25, 1944, the twenty-two prisoners on this august list,
identified by nationality, prison number, date of birth and place
from which they had come to Dachau, were ordered transferred
to the SS special camp at Innsbruck, where they were to be received as workers. The receipt was signed by the SS troop commander and leader of the work detachment.

As I walked out of the administration building, teams of soldiers
were trying to maintain some sort of order among the milling
masses of prisoners. Kitchen details working with medical teams
had established a rigid diet that would gradually increase the
survivors' food so they wouldn't die from over-eating.

On the morning of the third day I left Dachau. I had been away
from Rome only five days, yet I had moved so fast and seen so
much that it felt like forty. Munich had already fallen after a brief
fight. Resistance was crumbling quickly before troops who went
in with high élan, knocking over banks and camera shops as
though they were major military targets. The city appeared totally
destroyed. The rubble of tall buildings that had collapsed blocked
most of the streets. Bulldozers had cut a path through a few of
them. Those buildings that still stood looked ghostly and unreal,
their insides burned out by the tens of thousands of fire bombs
that had rained down on them. In some places block after block
of empty brick shells still stood, their fronts smoke-blackened and
shell-scarred.

As I sped southward toward the distant line of the Alps, it was obvious that the war would end in a matter of days. The only resistance came from isolated units, generally SS divisions, who still fought on.

Late in the afternoon I arrived at Innsbruck, deep in the heart of the Tyrolean Alps. The gingerbread houses of the lovely city had been badly damaged and the streets were littered with rubble and wrecked German vehicles. Because it was an important rail center at the north end of the Brenner Pass, as well as the advertised capital of the formidable southern redoubt into which the SS were going to withdraw and resist to the last man, it had taken an intense plastering from the air force.

From high on the eastern slope of the Hungerberg, where I found quarters, the scene below was still one of great beauty, with no visible scars of war. The towering, white-peaked mountains were separated by the broad, lush valley of the sparkling Inn River. It seemed incredible that a people so blessed by the Creator with talent and energy and a land of unmatched richness and beauty could store so much hate in their hearts. For this was a people most deeply attached to the nazi creed whose rabid anti-Semitism was more than just a political slogan. Hitler is gone, Innsbruck, returned to Austria, has been rebuilt, stone by loving stone, into its former beauty, but the roots of the nazi spirit, like a cancerous growth, still spread beyond the confines of the lunatic fringe of the city. Today it is a center of neo-nazi anti-Semitism. It is also the center out of which come the armed terrorists who operate in the Alto Adige section of northern Italy, where they are using plastic dynamite and machine guns to "liberate" the Austrians living here. From personal experience I can say that never has a minority people had it so good, both in political freedom and economic well-being. However, the fact that many of this minority do not want to be "liberated" doesn't deter the plastic bombers.

The commanding general in this zone was Major General

Anthony McAuliffe, who led the 103rd Infantry Division. He was
a peppery bantam of a man with a great gift for simple, direct
expression—a born leader of soldiers. His troops loved him and
followed him, even when the going looked hopeless. At Bastogne,
with his 101st Airborne Division completely surrounded, the
German commander had asked for his surrender. Tony McAuliffe
characteristically answered "Nuts," and fought on in what is regarded as one of the most thrilling chapters in American bravery.
He not only stalled the Wehrmacht's offensive, but within a week
actually captured the general who had asked for his surrender.

My seven-thousand-word article about this battle had been
mailed to him by his wife, and it had pleased him so much that
he had telephoned the press camp several times asking for me.
A war correspondent found his job much easier when he was
persona grata with the higher brass.

As soon as I was billeted, I sought out General McAuliffe and
asked him about the prisoners who had been moved from Dachau
to the concentration camp in Innsbruck.

"They were taken off by the SS before we got here," he told me.

"Do you know where?"

"My G-2 tells me that they are being held in a summer resort
hotel at Lago di Brais on the Italian side of the Dolomite Alps."

"Do you have anything down there?"

"No, that's out of my sector. I've got my men down as far as
Brennero, where we've been ordered to hold until units of the 5th
Army make contact. That should be in a day or so."

My intention was to get down there at once in order to beat the
war correspondents coming up from the south. Because Lago di
Brais was in 5th Army territory, I was faced with a serious prob-
lem. To be strictly legal about the matter meant returning to
Heidelberg, having new orders cut reassigning me to the 5th
Army, driving off to Paris, then flying to Marseilles and back to
Rome. From Rome, with luck, I could hitch a plane ride to Flor-
ence and then, if I was successful in scrounging motor transport,

arrive in Lago di Brais, which was less than fifty miles away from where I now stood, in about five days.

I was concerned with the legalities of the trip but I was even more concerned with the possibility that I might run into fighting Germans on the other side of the pass. Early the next morning I made arrangements for a car in General McAuliffe's motor pool and set out for the Brenner Pass.

The countryside was beginning to come alive. The collapse of the German military apparatus left units leaderless, and hundreds of thousands of soldiers, especially from the Eastern front, were fleeing westward in order to escape capture by the Russian Army. The doors of concentration and work camps were opened, and the forced laborers and prisoners found themselves without guards. Overnight their status changed from prisoners to displaced persons. There were four million of them in this area alone. Most were herded docilely back into repatriation camps, but one-and-a-half million of them, mainly Russians and Poles, headed eastward on their own. They were a motley crowd, the old women, bent with age and suffering, carrying large packs of household goods on their backs, the men struggling with bulging knapsacks and valises. Some rode in ancient trucks held together with baling wire, the vans groaning under the weight of people and goods.

In time they grew like a plague of locusts on the land, robbing, ravishing and murdering as they moved. These were people who had suffered every sort of indignity and torture that human cruelty could devise, and now they were repaying in kind. The German people were truly reaping a harvest of hate.

As I drove up the long, serpentine incline toward the Brenner Pass, a half-dozen German soldiers jumped in front of my car, and I had to slam on the brakes to keep from hitting them. One of them, dressed in a neat gray-green uniform, wearing a pistol hooked to his belt, announced in correct English that he was a captain in the medical corps and that he and his unit wished to surrender.

"How is it that a medical officer is armed?" I asked.

"Our regulations permit us to have a side-arm with only two shells."

"Let me have the gun." He handed it over. I stuck it in my pocket and put the jeep in motion.

"How about us?" the captain asked anxiously.

"You may officially consider yourself a prisoner of war," I shouted back.

The green valley of the Inn River grew narrower the higher I climbed and finally was lost from sight when I reached the timber line. The road snaked upward, and each sharp turn revealed views of awe-inspiring splendor. The straight, narrow street in the town of Brennero at the peak of the pass was covered with snow. Midway through the town stood an untended gate that marked the boundary between Germany and Italy. More important for me at the moment was the fact that it also marked the boundary between the 12th Army group, operating in southern Germany, to which I was currently accredited, and the 5th Army, which I had left just a short time before and which operated in Italy. To cross the line without military orders was considered an offense equal in gravity to entering the United States without a passport. My only document was a trip ticket for the jeep, signed by the motor pool officer of the 103rd Infantry Division.

As I skidded down the sharper descent on the Italian side of the pass, the mountains fell back from the road and the Isarco valley broadened. There was no traffic of any sort, nor were there any people about. A unit of McAuliffe's men had halted in Brennero, but the 5th Army, coming up northward through Italy, was still a day's travel away.

As an avid reader of world-war literature, I had been particularly moved by the story, in *All Quiet on the Western Front,* of the soldier who miraculously survived four awful years only to be killed the day peace was declared. It was a chilly recollection that stayed with me as I drove. At a fork in the road at Vipiteno, a lovely Alpine village, I slowed down, trying to remember whether I was to turn left or right. Tentatively, I tried the left fork. Almost immediately I ran head-on into the headquarters of a German military unit. A pair of burly sentries stood guard under a sign that read: "527th Flack Company SS."

The breath went out of me like a collapsed accordion while my mind raced for an answer to this predicament. In the space of seconds I examined the various courses of action. Should I run for it? And if so, where, since I was lost? Or should I walk? I decided to walk.

Without altering my speed I drove into the entrance of the SS camp, halted, stood up in the jeep. The sentries presented arms and I saluted them. In a minute an SS lieutenant came up to me and we saluted each other.

In the most fluent Yiddish I could muster I asked, "Which is the road to Dobbiaco?"

"This is the one," he replied politely.

"Are there any American units there?"

"A few troops arrived there this morning."

"And where is Lago de Brais?"

He took my map and explained the landmarks. I was to follow the left fork for twelve kilometers to a bridge that led through woods. If I followed that road up a hill I would be at the lake. On the other hand, if I wanted to go to Dobbiaco I needed only to follow this main road and I would run right into the town.

I thanked him for his courtesy, threw him a salute and received one in return, sat down behind the wheel and slowly drove off in the direction he had indicated.

I found the turnoff for Lago de Brais, crossed the racing stream and drove slowly through thick woods along a dirt road that climbed steeply up a hill to the lake on the mountain top. In front of a fieldstone hotel that was meant to resemble a chalet, I saw a few American soldiers and about a hundred men, women and children from a dozen lands. They were the Gestapo's richest

human booty, a prize they had jealously guarded in the belief that
it would insure their own salvation.

When the American troops had appeared a few hours earlier,
an SS officer, carrying a white flag, approached the commanding
officer. He wanted to know what concessions would be made to
the Deathshead guards if they turned over their prisoners unharmed.

He was told that no concessions at all would be made, but that
the guards could consider themselves prisoners of war of the
American forces and would be treated according to the rules of
the Geneva Convention.

"We will not be turned over to the Russians?" the SS man asked.

"No, you will be prisoners of the United States Army," he was
told, and with that the SS surrendered.

As I walked into the hotel, a man whose face I recognized from
countless photographs came forward to greet me. He was slim,
of medium height, dressed in a white shirt and a heavy Tyrolean
jacket. He was smoking a pipe that a soldier had given him. His
face broke into a happy smile as he shook my hand.

"I have waited many long years for this moment," Martin
Niemöller said.

"We worried about your safety."

"My heart is very full. Tell my friends that I am safe."

As he spoke about the dramatic days preceding his arrest, a
lieutenant came up and said that I was not to speak to Niemöller.

"Why not?" I asked.

"Because these are direct orders from General Mark Clark's
headquarters."

"That's the stupidest thing I ever heard," I said, turning back
to the pastor.

The lieutenant put his hand on his gun butt and said that this
was an order he intended to carry out, even if he had to use force.

"Don't you have to go to the toilet?" I asked the pastor.

"I think that perhaps I do," Niemöller replied.

So we went to the men's room and finished our interview standing at adjoining urinals.

I talked with Fritz Thyssen, the Ruhr industrialist who had financed Hitler's rise to power and who was ultimately destroyed by the Frankenstein he had helped to create. He refused to be drawn into any discussion about what had happened. "Right now I am worried about my family," he said. "I want to apologize for the poor appearance of my wife. She has had a hard time."

I visited Leon Blum, ex-Premier of France, and Kurt Schuschnigg, ex-Premier of Austria, in their rooms. They were too ill to come down and join in the general celebration. Schuschnigg's wife (her daughter, who was with her, had been born in a concentration camp and up to this moment had known no other life) spoke for him.

Prince Leopold of Prussia, nephew of the late Kaiser Wilhelm, was dressed in a khaki coat that brushed the ground. The white cross used by the Germans to identify prisoners was sewn on the back of it. "You didn't come a moment too soon," he said fervently. "They would have killed all of us like they killed poor General Delestraint. I was with him at Dachau when the guard came in to say that he was being freed. He was very happy. Then they just shot him down. That is what they had in store for all of us if you hadn't come when you did."

One of those rescued was the nephew of Vladimir Molotov, the Russian Foreign Minister. He hobbled off on his toeless feet to join the communist partisans he hoped to find in the area. Another one who escaped was Konrad Praxmarer, a nazi author who was jailed for writing poison-pen letters to Hitler, but who feared the Americans as much as his Gestapo prison guards.

The ex-prisoners milling about on the terrace of the hotel made up an international blue book. They included: General Sante Garibaldi of the Italian army; Dr. Hjalmar Schacht, nazi financial wizard; Richard Karl Schmitz, Mayor of Vienna; Prince de Bourbon, pretender to the throne of France; Josef Joos, Catholic Center member of the German Parliament; Fritz Cerini; Count

Peterman and his daughter, Countess Gisella; Johannes Van Dijk,
Dutch Minister of War; Johann Neuhauser, Canon of Munich;
General Alexander Papago, Commander in Chief of the Greek
Army, with his entire staff; Alexander Zamoyski, Poland; Dimi-
trije Tomalewski, Yugoslavia; Gabriel Piquet, Bishop of Clare-
mont; Karl Kunkel, Germany; General Fritz Halder, head of the
German General Staff who had planned the invasion of France;
Field Marshal von Thoma and General von Falkenhorst of the
German Army and Prince Kadley and Baron Schell, both mem-
bers of the Hungarian government. It was a reporter's field day,
but they were so hungry for news that they interviewed me.

Late that night I billeted in the Hotel Post, a *gasthaus* in the
small town of Brunico, a short distance from Lago de Brais. I
awoke the next morning early to find myself involved in an incident in which the similarity between the common criminal and
the nazi hierarchy was never better illustrated.

If the mass crimes of the Germans must be divided into sec-
tions, this one would come under the heading of robbery, sub-
division art. The loot involved was the world's most priceless
collection.

The cops in the case were a hard-riding, fast-shooting battalion
of the 339th Infantry Regiment. The tip about the stolen property
came from a German stool pigeon who, like our own garden
variety of underworld informer, had hoped that by turning in his
partners in crime he would be able to beat the rap himself.

A lieutenant brought him to me because I was the only American in the hotel who understood German. He said that certain
valuable paintings, earmarked to decorate Goering's Karenhall,
had been hidden in the small Alpine village of Campo Tures. The
informer didn't know whether the garrison charged with the defense of these treasures would lay down its arms, as a goodly part
of the German army was doing, or would continue to fight. This
last bit of information was all right with Major Minor, the unit's

C.O., because at this point in his career he had no love for the Germans.

"As long as they give me an excuse and as long as my government says it's legal, I'll kill them as fast as I see them," he said.

The major ordered two medium half-track troop carriers, fifteen riflemen in each, three jeeps with three machine gunners and a rifleman driver and a fourth jeep for himself. I sat beside him.

We set out at nine o'clock on a beautiful sun-bright morning, the major and I at the head of the column, along a dusty road through a green valley walled in by snow-capped mountains that converged miles ahead at Campo Tures. We passed camouflaged tank repair yards and gun positions that covered our route. The few villages we drove through swarmed with soldiers of the Wehrmacht, who watched us apathetically as we passed within feet of them.

"I hope they start something," Major Minor said.

"If they do, I'll have a better story," I said. "But maybe I won't be around to write it."

As we rounded a bend in the road, the town of Campo Tures appeared. Dozens of German soldiers stood in the town square. They dropped whatever work they were doing to watch the half-tracks move into defensive positions. The riflemen clambered down and stood with guns ready. The Germans stared with more curiosity than hostility as the major, his holstered .45 automatic swinging freely at his hip, strode up the stairs of the city hall with me at his heels and headed for the office of the town commandant. The guards in our path snapped to attention and stretched out their right arms in nazi salute. On the second floor a fat, round-faced German major named Wilhelm Damkohler rose hastily to his feet, gave the Hitler salute and looked questioningly at us.

"I have come to accept the surrender of your garrison," Major Minor said. "You will please give me the exact number and disposition of your men."

Damkohler didn't understand English so I translated into German. He didn't seem to understand my German either, so I tried Italian. This he understood perfectly, and the rest of the discussion was carried on in three languages: Major Minor spoke English, I put it into Italian and Damkohler translated into German for the rest of his staff.

The major didn't mince words. The Germans were to leave their positions in the hills and assemble in town. The officers were to disarm their men, but were to retain their own sidearms to enforce obedience within the ranks. Should any fanatic fire on the Americans, he, Damkohler, would be held strictly responsible. Minor said he would tolerate no nonsense on the part of any German. They were to remain in the garrison town until adequate arrangements were made to transport them to prison camps.

The preliminaries disposed of to his satisfaction, he demanded that the stolen property held in town be turned over to his men immediately.

"You mean the art collection," Damkohler said.

"Exactly."

"We have it in the building across the square," he said, pointing through the open window at a huge, gray, neo-Norman castle.

"What paintings do you have there?"

"Some rather nice ones," the German commander answered, in what turned out to be a masterly bit of understatement.

He sent for Dr. Hans Gerhardt Evers, a smartly-booted officer who bore the imposing title of Military Administration Counselor for the Fine Arts Section of the Occupation Forces, which, the nazi-occupied parts of Europe learned to their sorrow, meant looter-with-a-knowledge-of-art. Evers, introduced in a formal manner, clicked his heels and gave each of us in turn the nazi salute. Major Minor signaled him to get under way and we followed down the stairs and across the sunny piazza to the courtyard of Schloss Ottantal. Here he led us into a large, high-ceilinged room crowded with wooden crates. I asked Evers about the value of the paintings and sculptures they contained.

The fine arts counselor tilted his head haughtily and sighted me along the end of his nose. "You are observing the world's greatest collection of art," he said. "Its value is priceless." It was as though I had accused Jimmy Valentine of having committed a simple house burglary.

Evers' assistants opened the crates one by one and exposed the masterpieces. By the ambient rays of sun streaming through the high windows I saw Raphael's "Lady with a Veil," "Self Portrait" and "Cardinal Bibiani"; Peter Paul Rubens' "Holy Family"; Rembrandt's "Portrait of an Old Man"; Titian's "The Concert" and "Portrait of Andreas Vesalius"; Hans Holbein's "Holy Family" and "Portrait of a Man"; Andrea del Sarto's "Holy Family" and "San Giovanni"; Velazquez' "Philip IV" and "Portrait of a Princess"; Murillo's "Chicken Market"; Albrecht Dürer's "St. Philip," "St. James," "Madonna with Child" and "Crucifixion"; and Bernardo Daddi's altarpiece.

Fra Filippo Lippi, a priest who lived in the early 1400's, was a forerunner of the Italian Renaissance. In spite of the cloth he led a gay and dissolute life, but was forgiven by the various Popes because of his great talent. He was represented by his "Coronation of the Virgin" and a pair of tondi. His son, Filippino Lippi, born of an illicit relation between the painter and a nun, Lucretia Buti, was represented by "Adoration of the Magi." Botticelli, a student of Fra Filippo and the teacher of Filippino, had "Madonna with Child Enthroned." I found Michelangelo's sculpture of Bacchus in a manure pile in one of the stables of the castle.

These masterpieces, amongst the world's greatest, had been taken from the Pitti Palace and the Uffizi and Bargello Museums of Florence. Their cataloging took an entire day. In the mass of crated works were many paintings of the Dutch and Flemish 15th, 16th and 17th centuries, including Hans Memling, Brouwer and Terborch, and many French painters such as Clouet, Teniers, Boucher and Claude Lorrain.

Also from the Italian school, Credi's "Portrait of the Artist"; Agnolo Bronzino's "Portrait of a Florentine Lady"; Mazzolino's

"Murder of the Children" and the works of the 16th and 17th century painters Carracci, Correggio, Trevisoni and Salvator Rosa.

When the tabulation had been completed and an American guard posted on the castle, Dr. Evers came to me. "It is very important that you write about this correctly," he said. "We do not want the people of America to have the wrong idea."

"You mean about stealing the paintings?" I asked.

"You see how wrong you are. We were only taking them for safe-keeping. We always kept Mussolini informed as to where they were, and some day later on we intended to return them."

Major Minor, on overhearing this conversation, gave a throaty laugh and jerked his thumb in the direction of the soldiers already patroling the entrance to the castle. "These are the men who will return the paintings," he said.

Since that day I have made regular pilgrimages to Florence, and as I stand in the Uffizi Gallery and the Pitti Palace and observe again these works of art, the small part I played in returning them adds immeasurably to my enjoyment.

I was in Rosenheim, site of the 12th Army press camp, when the formal surrender was signed. It is a lovely town on the main road between Munich and Vienna. Its onion-shaped church spires and gingerbread houses make it appear like an illustration out of Hans Christian Andersen. It looks across the confluence of the Mangfall and Inn Rivers at the snow-capped Bavarian Alps that rise a short distance to the south. During the National Socialist years it lived in the ephemeral glory of having been the birthplace of Hermann Goering. Papa Goering, a minor official in the consular service, had met a young and pretty masseuse at the local *Bad* and had taken her, in his declining years, for his third wife. She was Jewish. One of the children born of this union was Hermann.

"Of course, nobody thought anything about it at the time," the mayor of Rosenheim told me. "But after Hitler came to power, I suppose it became a matter of embarrassment for the field marshal. Not that anyone would have dared mention it. You know, he never once returned to this city. We tried to get him to build an art gallery for us, feeling that this was the gift he would be most likely to give the city that wanted to perpetuate the historical fact of his birth, but he never sent replies to my letters. When we built one ourselves and asked him to dedicate it, he refused. Why, he wouldn't even loan us any paintings."

The fact that the shooting had ceased pleased the good *burgermeister*. "Isn't it wonderful," he beamed. "Now we have joined forces against Russia."

I politely explained that what the German Army was doing was not a sign of union between us, but an act of unconditional surrender. He didn't quite believe me—and only today do I realize how right he was.

So there I was in Rosenheim, and the war was over. It should have been a day of exultation for me, because henceforth it would be illegal for the Germans to try to kill me, and I could look forward to a renewed popularity with life insurance agents. But today was no different from yesterday, with the same bright sun shining and the same sharp snap in the air. I was working at the same job at the same typewriter in the same press camp. Somehow I felt let down.

I thought back to the days when, as a young newspaperman, I had covered the holiday ceremonies of Civil War and World War I veterans. I had watched them parade in the heat of July and had listened to their interminable speeches about the debt we owed the dead. Did we owe them any debt? And if so, what was the debt and how were we supposed to pay it? The orators agreed that those soldiers had died so that future generations would have a better world to live in, and that it was up to the living to see that the debt was paid. If this were so, then we were truly a nation of deadbeats, for no one in his right mind would have considered our world of the Thirties fair payment for the laying down of even one life.

And what platitudes would we think up for the dead of World War II? Did we owe them a debt, too? If so, could we find a better way to pay it? Only time could answer.

Part II
THE CITY REBORN

Chapter 6

Of Powdered Milk and Instant Money

M Y RETURN to Rome in the early summer of 1945 was made in
an elegant Auto Union. The motor pool of the 103rd Infantry
Division was bulging with civilian automobiles, and the commanding officer permitted me to make my own selection. The
Auto Union was the classiest and perhaps the fastest of the prewar German sports cars, with a dashboard that appeared to have
more gadgets than an airplane.

The roads I sped over were rutted by tank tracks and pitted
with bomb holes. All bridges had been blown. Some streams were
spanned with steel Bailey bridges and others were traversed by
tortuous by-passes. The countryside presented an unending picture of utter devastation, with mile after mile of damaged and
destroyed buildings littering a land scarred by the implements of
war. I had never seen any destruction as total as that visited on
the railway system. Every tunnel and bridge had been blown and
every inch of track twisted into a spiral.

It didn't seem possible that I, or the people who had lived
through this holocaust, could ever forget it. Yet nature is kind,

and even then I knew that a single spring could cover the earth's scars, and a single generation would bring forgetfulness.

Off in the distance, on the spires and saddles of the mountain ranges, were the typical fortified towns of the Middle Ages. Built in inaccessible places for defensive purposes, each one now clustered around a castle in ruins and a church in fine repair, eloquent testimony that the idea outlives the sword.

The car took so great a beating that I had to abandon it for it was barely limping as I drew close to Rome. In the distance were the umbrella pines, lofty trademark of the Roman *campagna* that surround the city. And, as it has in the hundreds of times I have since returned to Rome, it filled me with the warm, comfortable feeling of coming home.

I had to make an immediate decision. With the war over in Europe, Japan became the big military story. As a reporter, my place was with the invasion forces that were gathering on the islands of the Pacific. Should I pull up roots completely and hope to return when the Pacific war ended? This seemed logical, since there was no telling how long the war in the Far East would last or whether, with the high incidence of mortality in my profession, I'd still be around when that war was over. But I was afraid that if I closed shop completely, I might never get back. Like a coin deposited in the Trevi fountain, I left my belongings, which by this time had swollen to a considerable amount of furniture, house-furnishings and clothing, in the Corso Trieste apartment, kept on Maria, her daughters, Nello and the car and flew back to the U.S.A., en route to the Far East.

Ironically, VJ-day came in August while I was in the States.

Post-war Rome was bustling with the military activity of occupation troops digging in for an indefinite stay. The city, always a mecca for tourists, now had a new kind to contend with, all of them in uniform. The brown-out of the streets at night was as rigorously observed as it had been during the war, but now it stemmed, not from military directive, but from a simple lack of electric current. Water trickled from taps on lower floors while tenants on upper floors uncomplainingly took their jugs to the fountains in the streets. After all, it wasn't as bad as it was down south, where their poor Neapolitan cousins had to brave block-long lines of females waiting around Piazza Plebecito for a turn at the Allied water trucks, the only place where it was available. Women walked for miles, coming and going with water jugs balanced on their heads. Sophia Loren told me that she used to accompany her mother on the four-mile trek, and that in wartime, even during air raids, they would not run for shelter, lest they lose their place in line. Better a swift death than a lingering one of thirst.

Civilian vehicles were making their appearance in small numbers. Ancient buses and taxis run by methane gas contained in twin torpedo-shaped tanks on their roofs took their places alongside wheezing trucks of all descriptions and sizes run by enterprising owners who had taken over bus routes. If the particular route selected didn't pay, a new destination would be scrawled on a piece of cardboard and hung on the side of the truck, which would then cheerfully change direction in mid-trip.

It had been a hot summer, but none of the Romans went down to the beaches. Even if they could have found transportation, there was the danger that the sands still hid mines. Only a few narrow stretches that served the military had been safely deloused. Even the few public pools were not available, since they, too, had been requisitioned by the military.

The city bulged with Italians from all parts of the peninsula who had been uprooted by the war and had gravitated to the safety of the capital city. All the hotels and many houses were still under requisition, and it was not uncommon for families of ten to live in a single room. People lived in caves, in air raid shelters, in makeshift shacks on the fringes of the city. How did a population of one million, four hundred thousand inhabitants manage to live in space barely enough for half a million? The Italian himself explains it with quiet fatalism. *S'arrangia.*

A *Commissario d'alloggio* was given czar-like powers to correct a situation that, arithmetically, had no solution. He froze all rents and all leases, which made tenants happy but drove landlords mad. Reckoned conservatively, 90 per cent of the leases had been written before the war, when the value of the lira fluctuated between five and twenty cents. In prewar days a fine apartment in Parioli might have rented from two thousand to six thousand lire per month, or, in terms of dollars, roughly between one hundred and three hundred dollars. The rental on workers' homes was scaled at between two hundred and five hundred lire a month. With wartime inflation (today the rate is six hundred and twenty lire to the dollar), the rent on a worker's flat came down to between one and two dollars a month, and an elegant flat to from ten to thirty dollars a month. Many owners, unable to make repairs or pay taxes, abandoned their property.

The black market was now in a far better state of organization. Military supplies and foodstuffs were in abundance. Supply sergeants and higher ranking officers who once handed U.S. military supplies to their transient mistresses for love now learned the way to barter for profit. Fiorello La Guardia was named head of UNRRA, a massive United Nations project, almost wholly financed by the USA, designed to keep a large part of Europe from starvation, including both friend and recent foe for whose well-being we had assumed responsibility. So many thousands of tons of powdered eggs and dehydrated vegetables were sent over that they became a drug on the black market. It was an overwhelming act of generosity comparable to sending electric trains to a town that still used kerosene for illumination.

Dozens of political parties mushroomed, and their garish propaganda covered the walls of the city. One poster was an enlarged photograph of some twenty children gathered around a young friend of about four years of age who, by stretching the imagination, might conceivably have been addressing them. Out of his mouth came a cartoonist's balloon with the words (translated): "And Papa and Mama, if you don't vote right, we'll make pee-pee in bed." Other displays were in worse taste. Many who felt deeply about affairs expressed themselves on the walls. All it took was a bucket of paint and a brush.

Even the tottering monarchy took its message to the walls. Vittorio Emanuele had kept a tenuous hold on the sceptre by signing an armistice with the Allies, and now, by abdicating in favor of his son, Umberto, he hoped to save the dynasty. A plebiscite cut Umberto's reign to a bare month in the spring, earning for him the title of King of the May. Right now the walls were scrawled with contesting *M il re* and *W il re* ("Death to the King" and "Long Live the King"), with the former being in the majority.

There were some *W Maria Rossi* scattered about. She turned out to be an unknown movie extra with a head for publicity. Since there was no movie industry, she went quietly back into the shadows.

In Trastevere, across the Tiber, a quarter with cramped buildings on narrow alleys that considered itself old when Rome was new, someone had scrawled in dialect a pathetic plaint that mirrored the sentiment of the suffering Romans: *"Annatevene tutti, e lassatece piagne soli."* (Go away everybody, let us cry by ourselves.)

The side of the Aurelian Wall just off Porta Pia was plastered with votive offerings to the Virgin—flowers, crosses, photos, candles—in thanks for a miracle wrought during an American air raid, when a bomb struck a trolley car jammed with women and children. It was a dud. It didn't explode.

But despite the fervor displayed by the posters, most people were apathetic. They were neither pro-fascist nor anti-fascist. They neither hated Mussolini nor loved him. He was just a person who had been and now was gone. They worried about where the next meal would come from while they marked time, waiting for life to come back to a semblance of normalcy.

Shoeshine boys appeared, first by the tens, then by the hundreds, finally by the thousands. They crowded the bombed-out railway station, the piazzas in which soldiers collected, the street corners and the army posts. They were thin, ragged, stunted, an outward sign of the depths of Italy's defeat.

The movie industry took its first feeble steps. Mario Camarini directed Clara Calamai in a feeble thing called *Two Anonymous Letters,* while a director named Roberto Rossellini took over a bookie joint next to the Via Avignonese whorehouse and used it as a studio to shoot interiors for *Open City.* It aroused no more than a passing glance from the soldiers intent on more urgent business in the shuttered house next door.

Being the only professional revolutionaries, the communists got the jump on their opposition. In addition to gaining control of the labor unions and the best printing presses, they were on the verge of scoring their biggest triumph by taking effective control of the armed forces. Now that the fascist forces had been disbanded, the regular army consisted of the handful of men who had remained loyal to the king and who had joined the Allied forces in the war against the nazis. The communists proposed that the partisan forces be integrated into the national service with the same rank they had held as irregulars. Since the Communist Party had absolute control of these partisan forces, with the power to hand out commissions at will, and since the partisan ranks had swollen enormously after the war was over, it meant that control of the armed forces must surely fall to them. The partisans were heroes and the fascists were villains and the politicians dared not oppose this move because it enjoyed popular favor.

The daily press was intensely partisan and it was difficult to get an honest account of any event that had political significance. The Communists published *L'Unita,* the Socialists *Avanti,* the Republicans *Voce Repubblicana,* the Christian Democrats *Il Popolo,* and there were a dozen others. The most honest coverage came from lone independent, *Il Tempo.*

With the imminent arrival of my family I began to see certain inconveniences in the Corso Trieste flat. The elevator ran only two hours a day and even that was an iffy proposition. There was no telling when electric current would become normal again. My daughter was not yet four and my son barely six. I couldn't visualize them clambering up and down five flights of stairs. It had appeared a palace only when compared to a foxhole.

I had to look around for another place, and fortunately I found it quickly. It was a lovely flat on Via di Villa Sacchetti, a quiet street behind the Villa Borghese zoo. At the moment a group of Columbia Broadcasting System correspondents were living there, but they were about to move out. I asked one of them to let me know the exact date of their departure so that I could stake out my claim. After some profound hemming and hawing, he promised to do so.

Generally such a request would bring out the *esprit de corps* of war correspondents, so the hesitancy of my colleague made me suspicious. I checked further into the matter and learned that the broadcasters had made a deal with the proprietor, a Rumanian diplomat, to take over his flat on a rent-free basis on the promise that they would return it to him when they left. It was a good arrangement for the diplomat because the Allies would refrain from putting a flat on the requisition list if Americans were living in it. I could now understand why my presence at this moment was disconcerting to the radio reporters.

I went to the *Commissario d'alloggio* with whom I happened to be on good terms and had him assign the flat to me, fixing the rental at thirty-five hundred lire per month. Although the official rate of exchange at the time was one hundred lire to the dollar, on the black market in the Piazza Colonna one could get five hundred lire to the dollar. The press corps, along with all other holders of American currency, got it. This made my actual rent, for a beautifully furnished eight room apartment complete with linens, china and silver, seven dollars a month.

I pasted the local order from the *Commissario* on the door, and with this major problem solved, I departed for an assignment in Budapest with a clear conscience. A few days later I received a call from Sey Korman, the *Chicago Tribune* correspondent who shared offices with me in the Foreign Press Building, informing me that the diplomat had torn off the notice, changed the locks on the door and taken possession. I hurried back to Rome, gathered a jeep-load of MP's and Italian police and set out to correct the situation. They carried the diplomat out of the flat, ignoring his loud protests that he was covered by diplomatic immunity.

Two days later, still protesting from behind the bars of his diplomatic cell, he was visited by a civilian lawyer attached to the Allied Command Real Estate Section. The diplomat was informed that the crime of breaking and entering was punishable by a prison term of up to twenty years, and that a diplomatic passport, especially an enemy one, granted him no immunity whatsoever, as should be obvious from his present confinement.

If he was dissatisfied with the order issued by the *Commissario d'alloggio*, and it was evident from his actions that he was, then his recourse should have been to the Italian courts.

"But that will require ten years," he cried.

"Not nearly so long as the jail sentence for taking the law into one's own hands, as you have done," the attorney replied severely. "Now Mr. Stern will expect an apology from you. When he has it, he will not press charges and you will be freed."

The diplomat knew he was beaten. "But the price set by the *Commissario d'alloggio* is too low," he complained.

"Mr. Stern wants to be fair," was the reply. "How much do you want?"

The answer was ninety-five hundred lire a month. A contract was drawn up and signed by both parties. My rent had been raised to nineteen dollars a month.

My family was due to arrive in Naples aboard the old S.S. *Gripsholm*, which was making her last crossing before being returned to Sweden. Along with this first group of correspondents' families were the families of embassy and UNRRA personnel, priests, Protestant missionaries and their families, and several bishops who were to be elevated to cardinals at the forthcoming Vatican consistory. From what my wife had written, it was evident that a good part of the hold was filled with our possessions and that I would need a truck to cart it to Rome.

Since the army had called in all requisitioned automobiles, leaving me stranded, I had visions of human portage, with a long line of carriers balancing trunks, suitcases and children on their heads as they trekked to Rome. No other vehicles were available. Then, at the last minute, the army came to the rescue. It was announced that the tens of thousands of jeeps crowding ordinance depots from one end of Italy to the other had been declared surplus and were for sale, and correspondents were eligible to buy them.

I was driven to the depot at Aversa, a town just north of Naples, where I checked in with a friendly master sergeant. As he led me down long rows of jeeps, he said, "Pick out any one you want. Those marked 'A' cost nine hundred; those marked 'B' cost three hundred; those marked 'C' cost seventy-five."

I saw a "B" jeep that looked pretty good. "How is the motor?" I asked.

The sergeant lifted the hood. The motor looked dirty. "Hey, Silvano," he yelled at a civilian mechanic. "I want one of those new motors put in this one. Pronto."

I looked at the tires somewhat dubiously. "Don't they look worn to you?" I asked.

"And put four new tires on it," the sergeant yelled.

I came away with a new jeep. A great institution, our army, in war and in peace.

Chapter 7

Retribution: The Shooting of Anton Dostler

DURING THE WAR I had given a good deal of thought to the idea that criminals of war should be punished for their misdeeds. The thought was almost an obsession. It was not the bloodthirsty eye-for-an-eye concept of retribution, but a simple sense of justice. If an SS Colonel Kappler or Dollmann or Eichmann can slaughter innocent people with impunity because they deal in large numbers, how could I, truly believing in a concept of justice that is equal for all, feel that justice was being done when a sniveling punk in New York was hustled to the electric chair because he killed a cop during the commission of a felony? How could I ever return to the criminal courts, where I had served a lengthy apprenticeship as a journalist, and feel the same sense of outrage at their criminal misdeeds.

There is a criminal code on the books of all civilized nations, and in it murder is a most serious offense. There is much death in war, but what the Dollmanns and Kapplers had done had nothing

to do with battle. They had murdered the defenseless and innocent, and for that they should pay the penalty civilization has
prescribed. The nationality of these defendants didn't matter to
me. I didn't want to punish Germans *because* they were Germans
or *because* of their political views, no matter how odious to me,
but murder is murder in any time or place, and the murderers
must be pursued with the same assiduity that the FBI demon-
strates in its hunt for bank robbers and kidnappers.

On the battlefield at Malmèdy 129 American soldiers, prisoners
of war, were shot and killed in cold blood. An SS officer gave the
order and his men mowed them down. The ones who issued the
order, and the commanders who executed them, were guilty of
murder in the first degree. Those who took part in the cold-
blooded murder of the minority peoples of Europe committed
an outrageous offense in the eyes of God, and they were guilty
of premeditated murder. The crimes of a Eugene Dollmann,
whose whereabouts I did not know, and of a Herbert Kappler,
who had surrendered to the Allies, cried out for trial and punishment.

One German *was* caught and brought up on a charge of murder,
and I fervently hoped that his trial, as the first, would not be
used merely as an example, reserving for him the heaviest punishment and then sloughing off the others in the general let-down of
interest. As we shall see, I hoped in vain.

The German officer who stood before an American bar of justice
was General of the Infantry Anton Dostler. He was charged with
having issued the order to execute fifteen American prisoners of
war. The soldiers had been O.S.S. members of the Jinny Mission,
who had carried out a raid at La Spezia, deep behind the German
lines. The men, wearing their full uniforms, had been captured
before they could complete their task of blowing up a railroad
tunnel on the coastal line.

I was in the courtroom throughout the trial. The evidence was
overwhelming. The bodies had been recovered, still dressed in
U.S. Army uniforms, their hands still wired behind their backs.

Dostler admitted having issued the order for their execution, but said that he did so on Hitler's order. The "order" turned out to be a general *Führerbefel* which said that since American O.S.S. and British Commandos were largely recruited from prisons, and since their methods were criminal, they should, therefore, be exterminated without mercy.

It didn't take the court long to reach a verdict. General Jaynes ordered the prisoner to the bar and said, "It is my duty to inform you, as presiding officer of this military tribunal, that you have been found guilty." He waited for an interpreter to say *"schuldig,"* then cocked his head and looked down on the defendant. ". . . and it is the order of this court that you be shot to death by musketry." Dostler, smart in a freshly laundered uniform, clicked his heels sharply, gave a low bow and walked back to his seat.

The tech sergeant who ran the officers' mess in King Victor Emmanuel's summer palace at Caserta led me down the dim corridor to the senior officers' dining room. "There it is," he said, pointing to a table elaborately set for twenty. "All I know is that I was told to lay it on for the press."

I told him that as far as I knew only eight correspondents had come down from Rome.

"Christ, they'll do it every time," he said, "not telling me to get ready for twenty-eight." I repeated that so far as I knew there would be only eight, not twenty-eight, and he went away unconvinced.

Across the hall in the officers' bar, Lt. Colonel Graham Erdwurm, who had driven me down from Rome that afternoon, introduced me to a florid-faced, gray-haired major with whom he shared a sagging couch. The major asked me what I was doing in Caserta, and I told him that, while the matter was still in the hush-hush stage, I guessed that I would be witnessing the execution of General Anton Dostler. The officer who had briefed me that morning told me that he was under a pledge of secrecy not to reveal what the story in Caserta was, but that whatever it was, it would take place at dawn. He added that the correspondents who had been invited to witness it would be taken to the palace, where the "secret" would be revealed.

The major said, "Hey! I have to see it. I'm in G-2 and my colonel told me before he left that I was to witness it for him." Noting the peculiar look I threw at him, he added hastily, "It's not that I *want* to see the thing, you understand, it's just that the colonel ordered it."

For some reason the military command wanted the whole affair kept quiet until the sentence of death had been carried out, but the presence of eight war correspondents excited some comment. One officer asked Del Clark, a public relations colonel, what we were all doing in Caserta. Del replied, quite seriously, that we were down for the opening of the hunting season.

The PRO captain who was serving as guide told us that we would have to get up at 6:30 A.M. John Mecklin of the *Chicago Sun* commented that it was a hell of an hour to be getting up, and Ed Clark of the UP said he felt sure that it would be quite all right with General Dostler if the Allied authorities, out of deference to the press's desire to sleep, had scheduled the shooting at a later hour.

The gray-haired major from G-2 came in and asked the captain how he could swing it so that he could come in with us. "It's not that I want to see the thing," he apologized, "but when your colonel tells you to do a thing, that's all there is to it."

We spent the night in a villa on Via Roma. My room was a large, drafty affair furnished with a battered cot and one straight-backed chair. It had a single, large window which opened on a public toilet. In the early dawn hours we gathered around the gasoline stove in what passed for a living room until two jeeps and a command car came to take us to the summer palace. A damp, nasty wind whipped through the open vehicles as we twisted through the deserted streets back to the officers' mess.

At breakfast Colonel Leedam appeared and handed out a mimeographed release. On the first page I read that Dostler had been kept under twenty-four-hour guard by two men who stood in front of his cell, that every quarter hour the sergeant-of-the-guard phoned his headquarters and that if the call did not come through on the dot, a pair of investigators were rushed to the cell. Seventeen soldiers and an officer did nothing but guard the general. All these precautions were taken in spite of the prisoner's promise not to commit suicide or to attempt escape. Dostler was shot, the release said, using the past tense, in a freshly pressed uniform stripped of decorations.

The next page listed his background. He had been born in Munich where he began his military career, rising to the rank of lieutenant at the close of World War I. After the advent of Hitler and nazism, of which he had been a staunch supporter, he had climbed rapidly in the ranks. He had served in France, Russia, Finland and, finally, Italy, where he was named a full general and placed in command of the 75th Corps.

The third sheet listed the names and serial numbers of the fifteen Americans for whose deaths Dostler was convicted, and the final page detailed the manner in which the army prepares for an affair of this sort. At the prison stockade, a squad of twenty-four men are trained for the execution ceremony. (The word ceremony had an antiseptic quality to it.) They practice firing at two-inch disks at a distance of twenty-five yards, although in the actual execution a four-inch disk is used. The twelve men who are used are selected from names drawn out of a hat, and from one to four of the rifles they hold contain blank cartridges.

We were informed that the ceremony was to be solemn and dignified, with smoking and talking forbidden. The prisoner would be given the choice of wearing a black mask and would be permitted to speak a final word.

At a little past 8 A.M. Colonel Leedam told us that the vehicles were ready, so we filed into the courtyard of the summer palace. One of the reporters griped because his "general died at dawn" title was ruined.

"No fault of ours," an officer said. "We can't start without the press."

"You mean you're holding it up for us?" a correspondent asked incredulously.

"That's right."

"Well, that makes a better title," he said. "The General Dies at Press Time."

Our motorcade sped along the main highway toward Naples and, just south of Aversa, turned into the gate of the prison camp. An MP led us into the officers' mess. At the table, over hot coffee and doughnuts, we were told that the prisoner had spent a restful night and had had to be awakened in the morning.

Mecklin wanted to know if German war criminals were permitted to order anything they wanted for a last meal. Lieutenant R. B. Hoffer said sure, he had gone duck hunting for the final supper.

"Got him a mallard," Hoffer said. "The cook fixed it up and I shoved a red ping pong ball in the duck's mouth to make it look good. The general ate it, and the boys tell me that he enjoyed it. I got to admit, though, that I didn't shoot the bird. Didn't get a thing all day, so I went to a butcher shop and bought it."

A major came in and asked us to follow him. We walked about thirty yards down a neat path from the mess hall to a rectangular pit about five feet deep, seventy-five feet long and forty feet wide. The earth was soft and showed fresh rake marks. Hammered into the far end of the pit was an unpainted, sturdy six-by-six. It had a freshly-scrubbed look. A set of wooden steps went down into the execution ground.

Along a gravel walk that led from the pre-execution house to the pit, the firing squad stood in formation. At the near end of the pit, drawn up in two lines of six and snappily dressed in white helmets, white leggings and white gloves, was an honor guard of MPs. On the embankment, standing just to one side of the post, an army newsreel photographer waited. A layer of fog still remained in the pit giving it an eerie look. Near the steps inside the pit was a brown-stained gun rack with twelve Garand rifles arranged in two rows. We took our places along a flimsy green handrail that was too wet to lean on.

The husky, efficient looking major in command of operations was touchy. This was the first German war criminal to be executed by the U.S., and the major's every action showed that he was conscious of his moment in history. He called to a lieutenant to get that photographer out of there, pointing to the army news-reel man. "He's liable to get hit."

The lieutenant came back a minute later. "He says he doesn't want to move."

The major glowered. "Okay, then we'll have a double execu-tion."

An MP officer stepped forward to the press rail. "Do any of you fellows want to stop back for coffee and doughnuts after?"

It seemed embarrassing to be thinking about such small com-forts at a moment like this, and no one answered.

"Where's the doctor?" the major asked in the general direction of a group of men standing in the pit.

Captain A. N. Lieberman stepped forward. "I'm all set here," he said.

It was precisely 9 A.M. "Get ready everybody," the major said. He turned to the press. "When the prisoner comes out there'll be no smoking and no talking." A few butts were tossed to the ground. There was an embarrassed silence for a few seconds until the major said briskly, "Here they come."

I looked back and saw Dostler, flanked by four men, come striding down the path toward the pit. He was dressed in the gray-green uniform of a nazi general. There was gold braid on his shoulders and holes in his uniform where decorations had once been. The handout earlier in the morning had stated that he had been shot without his decorations, but I saw on his breast the Iron Cross. His stiff choker collar was open at the throat.

Actually, the first things I noticed were Dostler's gleaming black boots as he half goose-stepped along in front of his escort. The cadence seemed so snappy as to appear almost indecent in the face of death. A final bit of nazi arrogance, I thought. Then I saw his face. It was pasty and drawn, the jaw sagging and the puckered mouth agape like that of a man who has forgotten his false teeth. But when he neared the double line of soldiers between whom he was to march and saw the press, his head snapped up, his eyes came into focus, his mouth closed like a vise and every muscle in the lower part of his face became taut and rigid.

On his right was a German chaplain, a fellow prisoner, and on his left was an American chaplain. Dostler, a devout Catholic, was being prepared for his Maker in two languages. The group passed through the ranks of the firing squad and clumped down the wooden steps. The two MP guards touched Dostler's arm lightly in a guiding movement toward the stake, and he waded forward with as resolute a step as the ankle-deep dirt permitted. The fog in the pit had somewhat dissipated, but enough haze remained so that from the press rail the whole thing looked smaller, like a scene viewed through the wrong end of a telescope. A second pair of MPs, waiting at attention on each side of the stake, spun the general about, grasped his hands behind his back and tied them firmly together. Another MP looped a cord once around the ankles, once just above the knees and then tied him to the stake by looping the cord under the armpits. During this operation Lieutenant Lustig read the lengthy death warrant, calling out the names of each of the fifteen Americans who had been murdered. Photographers knelt in front of the stake, and flash bulbs illuminated Dostler's white face. Twice the jaw dropped, giving the mouth that same toothless, scared look, but each time it snapped shut and the cords in his neck stood out again.

The major moved up to the stake and asked Dostler if he had any last words. The condemned man shook his head. An MP standing behind Dostler lifted the army hat and another MP produced a black mask. As he raised it Dostler shouted what sounded like, *"Ich liebe Deutschland."* It had a reedy, strained quality and it must have sounded as unreal to him as it did to those of us who heard it.

The long mask dropped down over his head. Captain Lieberman put a stethoscope on the prisoner's chest and located the heart. An MP pinned a white cloth disk over it. All functionaries headed for the sides of the pit and then walked swiftly toward the rear. The instant the black mask went over Dostler's face, the firing squad turned smartly and in double file went down the steps. Rifles were thrust at them as they passed the gun rack. A master sergeant gave the preliminary order. They halted, left-faced and the rear rank executed a half-step right while the front rank knelt. Then a lieutenant spoke in a voice so low it could barely be heard ten yards away: "Aim! Fire!"

The rifles cracked and the firing squad, apparently without so much as a single glance at their handiwork, left-faced, replaced the rifles in the rack, marched back up the stairs and stood smartly at attention in their original positions.

Dostler seemed to stiffen for an instant as the bullets struck him. His blouse ballooned out in the back and the exiting shots carried with them what appeared to be bits of grayish cloth. His head and shoulders went forward; he hung in that position while his head gave a few convulsive upward jerks and then was still. The silence was broken only by the clatter of feet made by the firing squad as they left the pit. After a few motionless moments, Captain Lieberman stepped in front of the German and placed the stethoscope once again on his chest.

He faced the press rail and, in a voice which had as unreal a quality as Dostler's, pronounced the condemned man officially dead. A Graves Registration unit untied the body from the stake and laid it on the ground. It was then rolled into a mattress cover and placed on a stretcher.

John Mecklin said, "I wonder if we can smoke now?"

"È vietato," Ed Clark replied.

"That colonel is smoking."

"Then I guess it's all right." Clark took out a cigarette and lit it. The other correspondents followed suit.

The stretcher was carried up the steps and put down near the weapons carrier that was to bear it to the cemetery. The mattress cover was undone and the head exposed, so that a photographer could take a final photo for identification. Then the body was carried away.

A lieutenant who had been part of the twenty-four-hour-a-day guard over Dostler came over to us. "I'm God damn glad that's over with," he said. "He sure was a headache. Not that he gave us any trouble, but when you have an important prisoner like that you're keyed up every minute of the day. I'll be able to sleep nights now."

"Did he have anything to say before you took him out?" someone asked.

"He told me, 'I understand the American people believe in justice. Thank them for the courtesies you have shown me.' He took the whole thing very well. When we told him that he had to go, he said all right, but that his conviction was unjustified. He said he didn't mind being shot, but he hoped some day to have his name cleared. His only request was that we leave the handcuffs off when we marched him out. I told him he had a choice about whether to have the mask put over his head. He said it didn't matter, that we should do whatever was routine. He had only one final request. He wanted us to take a picture of his grave and send it to his wife and daughter in Munich."

As Chaplain Crimmins came by, Mecklin asked, "What was it that Dostler yelled before they put the mask on him?"

"He said '*Ich liebe Deutschland.*'" (I love Germany.)

Mecklin said, "I thought it was '*Es lebe Deutschland.*'" (Long live Germany.)

"I'll tell you what his final words were to me," Chaplain Crimmins said. "'I give my life to my country and my soul to God.'"

"It sounds stupid to me," Mecklin insisted. "I mean, why should he yell, 'I love Germany.' It doesn't make sense."

One of the MP officers called out, "Coffee and doughnuts ready."

As we headed toward the mess, Jack Begon said, "INS is going to say 'I love Germany.'" He dashed off for Naples to get out a quick story for the West Coast morning papers.

As a topic of conversation, the Dostler execution grew stale. A Graves Registration man came in to say that burial would be at ten-thirty for those who were interested, but he drew no response. The reporters finished their coffee and went to their portables.

Ed Clark typed:

"urgentpress unipress 01102 aversa wehrmacht general anton dostler shot viatwelve man unistates firing squad smorning proexecution without trial fifteen american ohessessers north italyward march fourtyfour para first general tried etconvicted viawestern allies as warcriminal dostler died number one stockade here stolidly etsoldierly covered clark"

Chapter 8

Reunion in Rome

THE GUIDE BOOKS say that there are special ways of entering a town in order to get the most striking impression. Florence must be approached from the north, Rome from the south. Venice is at its best in the heat of a summer's noon and seen from a gondola. Naples is disappointing unless one arrives by sea. Only then can one enjoy the harmony of its sweeping coastline, anchored at one end by a smoking Vesuvius and at the other by the beautiful hills of the Vomero and Posillipo.

This was true when an anonymous Italian poet wrote "see Naples and die" and when Goethe, on his first view of the city, said that he could understand why poets through the ages had sung its praises; that Rome, by comparison, seemed like a badly placed convent.

But all this was *not* true when the *Gripsholm*, with my family aboard, inched its way through the graveyard of sunken ships in the bay. Even from a distance gaping holes were visible in the landscape. The houses along the entire waterfront had been blown up by a variety of explosive forces—air bombs, artillery,

mines and dynamite—each leaving its distinctive mark of destruction. For as far as the eye could see, shore installations lay twisted
and rusting where they had fallen.

The children saw it all without surprise, as though it were the
normal order of things, but my wife was startled and a little
frightened. Sweating porters hoisted a dozen enormous steamer
trunks into the trailer, then piled on another dozen suitcases and
bundles. With the trailer groaning under the load, I placed the
family in the newly purchased jeep and tooled off toward Rome.

I had a tourist guide's patter planned and I gave it quickly.
Here alongside our dock is Santa Lucia and in the distance the
funicular railway. They were the inspirations for the two songs
that generations of children in the United States have learned in
school. The dust from the ruined buildings lay so thick it was as
though we were seeing through a cloud. I pointed out the San
Carlo Opera House, the royal palace and the *galleria*. Soon we
were out of the city.

I turned my attention to family matters. "Where did we get all
those trunks?"

"I borrowed some from my mother, some I bought and the
others we already had."

"I didn't know we had so much stuff to bring."

"We didn't. Four of the trunks are loaded with Klim. That's
milk spelled backwards. Macy's sells it for fifty-one cents a pound.
It's a powder. Add water and you have instant milk."

"Looks like you brought a five-year supply," I said. "Now if you
had brought that many cartons of cigarettes . . ."

"They would have gone stale before I could smoke them."

"You don't understand. Italy has a cigarette economy. It's a
medium of exchange, like gold."

"Do they pasteurize milk in Rome?" my wife asked sharply.

I admitted that they didn't.

"Then I didn't bring enough Klim—and that's milk spelled
backwards," she said.

By this time we had passed through Aversa. A three-car trolley moved slowly along the roadside. It was so crowded that people not only clung to the sides but crouched on every inch of the roof, their heads perilously close to the overhead high tension electric wire.

As we drove through Capua, I told them that this had been the site of the once famous gladiator school where Spartacus started his insurrection against Rome. From the road we could see the ruins of an old Roman amphitheater, the temple of Mithras and a fortress built on the banks of the Volturno River by Emperor Frederick II.

Antiquity fought a losing battle against modern ruins. We were passing through Formia, where Cicero lies buried. The lovely town, with its beautiful villas on the shore of the Tyrrhenian Sea, was reduced to rubble.

"What happened here?" Mike Jr. asked.

"This is where we were pinned down the winter before last. You see how the mountains come right down to the road. Well, the Germans held them, and if we had tried to move up along this road they would have zeroed in on us with their artillery. It was suicide to try to move unless we pushed them out. We tried to go around the valley behind this mountain, but Monte Cassino is there and again they held the high ground."

"Then why didn't we go around by sea?" he asked.

It was hard to explain that we had tried it at Anzio and it had been disastrous, not because of the strategy, which was excellent, but because of faulty execution and poor leadership. It frightened our high command to such an extent that it was afraid to try the same thing again.

"I guess they had their reasons," I said vaguely.

War damage was less visible in the province of Lazio, a fount of western civilization, in which Rome lies. I pointed out that in legendary times King Latinus, from whom the name Lazio is derived, had ruled here. He was a friendly type who gave hospitality to those Homeric heroes, Ulysses and Aeneas. King Latinus had promised his daughter, Lavinia, to Aeneas in marriage. However, for embarrassing reasons of state, he had also promised her to King Turnus of the Rutuli tribe. Aeneas helped him out of his difficulty by wiping out the Rutulis and killing their king.

In pre-Roman days Lazio was peopled by hundreds of independent, war-like tribes and it took longer for Rome to conquer them than to conquer the rest of the world. According to legend the city itself was founded in 753 B.C. by Romulus and Remus, probably on the Palatine hill which dominated the only crossing over the Tiber River at Tibertina Island. The bridge or *ponte* was so important a structure that a whole pagan worship grew up around it, and to this day the head of the Catholic Church is called Pontiff.

The fruitful fields stretching off to the sea, criss-crossed by canals, were once the infamous Pontine marshes, whose only crop was malarial mosquitoes. Mussolini had these marshes drained and turned them into one of Italy's richest agricultural areas, demonstrating that he, too, was good for something.

We drove into Rome at dusk. I pointed out the Palatine Hill with its ruins of the palaces of the caesars, then the Capitoline Hill and the Colosseum, standing perilously close to houses blasted by Allied bombs. The Italians now referred to the first as *Antica Romana* and to the latter as *Antica Americana*.

The children had already begun their on-the-spot classical education, and I couldn't help being stirred by the importance of the moment. "Are there any questions?" I asked.

"Yes, Daddy," said my son. "Do they sell comic books here?"

It was fortunate that the winter of 1945–46 was a mild one, for the Romans, living on the assumption that theirs is a tropical climate, overwhelmingly ignore an American nicety called central heating. Although our building, a new one, happened to have an excellent heating system, there was no fuel available for it. Almost all the coal went to feed the electric plants that were barely turning out enough power for a rationed four hours a day. The few scraps of coke and charcoal that dribbled into the black market were weighed out like precious metals.

Shopping was comparatively easy for an American. There was a PX on Via del Tritone and a black market in Piazza Vittorio. On her first day in the marketplace my wife saw pushcarts groaning under loads of cans of powdered milk imported in thousand-ton lots by UNRRA.

Her curiosity aroused, she approached an old woman who was loudly hawking her wares and asked, "How much?"

She saw the shrewd eyes of the old woman light up as she recognized a "rich American." (All Americans in that period were considered rich, and indeed they were, for they were practically the only people in the country who were certain of three meals a day.)

"Twelve cents," the old woman answered. My wife stared open-mouthed for an instant, then regained her composure and walked away, mumbling under her breath about milk spelled backwards.

"All right," the woman called after her. "How much do you want to pay?"

I had been told, and I took it for gospel, that it was only necessary to drop a young child in a foreign country and almost immediately he would be speaking the language fluently. At the end of the first month, neither of my two appeared to understand a single word of Italian, let alone speak it. At the end of two months there was no visible improvement. Midway into the third month I was beginning to think that I had fathered a pair of fairly good-looking idiots.

One day I returned from my office in the Foreign Press Building to find our downstairs neighbors and their weeping maid sitting in our kitchen, awaiting my arrival. It was quite evident that here was a crisis and that my wife's Italian was not yet up to coping with it.

"Your son should not have done such a thing," my neighbor

complained mildly. Italians, especially when they believe themselves to be in the right, love to complain loudly, but these were
days when they spoke very politely to Americans. The shouting
was to come later.

I asked what this terrible thing was that my son had done, and
everyone started to answer at once. After I had silenced them,
I said that since the maid had been the victim, I would listen to
what she had to say.

"Your son is going to get me in trouble," the maid sniffled. She
was an illiterate peasant, a couple of steps lower even than our
own illiterate Maria. "He said that he is sending the whole
American army to arrest me and put me in jail. And I didn't do
anything. I only asked him not to play with mud where I was
washing clothes."

"He said all of that to you?" I asked in amazement.

"He said a lot more," she added emphatically. "He said even if
I tried to hide it wouldn't do any good, because the Americans
have a special bomb that they can throw and even if I wasn't
near the explosion the rays would wipe me out."

"And all of this he said to you in Italian?"

"Yes, sir."

I looked at my son with fatherly pride and heaved a sigh of
relief.

Finding a school for our offspring presented something of a
problem. I had very much wanted them to attend a local one in
order for them to become acclimated more quickly to their new
environment. But the terrible state into which the Italian school
system had fallen precluded this, at least for the immediate future. We finally enrolled them at Marymount, a private school
run by the Sisters of the Sacred Heart of Mary, with Margaret
entering kindergarten and young Michael the first grade.

There were problems each step of the way. Even so simple a
matter as securing uniforms for them became a challenge. Cloth
had disappeared from the Italian market and the small amount

that filtered in was very expensive and of inferior quality. So we gave the dressmaker a long evening coat of my wife's to make the short, double-breasted, navy blue jackets. The white blouses were cut from bedsheets. Over the uniforms the children wore *grembili,* the button-down-the-back cotton smocks so common on the Italian scene.

Marymount, staffed and administered by American sisters, maintains many schools throughout the world, but these are for girls only. Except in Rome. Here the nuns accepted boys up to the fifth grade. They did, that is, until one day a sister came upon a small-fry pair of opposite sexers holding hands. Now they only take boys through the third grade.

An important part of the curriculum is good manners, a subject of little importance in the rough-and-tumble New York schools of my day. In fact, I was not even aware of the need for it until I saw how it paid off in assurance and poise. The Italians are the best mannered people in Europe, and this is responsible for a good deal of their charm. The girls curtsy and the boys bow when they meet their elders with as much ease as an American youngster would say "hi."

Still the Marymount of that day didn't quite fulfill our requirements, so during the summer my wife looked further, but without success. One day she remarked, "What would you say if we started a school of our own?"

"Who is we?" I countered.

"Sylvia and I and a few other women."

Sylvia Horwitz, a tiny, bright, energetic woman, had come over on the *Gripsholm* with my family and had become a good friend. She is married to a dedicated social worker who was then employed by UNRRA. Her son, Paul, who was the same age as our Mike, had tried a semester in an Italian school in Milan with unhappy results.

"I would say you're crazy," I told my wife.

"Would you have any objections if we tried?"

"You'll try it anyway, whether I object or not."

The next day, while Charlie Dasher and I were on the Acqua Santa golf course, I mentioned my wife's conversation. "It's a crazy idea and I tried to talk her out of it," I explained. "But you know women."

"I don't think it's so crazy," General Dasher said.

"You will when you find out what they want from you."

"You tell them to come in and see me." We went on to other subjects as we continued our game.

Sylvia went to the office of the Rome area command in Piazza Venezia. The first request was for a rent-free building that would be suitable for a schoolhouse. Since most of the public edifices were still under military requisition, it was within his power to grant it.

"I'd like to make a deal with you," General Dasher said. "The families of our military personnel are beginning to arrive. We expect quite a number of them. If your school will accept the children of our dependents, I'll not only give you the building, but I'll also let you have as many school supplies as I can lay my hands on. And if I find any teachers in our ranks, I'll also help with the staff."

Thus was born the Overseas School of Rome, today one of the largest private schools in the country, ranking high both scholastically and socially.

The present quarters are a complex of well-designed modern school buildings at the eleven kilometer marker on Via Cassia, the ancient road to Florence. The headmaster is a distinguished educator brought from the United States. The student body exceeds six hundred and consists of pupils from thirty different countries. It opened for business the autumn session of 1946 in seven rooms of the American military rest center in the Mussolini Forum. (Although this has since been renamed the Italian Forum, it is still dominated by a sixty-foot obelisk on which is sculpted "Mussolini-Dux.")

General Dasher found two Wacs with teaching degrees and impressed them into the service. One Englishwoman and two

Italo-Americans completed the staff. School was on a five-day-a-week basis, rather than the Italian six, and the curriculum followed the one laid down by the New York State Board of Regents.

Classes went through the sixth grade only, but this worked no hardship on anyone. Wars are fought mainly by the young, and the children of the military tend to be of tender age. Even the diplomatic and foreign press colonies were young. Fortunately, these pioneer women were able to handle that first, rough year, though they required much benevolent assistance from Charlie Dasher, who was able to find supplies of paper, pencils, and books, not to mention desks and benches, all unobtainable through normal civilian channels of supply.

The first year was hard, but it concluded so happily that the pioneers decided to cut out on their own. Sylvia, my wife and several other mothers advanced the first year's tuition of two hundred dollars per child, which gave them fourteen hundred in operating funds. Ownership of the cooperative school was vested in, and administered by, a board of directors elected by the parents of the children. Sylvia was president and my wife was treasurer.

The new site was Villa Torlonia, Mussolini's fabulous home practically in the center of Rome. The school itself was in the twelve-room *dependance* in which his son, Bruno, had lived. Classes were extended through the eighth grade. A kitchen was set up so that students could eat a hot lunch. A ball field took over part of the lawns.

The leading events on the social calendar of the foreign colony were the annual ball and the bazaar, which were designed to bring in enough cash to balance a budget no longer padded with military assistance. The Wac teachers had already been shipped home, and their places were taken by a group of mixed nationality. The new headmaster was a young English ex-army officer. By the end of this second year, the enrollment had risen to one hundred and twenty.

The time came when classes had to be extended beyond the

eighth grade. Because of the additional expenses involved, the board decided to ask for a loan of five thousand dollars to be repaid at 6 per cent interest. As treasurer, my wife ran the finances of the school as she did those in her home. Her maxim: "Never borrow what you cannot pay back out of income."

At this time the Marshall Plan was in full swing. Its announced purpose was to grant money and goods to the nations of the Free World to help them get on their feet, and aid to education was considered an important part of the program. Since the Plan had given Italy billions of dollars, my wife had few doubts about the outcome of her request. Confidently, she filled in the application and left it in the office of the administrator, James Zellerbach, a successful businessman and distinguished diplomat.

Eventually a decision was reached. The school's appeal was turned down. At the same time a $75,000 loan for a night club was approved.

To make matters worse, the school now faced the loss of its building, the improvement of which had taken all its money. It seems that Villa Torlonia, rented from the Italian government by the school for a nominal figure, had been seized as part of the Mussolini assets. Now, however, Prince Torlonia filed suit against the government asking that the property be returned to him on the ground that he had not spontaneously given it to the dictator but that it had been taken from him by coercion. He won his case, and the school was notified that it had better move elsewhere at the conclusion of the academic year. With the military gone, the loan denied, costs mounting and the exchequer slim, disaster faced the pioneer mothers.

Fortunately for the school, there was a new and hardy breed of public servant whose children were attending and whose wives sat on the board of directors. These were our high-ranking embassy and aid program officials. One of them cut to the heart of the problem. "We'll get a loan for a hundred and fifty thousand," he stated flatly.

"But they turned us down when we asked for five thousand," my wife said.

"That's because you didn't ask for enough," he answered.

"But we can't even keep up with the interest on a loan that size."

"Who said anything about paying any interest?"

"But the principal—we can never repay it."

"That's just it," he said merrily. "We won't."

He was as good as his word. The money came from the Italian Ministry of Education, which didn't care about getting it returned because the American administrator advanced that additional amount to them. And the Marshall Plan never got the money back from the Ministry of Education because it has a full-time job giving and no time left for getting back. The frugal house-wife treasurer was so shocked she still hasn't recovered.

Chapter 9

Bandit with a Dream

THE CUSTOM of the midday siesta found its firmest adherent in me. I, too, would hurry home to an ample meal of spaghetti, meat, fruit and cheese, all of it washed down with at least a half pint of dry Frascati white or Chianti red. Then a snooze to sustain me through an afternoon's work, evening cocktails and late dinner. (On a warm day there is no better soporific than a glass of wine and a substantial meal. It's better than a sleeping pill.) Or I might go to the country club for lunch, a half hour's nap in the sun and nine holes of golf and still be back at the office by five. The siesta for the ordinary worker lasts from one to four in the afternoon, but the boss can stay out until as late as six or seven.

In a country where divorce is impossible and extramarital love affairs commonplace, the siesta assumes a new dimension. In Paris it is the *cinq à sept;* in Rome it becomes one to seven. A serious Italian business executive would never dream of taking his mistress out at night. This time is reserved for his family. He uses his siesta for dalliance. If the relationships are casual, he keeps a *garconière.* If the relationship is a serious one, he sets up a second home, an afternoon one, as opposed to the official, or night one.

One immensely wealthy industrialist was importuned by the beautiful brunette of his afternoon ménage. She insisted that he buy her a fifty thousand dollar necklace that they had seen in the jewelry shop owned by a friend of theirs. The wealthy boy friend said it was too expensive. But his mistress, with rare cunning, figured out a way of getting it. She withdrew fifteen thousand dollars from her bank account, all the cash she had accumulated from a four-year relationship, and took it to the jeweler.

"You know that Giovanni can't resist a bargain," she told him, "so here is fifteen thousand dollars. You call him and tell him that you will let him have the necklace for thirty-five thousand."

The jeweler did as he was bid, and Giovanni, who truly recognized value in jewelry, bought it instantly. That night, at his official ménage, he presented the necklace to his wife for her birthday.

The siesta habit is not only ingrained in the Roman character, but it also gets a legislative assist from an ordinance that forces shops to remain closed during the one-to-four period. Business offices follow suit. Every once in a while an American go-getter throws himself into this placid life convinced that his money-making ideas, if presented with western vigor, will make a change, at least in his own case. After swimming upstream until exhausted, he finally relaxes and moves with the Roman current.

The architecture of the Foreign Press Building is a classic example of Mussolini modern. It was, indeed, built by the dictator, who staffed it with his own personnel whose job it was to serve, and incidentally to keep an eye on, the foreign correspondents. It is on Via della Mercede, across the street from the central post office and telegraph building. Since there were no available building sites in the center of the city, Mussolini ordered that its stucco walls be wedged into the courtyard at the angle formed by Via della Mercede and Piazza San Silvestro.

I shared a three room office in the building with Korman of the *Chicago Tribune*. Our neighbor was *TASS*, the Soviet wire service, and it was fortunate for my friend that Colonel McCormick didn't visit his Rome bureau. For he would have been shocked by the proximity of the names on the adjoining doors. To one accustomed to the easy camaraderie of western foreign correspondents, the secretive Russian newsmen seemed like conspirators.

I suppose they must have considered me the most corrupt of capitalists, because I arrived at the office each morning in a chauffeur-driven American car. Although it was only a Ford, it was the first post-war civilian vehicle to appear on the streets of Rome, and awed crowds used to gather around to gape at its elegance. Two years later, when I sold it to make way for another car, I was paid three times as much as it had cost me.

On a warm spring day in 1947 I decided to lunch in town. I dismissed the car and strolled down Via della Mercede. Although it is in the very heart of Rome, the cobblestone street had no sidewalk. There were few autos to worry about, but the traffic in the streets was beginning to thicken with bicycles. It was just past one, the hour when all Romans were heading homeward for lunch and siesta.

I purchased *Il Messaggero* at the newsstand in Piazza San Silvestro, folded it under my arm and strolled down the Corso to Piazza San Ignazio, an architectural jewel that was designed and built like a theater backdrop in 1728. I seated myself at a table at the outdoor pizzeria. Here was an air of peace and tranquility. Movement was strictly in slow motion. I had often come here during the war, when the place had been a favorite of war correspondents and taxi drivers. The pizzas were a gourmet's delight, each one a meal in itself. They had cost all of four cents in the war days, but now, with inflation setting in, the price had gone up to nine cents.

I ordered a bitter Campari and unfolded my paper. In it was an article about a Sicilian bandit named Salvatore Giuliano. The two-column lead article on the front page was poorly written, and its few facts were somewhat overblown, but it purported to detail the crimson career of a bandit who had already committed one hundred murders but who was, withal, a gentleman. Notorious as a robber, kidnapper and murderer, he was the peasant's hero because he robbed from the rich and gave to the poor.

Giuliano's charity, while freely distributed, was done on a personal basis and, quite naturally, it won for him the affection of the receivers. An old woman, dying because she could not afford an operation, would wake to find fifty thousand lire under her pillow. Families facing starvation were helped without the annoying red tape of public charities. When a town had its spaghetti ration cut off, two truckloads of government supplies were hijacked and distributed free of charge in the piazza. It was the sort of philanthropy that found little favor with the Italian authorities, but the peasants loved it.

According to the article, Giuliano's reputation as a gentleman bandit came from the exaggerated courtesy and deference he accorded his titled victims. For example, when he invaded the ancient castle of the regal Duchess of Pratomeno, he kissed her hand and invited himself to tea while his men rifled the castle from dungeon to tower. Only once did the duchess complain. That was when the bandit pointed to a large diamond ring she was wearing. "Please don't take it," she begged. "It is the engagement ring given me by my husband. It is a reminder of my youth, of my first and only love."

Giuliano bowed courteously. "Knowing the story behind the ring will make me treasure it even more," he said, relieving her of it.

In addition to his elegant deportment, he was a killer with political aspirations who had declared himself the commanding general of an army that was sworn to fight for Sicilian independence. In a country of colorful and flamboyant politicians, he was the flashiest. He made the mainland variety look colorless by comparison. If he had carried his political ambitions to the point of running for public office, a distinct possibility under Italian law, which permits an outlaw to run for office from his hide-out, we would have had the spectacle of a sort of Al Capone for senator.

It was all very interesting. A Twentieth Century Robin Hood had been dumped right in my lap. Well, if not exactly a Robin Hood, at least a Dillinger with a press agent. It had all the elements of a fine story, but just to write about him was not enough for me. To make good copy I had to reach him, get an interview and photograph him. The adventure involved in getting to him would highlight the story. By a happy coincidence, it happened that I was leaving for Sicily the next morning to cover and photograph the new and frightening eruption of Mt. Etna.

At three-thirty, I strolled back to the office and wrote out a message to the late Bill Williams, a two-fisted editor whose capacity for distilled liquids is already legendary.

> via radiostampa press collect
> williams fawcpub ny
>
> shall eye attempt outsmoke sicilys socalled bandit king whose killed one hundred etregarded romantic figure stop expenses procoverage small bandits lair near mt etna stop trying interview etpix stop cable soonest
>
>   mike

The answer came two hours later:

> stern fawcpub rome
> yes stop dont get shot
>   bill

Early the next morning I dressed in army khaki, strapped on a shoulder holster with a loaded .45 Browning automatic and slipped a battle jacket over it. I loaded my camera equipment and baggage into the back of my jeep, sped down the Appian Way to Naples and from there bounced over the unbelievably bad roads of Calabria to the toe of the Italian boot. There I ferried across the Strait of Messina to Sicily and raced through the Mt. Etna assignment. The following day I was bumping slowly across even worse roads in the mountainous backbone of Sicily toward Palermo.

By now the difficulties that faced me appeared enormous. It was up to me to find and speak with a killer who was being actively hunted at the moment by some ten thousand police and troops. Then, if lucky enough to find him, I had to manage to stay alive long enough to write the article. And, having written it, protect it while waiting for my publication to go on newsstand sale.

I kept figuring ways and means of meeting with Giuliano. The fact that I had been a competent crime reporter in New York City would be of little help to me now. There was no purpose in calling on the local newspapermen, because if they knew how to reach Giuliano they would be doing that very thing for themselves. The same was true of the police. Twenty of them had succeeded in making a sort of rough contact with the killer, and these had been buried with full military honors. Trying to approach elements of his band, if I could dig them up, might be a possible answer, but this could have unpleasantly fatal consequences if the mobsters became nervous during negotiations.

I checked into the Hotel delle Palme in Palermo and, after a good night's sleep, rolled out of bed in the morning with the solution. It was so simple that I could have kicked myself for not having thought of it sooner. Who were the people in whom he had the greatest confidence? Why, his family, of course. That being the case, I would make my approach through them.

First, though, I dropped into local police headquarters to get an official fill-in from Inspector General Messana, the stout, bald-headed chief of the Public Security forces. I made a note that if Giuliano was Robin Hood, then this man was the Sheriff of Nottingham. He told me that he was angry because the Italian newspapers were glamorizing a person who was nothing but a cold, scheming killer. He seemed to speak with a good deal of personal malice, not only because a score of his officers had already been killed, but because on one occasion, on orders from his superior, the minister of interior, Inspector Messana had plastered Sicily with posters offering a million lire reward for the capture of the bandit king, dead or alive. A week later Sicily was plastered with a second manifesto, signed by Giuliano, offering two million lire for the capture of the minister of interior. This was a mortal insult.

"And I suppose that now you would like to interview him," the inspector general snickered.

"Yes," I told him.

"So would I," he said, throwing back his head and roaring at his own humor.

I was passed on to *Commissario* Nick Albertini, who was happy to talk to an American correspondent because he had a brother-in-law in the U.S. (I don't think there is a single Sicilian who doesn't have at least one close relative somewhere in the United States. If there is one, I haven't met him.)

"Here, I'll write his name for you," the *commissario* said, writing out "Sam Mangiapani, 6669 Raymond Avenue, Detroit, Michigan." He pulled out the Giuliano file and ran through the list of murders. It took the better part of the morning. Then we went through the kidnappings. This was an art which Giuliano had developed to such perfection that it was no longer necessary for him to make the actual physical snatch. All he did now was to write a letter to the prospective victim saying that he was next. The victim avoided unpleasantness by making an immediate deposit in favor of the bandit.

"If you have any idea of getting to Giuliano you had better forget it," the *commissario* advised. "The last word we had on him is that he has fled to France to recruit an army for the separatist movement. You see, he has become a politician now. He wants Sicily to secede from Italy and become the forty-ninth state of your United States."

"Then he must be very popular with the peasants," I said.

"It's easy to give away someone else's land."

"And he hands out a good deal of cash."

"It's easy to be generous with somebody else's money, too."

Despite this discouraging news, I went ahead with my plan. A foreign correspondent learns to take an official pronouncement with a generous sprinkling of salt. The next morning I took off in my jeep across the flats southward from Palermo harbor toward the towering gray cliffs that rise sheer and forbidding from the plain. Twenty miles further inland, in the center of this almost impassable rocky mass, is the town of Montelepri, capital of the bandit king's empire.

At the end of the flats was a roadblock controlled by six *carabinieri* and soldiers. They checked my papers and waved me on. I snaked up the hairpin turns of the gray mountain, drove inland a few more miles and finally made my way into the central piazza of the town, where a crowd of curious peasants immediately surrounded my jeep.

"Where," I asked, "will I find the home of Giuliano?"

There was an embarrassed silence, then an old man piped up. "There are many Giulianos in this village. It is a common name."

"Salvatore Giuliano, the bandit," I said.

There was a sad shaking of heads, as though they had never heard of this particular Giuliano. An old Sicilian joke came to my mind. A teacher asks one of her young scholars, "Who killed Julius Caesar?" No reply. "Stand up, Giovanni," orders the teacher. "I know that you know the answer."

"Sure, I know," Giovanni sneers, "but I ain't squealing."

I finally impressed on one of the youngsters that as an American I was a worthy object of trust, and he said he would guide me to the home of the parents. The old man who had denied ever hearing of Giuliano climbed into the jeep. I told him to get off. He ignored me. I shrugged my shoulders and drove down shabby Via Castrensio di Bella to number 189, the modest two-story plaster abode of the bandit king's family. The old man followed me into the house.

I introduced myself to the gnarled old woman who was the

bandit's mother and talked myself into an invitation to lunch, then turned to the old man. "You don't have to wait for me," I said with annoyance. "You can leave now."

"He's all right," Mama Giuliano said. "He's my husband!"

After a fine luncheon, I leaned back in my chair. "Your son is interested in what America thinks of him," I said. "Yet when I leave here, I must write that he is a common criminal, a cold-blooded killer—all because I know only what the police have told me. And so, unfortunately, that will be his reputation in my country."

"It's a lie," Mama said hotly. "He is a patriot."

I pulled out my notebook. "The police say he killed Terranova."

"Because he was a usurer."

"And Salvatore Abate, the postmaster?"

"Because he kept part of every American money order that came from American relatives. Why, he even did it to my daughter-in-law."

A fatal error, I agreed. "And Candella and Giacomo?"

"Because they robbed the poor people, and said they were sent by Giuliano. And, besides, he gave them a fair trial, which is more than the police do."

"More than fair for such criminal libel," I murmured. But hearing it from Mama was not good enough. I had to hear it from the head man, her son, just as I had heard from the head man on the other side, the inspector general. And there it was: killer or patriot? What would be the American verdict? The answer depended on Giuliano.

My greatest aid came from Mama's shrewdness. She reasoned that with American approval, Giuliano could run for senator. And if he could get elected, which seemed reasonable in view of his popularity with the peasantry, he would gain immunity for his criminal offenses as long as he sat in the legislature. I did nothing to weaken the notion that such approval could stem only from me.

From then on events moved swiftly. A rugged youth with a Colt .45 strapped to his waist came down from an upper floor, took me by the arm and hustled me into my jeep. We drove to the lip of the cliff overlooking the police roadblock that I had driven through a few hours before. Here I halted to permit another armed figure to climb into the back of the jeep. A peasant leading a mule up the cliff passed us wordlessly. The men in the jeep touched two fingers to their right brows, evidently a signal that all was well with them. The man with the mule tugged twice on his hat brim and continued climbing.

Now I was ordered to start the car and ride down to the plains, then cut back through an olive orchard to the base of the mountain. The men flanked me as I jumped out of the jeep at the designated spot. Two hundred feet in front of me, alone, stood a heroic figure of a man, tall, broad-shouldered and handsome in a dark, swarthy, Brando-cum-Valentino fashion. Hanging from his belt was a Browning automatic.

My first impression was that this was a person of tremendous physical strength. His thigh muscles filled out the corduroy work pants. His swarthy face was marked by more than a dozen small scars, but he had level brown eyes and carefully groomed, curly black hair. It was the frank, open face of a man who inspires confidence. He wore a GI suntan shirt open at the throat and a green corduroy hunting jacket. This first glimpse of the bandit king was a stirring sight.

We shook hands; then we stretched out on the ground under a tree and talked for the remainder of the afternoon. Around us henchmen, armed to the teeth, were deployed in strategic positions. From where I lay on the turf I could see the *carabinieri* at the roadblock. They were part of the army looking for Giuliano.

As we talked, he told me how he had become a bandit. As the son of a poor peasant—and in Sicily the peasants are rarely far removed from actual starvation—the burden of support had fallen upon his shoulders. One day when he was nineteen, he was taking a horse-load of grain to Palermo to sell in the open market. On the way he was stopped by three inter-province customs guards who confiscated the horse and grain and placed him under arrest. He broke away and tried to escape. The guards fired and he went down with two bullets in his back. As he sprawled on the ground, he whipped out a small caliber pistol, conveniently tucked inside a sock, and fired six shots. Two guards toppled over dead, and the third was wounded.

Now that the life of a bandit had been forced on him, Giuliano said, he decided to be a good one. He wouldn't rob only for himself, but for all the suffering people on his unhappy island. He robbed prodigious amounts of money from the rich and spread his gains lavishly amongst the poor. One newspaperman wrote that it was feudal Sicily's first redistribution of wealth. Another critic noted that Giuliano's policy of robbing the rich came less from social conscience than from a fine sense of double entry bookkeeping.

"The police say that I am a criminal," he continued bitterly. "You tell me who is the greater bandit, the policeman who squeezes money out of the poor to put in his own pocket or I, who rob from the rich in order to give to the poor. Why, if I was interested in myself, I would merely have to keep the proceeds from a single kidnapping and with this I could live like a gentleman for the rest of my life."

He was bubbling over with political plans. "I have a matter of great importance to discuss with you," he said. "Here is a letter I have written to President Truman. I would appreciate it if you would read it."

A most logical document it proved to be. It pointed out that the United States had spent more than a billion dollars in Italy, Greece and Turkey to keep communism from growing in the Mediterranean area. Yet here in Sicily, in the forthcoming elections, the communists might very easily come into power. This victory in itself would nullify the entire Truman Doctrine. Therefore, as the leader of the only armed force in Sicily that was actively fighting communism, he asked for aid as a co-equal with these governments. He alone was the bulwark that could protect American foreign policy. And he wasn't coming to the president with empty hands. He was offering Sicily as the forty-ninth state of the American union. He didn't want any money from America, he told me with a boyish grin. There were enough rich clients on the island to finance his program. What he needed was modern machine guns and heavy caliber field pieces.

I folded the letter and put it in my pocket, promising him that I would translate it into proper English before mailing it to our president. I told him not to be offended if there was no answer because, after all, our chief executive was a very busy man; also, a direct response might give offense to Italy, with whom we were on friendly terms.

The matter of military aid was of great urgency, he pointed out. Would I explain to President Truman that the island of Sicily had just been granted regional autonomy by the mainland government of Italy as a cunning move to destroy his separatist movement. In the first vote for the local assembly an electorate that only a year before had voted overwhelmingly to retain the monarchy had now given the majority of its votes to the Communist Party. The bandit, who was determined to do something to remedy this situation, felt that the American president could readily see what all this meant. Giuliano's personal response to the communist challenge had been most violent. He had led a group of masked horsemen across a ridge near the town of Porta della Ginestra, where a communist May Day celebration was being held. His men opened fire with machine guns, and when the smoke lifted, eight townspeople lay dead and another thirty-three lay wounded. Labor unions called a general strike, which paralyzed the country and almost overthrew the De Gasperi government. The price on Giuliano's head was raised to seventy thousand dollars. This had no effect on the bandit leader, and a few weeks later, using dynamite, he struck again. Communist Party headquarters in half a dozen towns were blasted out of existence.

During our conversation I told him that he reminded me of Pancho Villa.

"Who is this Pancho Villa?" he asked suspiciously.

"A Mexican bandit and killer who rose to great heights. You know, Wallace Beery."

"Never heard of him."

"You're sure you never heard of Villa?" I asked cautiously.

"I never did," he said with assurance.

"In that case let me tell you about him. He was a murderer and a kidnapper and the government of Mexico called him even worse things. He, too, robbed from the rich and gave to the poor, but the people loved him and he became ruler of his country. He made only one mistake. He killed an American. Very foolish of him because it served no purpose. The whole of the American army came after him and hung him, and that was the end of Pancho Villa."

Giuliano nodded sagely, and I could almost see the little wheels in his mind turning slowly as they assimilated the obvious moral of this fabrication.

The existence of a Giuliano is easily explained. He was produced by a combination of war and geography. The Allied invasion of Sicily left the island a physical and economic wreck. It pried loose Mussolini's dictatorial hand and replaced it with a political freedom that bred self-seeking parties and grafting politicians. The word "liberty" was bandied about freely, but to the peasant it was a meaningless concept. More real was the bitter poverty in the villages; the hunger of the shepherds in the *busambra;* the isolation and squalid loneliness of the *latifondo;* the misery of the sulphur miners, whose families couldn't afford a normal meal on the earnings of a ten-hour day of toil in the torrid sun.

I had come to Sicily to scoff at a pretentious killer. I left with mixed feelings. Giuliano was a Sicilian, and the Sicilians are a proud people who have suffered every possible inequity through the centuries. This unlettered youth—he was twenty-five years old when we met and had barely finished the third grade in elementary school—was trying to right these wrongs. His methods were illegal and immoral. The code by which he lived was criminal. But in his own fashion, and in his own dreams, his goal was pure.

There wasn't a shadow of a doubt that the eventual outcome of his battle with Italy would be death for Giuliano, but in our conversation he was confident in his own prowess. "The winner will be the one with more *fegato*,"* he said. "So far I have not lost a single battle."

I mentioned that the police did not regard their hunt for him as a political matter, but a criminal one. As for catching him, there were other ways besides fighting pitched battles. Through a woman, for example, as was the case with Dillinger, or through the treachery of a confederate. He smiled at my naiveté. The way he lived gave him no time for girls. And as for his gang, he had men like his cousin, Gaspare Pisciotta, who was sitting with us, to protect him. Pisciotta, mustached, swarthy and shifty-eyed, smiled at the words of praise. He was Giuliano's "blood brother," which meant they had performed the ceremony of cutting their wrists and holding the wounds together so that the blood from one would supposedly flow through the veins of the other.

Two years later Giuliano was shot to death while he slept at the side of this blood brother, who had made a deal with the police for the seventy thousand dollar reward.

Back in Rome, word got out somehow that I had secured an interview with Giuliano, and reporters raced to Sicily. In the first group were Sey Korman and Camille Cianfara of *The New York Times*. If they succeeded in reaching the bandit, my scoop was a dud, since a daily is much faster than a monthly publication. I sent off a telegram to Giuliano's home, informing him that I had just uncovered a plot on the part of the *carabinieri* to trap him by sending down secret agents disguised as American correspondents. The more perfect their American accent and the better their identity papers, the more chance there was that they were police spies.

* *Fegato:* literally "liver." The word is used as Americans use "guts."

In an ironic double double-cross, Pisciotta, who had sold his blood brother's life to the police, was convicted of Giuliano's murder and sentenced to life imprisonment. This caused him great unhappiness, especially since he had been promised in writing by responsible members of the Italian government that if he would eliminate the bandit king, he would be guaranteed his freedom in addition to the reward. While Giuliano slept one night, Pisciotta shot him in the back, although the police, dragging the body into a lonely village courtyard and shooting it with machine guns, made it look as though Robin Hood had been killed in a running gunfight. Pisciotta, in short, had kept his part of the bargain. But here he was, without the seventy thousand dollars and sentenced to prison for life. No wonder he was unhappy.

He issued an ultimatum to the government authorities who had made the promise that if he wasn't sprung, he would blow the whistle on all of them. As Pisciotta sat in the cell he shared with his father, also a long term prisoner, he was handed his morning cup of coffee, differing in the brew he had received on previous mornings in that this one contained enough strychnine to kill twenty men. He drank it and fell dead.

Giuliano was a peculiarly Sicilian phenomenon, a product of the same forces that produced and nurtured another far more famous extra-legal organization—the Mafia. "Mafia" is among the most misunderstood terms in America, but on this impoverished, unhappy island it is a grim reality. Since it figured very much in the aftermath of the Guiliano story, and since I was to become involved thereby in some of its bloody manifestations, some attempt to explain it is in order. Actually, the Mafia is difficult to define except in negative terms, but perhaps a partial picture will emerge from the following episodes:

Fanuzza, a dark, fiery Sicilian maiden, was made for love. Several times in such diversely romantic places as olive orchards, haystacks and two-wheeled carts, she fulfilled her natural function with the son of a wealthy landowner. As a consequence of these sentimental adventures it was not surprising that she found herself in what Victorian writers called an interesting condition.

It was even less surprising that the young man, far from having any thoughts of legitimatizing the situation, was off in search of other hot-blooded maidens. Now if all this had taken place in America, the girl would go to court to seek relief. But Monreale, where the event occurred, is in the heart of Sicily. It is a beautiful village on a hilltop where the inhabitants have been taught from the cradle, indeed have breathed in the very air, that it is dishonorable to appeal to the authorities.

News of the girl's condition was brought to old Don Caló, a short, pot-bellied man with white hair and soft blue eyes and an even softer voice. Don Caló listened quietly to the report, but made no comment. A few days later he visited the young man's family. After a lengthy and flowery greeting he turned his attention to the young man, a law student, and, begging pardon for his own ignorance, asked whether the law permitted a gentleman to walk into a private garden and pluck a rose. The young student at law advised him that this was against existing regulations. Thereupon Don Caló asked what would happen to the rose-plucker if he were caught. He was informed that the culprit would have to pay the penalty prescribed by law.

With an air of quiet triumph, Don Caló turned to the young man's father and said, "I offer you my congratulations. You have heard your son quoting the law. He is willing to pay."

The young man's jaw dropped as he asked, hesitantly, how he came into the act. The white-haired gentleman drew a parallel between Fanuzza and the rose in the private garden.

"But she is of age," was the protest.

"So?" the white-haired man said.

"I have done nothing wrong in the eyes of the law," the youth replied.

"You speak of laws that were made by man and I speak of the laws that were made by God," he replied. Although spoken without emphasis, the verdict that was implicit in Don Caló's words carried more weight than a court order.

The young man's father bowed his head slightly. "Don Caló," he said with feeling, "it will be my honor to ask for the hand of Fanuzza in marriage for my son."

This is the Mafia in action.

Roccu Lombardi, a poor farmer, working a miserable piece of land near Caltanissetta in the interior of Sicily, tried after a particularly tough year to get a loan of a hundred thousand lire, roughly a hundred and sixty dollars at the present rate of exchange, at the local bank. But, having no security, he was turned down. The following day the banker received a visit from a roughly dressed though very respectful individual who introduced himself as an *amico degli amici*.

"Although we realize how unworthy Lombardi is of any trust from so great and powerful an institution as the one you represent," the roughly dressed one said, "still may we point out what grave hardships it would work upon him and his family not to have this loan. And may I also respectfully say how pleasing it would be to Don Caló if Lombardi's request were to be honored."

"You may inform Don Caló," the banker said, "that it will be an honor for this institution to extend credit to Roccu Lombardi."

It would have been unthinkable for the banker to refuse the request made by a "friend of friends," as the Mafia refers to its faithful. Although coercion had prompted the banker to part with the cash, he did so without qualms, because the Mafia, having prompted him to make the loan, was honor-bound to see that it would be repaid. If anyone had suggested to Roccu that he was a member of the Mafia, he would have been astonished. He had never joined the Mafia because there is no organization to join; he had taken no oath because there is no oath to take; he had attended no meetings because meetings do not occur. But if Don Caló had told him that it was necessary to walk to the next village and sink a stiletto into the back of a totally unknown person, Roccu, though he might never dream of committing a crime for personal profit, would obey without hesitation. If Don Caló wanted this done, then it was a worthy act that he, an ignorant peasant, would not even try to figure out, for Don Caló was a kind and a just man who had the respect of all the people in the community.

This is the true Mafia.

Don Caló's full name was Calogero Vizzini.* He was a small landowner of moderate means, who wore the rough corduroy clothing of the countryside and who moved about, on the rare occasions when he left his hearth, on the back of a donkey, or in a rickety car. He lived modestly in the town of Villalba with his brother, who is a priest. The injustices, the angers, and the criminal enterprises of Sicily were brought to him and he listened patiently. When he said: *"È cosa mia,"* it meant that he had accepted whatever matter was under discussion as a personal obligation. He carried no arms and rarely made threats, but his decisions were rigidly enforced. He had no kingdom, but he reigned. He had no court, but the peasants in the countryside were his vassals. He rarely raised his voice above a whisper, never threatened, was always respectful, and had never heard of Frank Costello and Joe Adonis. He knew Lucky Luciano only because the deported racketeer put in an appearance in Sicily. Don Caló treated him with the same respect he would have shown any peasant in the area. Neither more nor less. As long as Luciano behaved himself, he had nothing to fear from Don Caló.

Such information as this might come as a surprise to many who, if they ever gave the subject of the Mafia any thought at all, have concluded that Joe Adonis, Lucky Luciano and Frank Costello headed this organization.

---

* Don Caló died at a ripe old age and at his funeral, which was attended by hordes of people, not a single American gangster was present. He was succeeded by Giuseppe Russo, called Zi Pepi (Uncle Pepi), an evil-looking, swarthy, mustached figure who comes from the drab mountain village of Mussomeli. At Don Caló's funeral he carried one of the casket cords. I visited Zi Pepi shortly thereafter and he told me, "I have inherited the teachings of Don Caló. Nobody can inherit his command."

Don Caló, like Guiliano, had definite political opinions, among
them a bitter antagonism to the Communist Party. The manner in
which he expressed this sentiment was likely to be as direct as the
bandit king's. On one occasion Senator Giralamo LiCausi, the
island's communist commissar, who was trained for the job by a
careful indoctrination in Moscow, announced that he was going to
hold an open air mass meeting in Villalba. (The communist senator
happens to be a real firebrand as an orator, a fact which is painfully apparent to this writer, for the honorable senator from Sicily,
wrapped in a cloak of legislative immunity, has made me the
subject of several inflammatory speeches.)

In any event Don Caló, anxious to keep LiCausi out of Villalba,
did what any good Mafia chief would do in like circumstances. He
let it be known that LiCausi's presence in Villalba would dis-
please him. The fiery communist appeared anyway. As he began
to speak in the crowded town square, there was a blaze of gunfire from the roofs of surrounding buildings. The crowd scattered
like magic. Senator LiCausi, wounded, lay writhing in agony. An
old man ambled across the now empty square toward him, leaned
over and asked if there was anything he could do to help.

It was Don Caló, in the finest tradition of the Mafia, offering a
hand to a fallen enemy.

What, precisely, is the Mafia? It is a deeply rooted tradition, a
similarity of sentiment and spiritual temper. There are no elections
for chief of the Mafia, and a person does not achieve this title by
the use of a gun, as he does in the American underworld. A
Mafia leader gains his position through the respect in which his
followers hold him. This is the keystone of his power. If he were
to use violence in the interest of what Sicilians would term injustice, or for the purpose of enriching himself, he would rapidly
lose the respect of his followers, and this in itself would mean the
loss of his power. No sign of recognition between members is
necessary, because they know each other from infancy. The Mafia
needs no statute because it has a tradition that is eight hundred
years old, and the key to this tradition is *omerta*.

A brief glance at Sicily's history, at the injustices that her people have suffered through the centuries, makes the peculiar institution of the Mafia understandable, even if it is not forgivable. Since the fall of the Roman Empire, Sicily has been the prey of Greeks, Turks, Normans, Spaniards, French and Neapolitan invaders, all of whom came with the idea of taking out as much wealth as they could. The police were always the executive arm that the various conquerors used to enforce their depredations. There was barely a household that didn't have its women folk raped and its money stolen by the upholders of law and order. This built a feeling of hatred and distrust of established government which has extended through the Savoy kingdom and Mussolini into the present democratic regime.

The Mafia took form in the Thirteenth Century as the only force that permitted the weak and the poor to gain a certain measure of respect and dignity for themselves. Since they could not appeal to outsiders, which meant the local government in force, they took on themselves the administration of justice, and they performed such services as bushwhacking the more obnoxious of the cops and slitting the throats of those compatriots who cooperated with the surviving police.

Through the centuries the tradition of the Mafia and of *omerta* grew stronger. The origin of both words is obscure, although their meaning is clear. Mafia is believed to have been the name of an old and adept killer (although other Italian experts say it is a Turkish word or that its letters are the initial ones of a phrase demanding death to the French). Omerta means man with a capital M, and in Sicily this has come to have special significance. A Man never reports a crime to the authorities, but regards it as a personal offense that must be wiped out with blood. Aid must never be given to the police, even though justice be served by it; and, conversely, aid must be given to fellow Mafiosi, no matter how grave the crime they commit and no matter how perilous the risk. The Sicilian applauds the man who knows how to talk, but his love is for the one who knows how to keep quiet. He respects the man who knows how to pardon, but he prefers the man who knows how to take revenge.

The Mafia is a power in Sicily's rabid politics. It has reached a compromise with local politicians whereby the latter make use of the Mafia in order to achieve their ends, in exchange for which they submit to certain impositions by the Mafia. It has become a Tammany Hall—with stiletto. Just how powerful a force it is can be judged by the fact that Vittorio Emanuele Orlando, grand old man of Italian politics and one-time premier of his country, ran for Congress with large election posters reading "*Votate per Vittorio Emanuele Orlando—l'amico degli amici*," thus openly advertising that he was kin to the Mafia. In another election on the island in which the Mafia had a keen interest, the local leader tapped the opposing poll-watcher on the shoulder and politely invited him for a cup of coffee. To have refused would have been a mortal insult, so the watcher crossed the square, gulped a hasty drink and hurried back to the poll. He wasn't fast enough. In a town of three thousand souls, twenty-four hundred of them had just dropped their votes for the Mafia's favored candidate. Obviously, if the Mafia was powerful enough to elect others, the day would have to come when they would elect their own candidate. And there have been several legislators and at least one cabinet member who were part of the Mafia.

The Mafia's love for intrigue and cunningly contrived vendetta is best illustrated by what happened to an individual named Francisco Paolo Coppola, alias Angelo Vota, alias Frank Lomondo, alias Frank Lorconio, alias Jim Cabrera, alias Frank Loicono, alias Gimi Barbera, alias Frank the Cripple, a character who needed all of these aliases because he had been arrested some fifteen times in the United States for such diverse activities as murder, dope peddling and kidnapping. He was a truly tough mobster who had been involved, directly or indirectly, in ten homicides. Coppola made his headquarters in New Orleans, where he had been part of Frank Costello's mob in the slot machine business. Because Coppola happened to have been born in

Partinico, Sicily, which is the very heart of Mafia country, and because he was a full-time criminal closely associated with Frank Costello, that section of the press which wrote about him in America found it a matter of simple logic to name him one of the chiefs of the New Orleans branch of the Mafia. The error in the seemingly impeccable logic was proved by Signor Coppola's subsequent misadventures.

Coppola had smuggled himself into the United States, a fact that came to the attention of Commissioner Harry Anslinger of the Federal Narcotics Bureau, who suspected Coppola of dabbling in contraband. The result was that narcotic agents harried him with such determination that it left him little opportunity to practice this profitable racket. It was Anslinger's desire to rid the country of this undesirable alien, and he pressed the case on the immigration authorities. It proved no easy matter to get rid of Signor Coppola, for coming to his aid were such politically important persons as Congressman James Domengeaux, Louisiana Attorney General Fred S. LeBlanc, Baton Rouge Chief of Police Fred C. Parker, and a few assorted district attorneys. Their assistance was so effective that the Board of Immigration reached the conclusion that Coppola had established a "good moral character."

This was a barren victory for Coppola, however, because the narcotics agents continued to make his life miserable, and he decided to leave the United States of his own volition. He returned to Sicily.

In the Mafia, the tougher one is, the softer one speaks. But Coppola informed all and sundry that he was a person of great importance and expected to be treated as such. The Mafia ignored him. It was then that he made a serious error. In need of some funds, he and two pals put the snatch on a local gentleman named Don Lucio Tasca and Tasca's nine-year-old grandson. This was an act that even a Sicilian idiot would have avoided, and it clearly indicated that he didn't know the first thing about the Mafia.

Don Lucio, a man of haughty lineage and massive wealth, is

one of the progressive land barons on the still feudal island. His liberal attitude toward his peasants has earned him their affection. More important, he has the undying respect of the Mafia. They tip their hats and bow low before Don Lucio. An insult to his person is an affront to the honor and dignity of the Mafia. In the case of the unfortunate Signor Coppola, retribution was not long in coming. Two days after the kidnapping, both Don Lucio and his grandson were released, unharmed and without the payment of ransom. Unknown gunmen grabbed Coppola's two henchmen, shot them through the back of the head and dumped their bodies in a ditch beside a lonely mountain road.

The murder of Coppola's pals was the work of the Mafia. Their way of punishing him was to plant enough evidence around to make it look as though he, Coppola, had murdered his own men. And, indeed, if you examine this case in a nonlegal light, he had. Coppola was picked up on a murder charge. To add to his woes, agents of the Italian customs police received an anonymous tip, raided his villa in the town of Alcamo and found a trunk, the false sides of which ingeniously concealed six hundred thousand dollars worth of pure heroin, addressed and ready for shipment to the United States.

It is necessary to have this background on the Mafia and to realize the enormous impact that Giuliano and the May Day massacre had on the country to understand the events that now took place.

The Sicilian communists, who breathed the same Mafia air and possessed the same traditions as other *mafios,* were not going to take Giuliano's oppressive tactics without fighting back. Nor, for that matter, were they letting me go unpunished for the supposed support I had brought Giuliano from the American government. (The only explanation they could make for the ease with which I contacted Giuliano was that I was an American spy, and because America was anti-communist, I had, therefore, induced Giuliano to bomb their meeting places and kill the May Day paraders.)

The opportunity to punish me, destroy Giuliano's influence and add to the stature of the Communist Party was soon forthcoming.

One day a young member of the Giuliano band walked toward a mailbox in downtown Palermo. In the breast pocket of his jacket he carried a letter written by Giuliano and addressed to Signor Michael Stern, Via Mercede 55, Rome, Italy. As he approached the box, communist assassins fired point blank at him with sawed-off shotguns. The young hoodlum was killed outright. The pellets perforated the letter, staining it with blood.

The communists knew the contents of the letter. It was meant to be found on the body of the dead man, for its publication was meant to discredit the bandit as the agent of a foreign power, one that sent billions of dollars of aid with one hand and death with the other.

I knew nothing about this "explosive" letter. I didn't even know about the murder. I missed the story because it only rated a few lines in a Rome daily. It seems there was a slight hitch in the communists' calculations. The police officer who found the letter did not make it part of the criminal file, for it is not to be found there. One theory is that he found it so hot that he dispatched it to Rome, where it was impounded by the minister of interior.

The Communist Party organ, *L'Unita,* used it as a basis for accusing me of being an American spy, of using the cloak of journalism to mask these nefarious activities, of having furnished Giuliano with arms and of having given the orders for the "pogrom" at Porta della Ginestra on May Day. It was this last charge that I found ironic, for my grandparents had fled to the U.S. to escape the pogroms of Europe. Now, according to the communists, I was back in Europe starting new ones.

I read into these vitriolic attacks an invitation to a party faithful to become a hero by slipping up behind me and putting a bullet in my head. I defended myself by filing criminal libel charges against the two writers of the article and the editor of the paper and by sleeping with a .45 caliber automatic under my pillow.

All three were convicted, sentenced to prison and fined. Then I sued them civilly and was awarded seven million lire in damages and interest. Such are the ramifications of Italian law, the power of the Communist Party and the weakness of the U.S. Embassy in Italy that they served not a single day and paid not a single lira in fines or civil damages.

The honorable LiCausi, in a speech in the Senate in 1951, spoke about these letters: "There exists a letter which Giuliano wrote to Major (sic) Stern on his return to Rome from Montelepri. It was found in the pocket of a bandit who fell in a gunfight, and the police immediately sent it to the minister of the interior. Two years ago I asked Minister Scelba whether this letter existed and the minister did not even bother to answer."

The Communist Party and its press never gave up the search for the letters, and in the end they were rewarded. The communist daily, *Paese Sera*, managed to secure photostatic copies, and its issue of November 26, 1960, devoted two full pages to them. The headline ran across the full nine columns:

FOR YEARS IT WAS HUNTED: PAESE SERA PUB-
LISHES IT FOR THE FIRST TIME—THE TWO LET-
TERS FROM BANDIT GIULIANO

In the First, Addressed to the American Journalist Stern, the King of Montelepri Has Attached a Letter Destined for the American Command. What Did the Outlaw Ask a Few Days before the Massacre of Porta della Ginestra?

The Two Dramatic Documents Were Found in the Pocket of a Bandit Killed by Shotgun Fire. An Envelope Lacerated by Bullets, the Original is Missing: Who Stole It? The Journalist Stern, Perhaps, Can Still Help Justice To Illuminate the Grave Political Background of the Bloody Actions of the Giuliano Band.

In the eighteen columns devoted to the story I read the following facts about myself:

Signor Stern was in the American army with the grade of major during the war and it appears that he was assigned many delicate duties. He has always publicly admitted his personal relations with Giuliano and has given a comprehensible explanation, exhibiting his excellent reportage on the Sicilian bandit. The letters that we are now publishing never reached the hands of Signor Stern, even though they were addressed to him. They were found in the pocket of a bandit lying dead on the ground.

Here are the letters:

Signor Stern,
     With my best wishes I send you warmest regards. I ask if it is possible to have the enclosed message given to the American command. With infinite thanks.

(signed) *Giuliano*

Dear Sirs,
     Some days ago I sent a young man to inform you of my effective position and he, on his return, informed me of certain things, but nothing concrete. Please don't think of me as the bandit that the Italian government must naturally call me. Please believe me to be one who knows how to fight against the vile Reds. I ask that you send somebody to me so that he take note on the situation in Sicily that I, myself, will illustrate. I ask you to note that many political parties have wanted to help me in all ways that I wish, but my pure and honest sentiment has not moved one inch from that principle that I will follow until death.
     My feeling is that any attempted resistance on my part will be in vain, because the Italian government has decided

to put me out of the way no matter what the cost. This does not frighten me but it saddens me that only with my machine gun must I affront their tanks. I beg you to send somebody because most certainly I can be useful. This is my address: Via Castrensio di Bella N.189, Montelepri.

If one of you should come I ask you not to wear your uniform but come in civilian clothes and for major security be accompanied by Signor Stern so that my family can remain more tranquil. Accept my best wishes.

(signed) *Giuliano*

Part III
AND EVER AFTER

Chapter 10

Master of Villa Spiga

I FOUND A NEW HOME. Although the Via di Villa Sacchetti apartment was a comfortable, elegant one in a fine section of the city, the new residence can only be described as fabulous. Its name is Villa Spiga. It is located on Via Trionfale where the road snakes to the top of Monte Mario, the highest point in Rome, on the northern edge of the city. Finding the villa was an important event, because I knew that finally I, an October 1st gypsy from New York, had found a home.

An eight-foot, massive stone wall bounds the grounds on the street side. Built into it is a long, low, one-story caretaker's cottage. Where the cottage ends, a pair of heavy oaken doors, painted green, swing inward on enormous hinges. Here a broad courtyard leads into a wide graveled drive that curves gently uphill for two hundred yards under a canopy of eucalyptus trees. The house itself has eighteen rooms on five levels, and it is surrounded by some thirty acres of park, gardens, orchards, stables, greenhouses, a swimming pool, fountains, grottos, ancient Roman statuary, palm trees, wooded groves and a dozen umbrella pines, which have always filled me with a warm feeling of nostalgia. Each city has an individual landmark that identifies it to an inhabitant or visitor. Some get the feel of Rome when they see a photo of the Colosseum or the Forum or St. Peter's. In Paris it might be the Champs Élysées, the Eifel Tower, or the Seine; in London, Piccadilly, the Strand or London Bridge. For me the umbrella pines spell Rome, and perhaps some psychiatrist can make something of it.

Around this new home of ours, rose bushes bloomed from April to December; poinsettias and orchids flowered in the greenhouses and mimosa trees spread their sunny yellow hue in the closing days of January; almond blossoms flowered in the soft rains of February while March, April and May were rampant with the blooms and scents of the fruit trees. Each terrace had its particular fragrance: the one adjoining the dining room was gardenia, the living room had the spicy geranium and the master bedroom, orange blossom.

Supervising so large an estate was quite an undertaking, and the very idea was both heady and somewhat frightening. It required a large staff, so we started with seven. First there was Pina, the cook from Treviso who made eating a delight rather than a habit. I understand and appreciate good food, so I can be objective when I say that no restaurant made a pizza as good as she did; so good, in fact, that the thousands of American friends we have wined and dined over the years have given it a name—Pizza a la Stern. She hit upon the recipe by accident. There was no fresh yeast on sale at our local *drogheria,* so she used baking powder instead. With this, she achieved a crisp, wafer-thin crust instead of the soft, doughy one. And she doubled the amount of tomato and mozarella cheese. Try it yourself. It makes a mouthwatering morsel, if such a small word can be used to describe her gigantic cartwheels.

Pina looked after the family with the ferocity of a lioness protecting her cubs. During her first month in service my wife gave her a coat with a fur collar that had belonged to my mother-in-law. It would have taken two years of her salary to purchase a cheap replica. She had left her last position after thirteen years because she could not make ends meet with the eighteen hundred lire per month salary she received, a good part of which went to support her brother's large family. She asked us for three thousand lire as a start and perhaps later, if we were satisfied with her service, she would like to be raised to thirty-five hundred lire. The local scale at that time was twenty-five hundred lire a month for a cook. The free market exchange, which I received, fluctuated between five hundred and seven hundred lire to the dollar, making her salary about five dollars a month.

When Pina discovered that the food served in the kitchen was the same as that in the dining room, her loyalty knew no bounds. Her amazement on discovering that the refrigerator and the pantry had no locks for which the mistress of the household jealously guarded the keys would be difficult for an American to understand. Because of this manifest trust in her, she maintained a fierce surveillance over everything these repositories contained. Woe betide the servant who tried to pilfer!

Having come from a job with a titled family, where meat was allowed the servants just once a week and where the rest of the menu was sharply limited as well, common treatment for servants of the time, she regarded her residence in Villa Spiga as a paradise in which I was the leading angel. This heaven remained hers for ten years, until one day I shipped her off with my family to the United States for a winter. By this time her salary had gone up to twelve thousand lire, and it was doubled for the time she spent abroad. This was not enough to blind her to the larger paradise for domestics that exists in the U.S.A. and, alas, she is still there.

The nursemaid was Rina, an attractive girl of twenty who had just returned from France, where her émigré parents had raised her. I still have before me a mental picture of my son, age ten, stretched out on his bed reading a comic magazine and Rina, leaning over, trying to divest him of a pair of trousers. In the picture the boy is saying, politely but firmly, from behind the magazine which he never lowered for an instant, "Please be careful. You know I don't like to be jiggled while I'm reading."

Then there was Aldo, the chauffeur-butler, and his young, attractive wife, who was the upstairs maid. Impeccably dressed in chauffeur's uniform, Aldo drove the children to school each morning and home again in the afternoon. In the house when he served he wore a white jacket with gold buttons and gold braid on the shoulders and white gloves. The upstairs maid brought breakfast, which, like the normal Roman family, my wife and I ate in bed. Aldo was the perfect servant in every respect except one. He was light-fingered. The first time I caught him lifting a few packages of cigarettes, but he was too good a servant to be fired for so petty a theft, so I merely lectured him. He seemed very contrite. The next time I caught him stealing several jerry cans of gasoline. This was still very petty, so I lectured him a second time, and he was even more contrite. At the third theft I fired him out of hand, giving him ten minutes to collect his belongings and be off. A month later a headline on the crime page of *Il Tempo* caught my attention. It stated that the perfect Jeeves had absconded with the jewelry, silverplate and even precious paintings of the employer to whom he had gone after I had thrown him out. In the body of the article I read that he had been secretly maintaining a mistress and that he had fled with her, leaving his wife behind to face the music.

Aldo was replaced by Giovanni, a young man of decided feminine tendencies, which I was inclined to overlook. With so many attractive females in the household, I didn't want sex to complicate matters backstairs. Like Aldo, I permitted him to sleep in the main house. One day while starting the coal furnace in the basement, he tossed in a bucket of gasoline to speed the fire along. The explosion blew him into the hospital and out of my service.

Gerhardt, who replaced the effeminate Giovanni, was an entirely different sort. He held an engineering degree from a good university in Germany and was well proportioned, blond and good-looking. He was bedded down in the chauffeur's room in the lower level of the gardener's cottage, approximately two hundred yards from the villa, but that, too, turned out to be a mistake.

Gerhardt had been a nazi, a captain in the Wehrmacht and the highest ranking officer in the German prisoner of war camp in Rome. He had not been repatriated because his home was in East Germany, and the Soviets were tempting him with the rank of major if he would join their new army. My good friend, General Charles Dasher, the last commanding officer of our forces in Rome (he later commanded our troops in Berlin), asked me to give Gerhardt a job. This would permit us to liberate him from the camp and would also serve as an excuse for not returning him to Germany. What neither General Dasher nor I knew was that politics had nothing to do with Gerhardt's desire to stay out of the Soviet zone. It seems that he had a wife and two children waiting for him there, and he had no particular desire to return to them. He had, also, a German girl friend who had managed to make her way to Rome. He was an excellent chauffeur and he even learned how to wait on table, though he acted more like a Prussian officer than a Jeeves. I never did learn how he felt about serving the Cohens and the Schwartzes, who on occasion dined with us, for he never betrayed by so much as a single sign that all of this wasn't the most natural thing in the world for him.

I was the last one in the villa to find out that his girl friend had moved into his room and was a happy member of our ménage. Eventually his papers were validated by the Argentine government, and he and his girl emigrated there. I was not sorry to see him go.

A laundress and two gardeners rounded out the staff. Salaries in Italy are paid on a monthly basis, and the combined amount for the seven of them came to well under one hundred dollars. The rent was twenty-five thousand lire a month, or about fifty dollars. Since the contract had been signed before January 1st, 1947, I benefited by the Italian blocked rental law. This meant

that the rent could be raised only by law and that the term of the
lease was automatically extended for as long as the law was on
the books. It still is.

I would be less than normal if I didn't say quickly that this was
a phase of life in Rome that I found very much to my liking.
So many of us struggle for years, making compromises, in order to
earn enough money to be able to afford to live like this. Most of
us don't quite make it. Yet without any merit on my part, merely
by being in this particular place at this particular time, I made it.
When Spyros Skouras visited Villa Spiga, he wrote in the house
book, "You're a liar. No newspaperman can live like this." Sinclair
Lewis was our house guest. Before he had seen the villa, he
lectured me about becoming a European beachcomber and
warned me to return home and give fuller play to my writing
talents. After staying at the villa, he retracted his warning. "Stay
where you are," he said. "I can't afford to live this way in
America."

Certainly economic ease played a part in my love affair with
Rome; it is a wonderful feeling not to have to devote one's full
energy toward earning money. But there was another kind of
ease I appreciated even more. During the last years before the
war, I lived in the suburbs of New York. The famous Long
Island Railroad required an hour to transport me to Pennsylvania
Station and another hour to bring me back, and I thoroughly
hated every second of the two hours given over daily to the ride
and felt dominated by the regimentation of a train schedule. I
remember that I would arrive home breathless, even when I
didn't have to race for the 5:17 express. I love music and art, but
there was little time or energy left for concerts and exhibits.
Distance and traffic were making me lead a life that was not of
my choosing.

In Rome my office is close at hand. When I leave it, I can be
at a dozen galleries in five minutes. If I lunch at Capriccio, I
often stop in at the Odyssia Gallery and look at some Fabbri

and Somaini sculpture or Morlotti abstracts. (In order not to destroy a beautiful old tree whose branches shade part of the Capriccio terrace, the gallery was built around the trunk, which takes up almost half its space. Only in Rome would an architect plan his structure around a tree.) When in the mood I can make a one-minute detour and see a Nino Caffe or Bruno Caruso exhibit at the Obelisco, or catch an Omicciolli, de Pises or Capogrossi show as I walk back to my work. For eight months of the year I make appointments at sidewalk cafes and conduct interviews over an *aperativo*.

When I worked for the Middletown (New York) *Times-Herald,* I loved the pace of small-town life and couldn't understand how I ever could have been happy working for a metropolitan newspaper. But when I returned to the big city I was shocked that I could have been beguiled away from pursuing a journalistic career in this more important environment. Because I was ambitious, I needed a big city, but it didn't keep me from pining for the tranquility of a Middletown. Rome furnished me both. It is a world capital of religion, music and art. It is a communications center that has become as important in the post-World War II world as Paris had been in the post-World War I. And in addition it has become the world's film producing center. Yet in spite of all this, Rome has managed to keep the pace of a village.

When my wife and I attended Syracuse University during the depression years, it was our dream to visit Rome, but "Not as a tourist," I kept insisting. Of course, these were idle dreams, because in those early Thirties it didn't seem likely that there would even be enough money for us to finish our schooling.

To put the frosting on the cake, I learned after I came to Italy that the U.S. government levies no income tax on the earnings of foreign correspondents who establish bona fide residences abroad. The Italian government didn't get around to levying taxes until much later, and then it did so by profession rather than by individual earnings. Foreign correspondents were divided into three categories, all the Americans being put in the top bracket and charged a flat thirty-six dollars per year. It has now been raised to $110.

Villa Spiga has an interesting history. It was originally the home of Field Marshal Diaz, Italy's hero of World War I, whose heirs sold it to a wealthy Jewish department store owner who, when the enforcement of Mussolini's racial laws appeared imminent, sold it to a Milanese banker. The latter spent a fortune converting it into its present form. He installed the walnut-paneled library, the modern heating plant and the swimming pool and lovingly furnished the house with Louis XV and Louis XVI period antiques. But before he got a chance to live in it, it was requisitioned for the use of a German field marshal. Anti-aircraft batteries were installed on the grounds below the gardener's cottage, and the soldiers who manned the guns were quartered in the cottage. When I took up residence the steep wooden steps leading to the batteries were still there, as were the two wooden shacks that had housed the ammunition. I had them all torn down.

When the Germans fled, they took with them every pillow and mattress, although they left behind valuable books, paintings and furniture. After them came a line of high-ranking American officers, the final one being my good friend Admiral "Egg" Mentz, a heroic naval officer who had headed one of the many Allied commissions in Rome. When friends ask me how I was able to get the villa away from him, I reply that I won it on the golf course. Like all good stories this one contains just enough truth to be almost completely false. I knew the villa, having dined and wined there under its various Allied tenants. During a golf match with Egg and Charlie Dasher, Egg asked for my opinion about his moving out of the villa and into a suite in the Hotel Excelsior. I said he'd have to have his head examined.

"It's too much for me," Egg said. I knew he couldn't be referring to the rent or upkeep, because it all came out of Italy's cost of occupation.

"What is?"

"Everything. Like ninety-six pounds of sugar a month. That's excessive, no?"

"That's excessive, yes. Unless you have a very large sweet tooth."

"What makes it worse is that I don't even use sugar in my coffee. And I eat most of my meals out. You should see how much meat, spaghetti, coffee, canned goods, C-rations, ten-in-one rations and God-only-knows what else we consume. I could provision a regiment. I'm just too busy to cope with loose-fingered help."

"My advice, which is purely non-objective, is that you move immediately—because the day you go out, I go in."

And that was how I found our new home.

I was the lord of the manor and I played the part with what I hoped was quiet dignity. I took long walks within the villa walls, always carrying my *burgenstock*, a mountain walking stick I had liberated from the home of Franz Hofer, the nazi gauleiter of Innsbruck, and always accompanied by Duke, a black cocker spaniel. The household help, the gardeners and the local peasantry tipped their hats respectfully and brought me their problems.

Before long I found myself putting in an eight-hour day just trying to keep the house running. Take the time the lights failed. Just call an electrician, you say? Being a person of ordinary intelligence that is exactly what I did the first time. I had the cook find an electrician in the neighborhood. He would be along soon. In three days he arrived, did his work and was paid. When I came home, the house was still in darkness. It seems he was not really an electrician, just somebody who tried to be helpful. Quite naturally, he couldn't be turned out empty-handed because after all, he had put in a day's work, and we couldn't condemn him to starvation even though he was a fraud.

So we lived by candlelight and cooked on a primus stove while I scoured the town for an authentic electrician. This required a week, but it was worth it. This man was a professional, and in no time at all the repairs were made. At the very next failure, I sent the chauffeur to pick him up by car. Back came the driver, empty-handed, with the news that our man had left Rome for his native village. The hunt for an authentic electrician started all over again. This same routine was true for plumbers, carpenters, radio repairmen, painters, bricklayers, tree surgeons and professionals in almost every other field of human endeavor.

Just above the swimming pool, carefully landscaped into the side of a hill below the terraced vegetable gardens, was a cement hut with two electric motors. The larger one drew water from an artesian well to fill the pool, the smaller one emptied the pool by pumping the water through a complicated series of underground pipes, which served as a sprinkler system for the park around the house as well as for the gardens and orchards below the twenty-foot-high retaining wall of the driveway. Both motors were burned out when we moved in, but fortunately Colonel Ben Camp, a physician in command of the Allied military hospital in Rome, knew of a repair shop near the bombed out San Paolo freight yards. By this time I had learned that if I wanted work done properly, I would have to see to it myself.

In a week the pumps were fixed, remounted and working beautifully. In a month both were burned out again. I repeated the routine and once more, after a couple of months, they were out of use. Having repaired them for the third time, I resorted to what I thought was a secret weapon. I had learned that the fruits of my vegetable gardens, which were cared for so lovingly by the head gardener, were not arriving at my table, but were being sold in the local market for his sole profit. I told him, "If these motors burn out once more I am not going to have them repaired. You will just have to carry the water for the vegetable gardens on your back."

Sure enough, the motors burned out again. And sure enough, I kept my word. When he tried to argue with me, I ordered that henceforth he could not address me directly. He sent word through the cook that it wasn't his fault. The reason the motors burned out was that the safety device was broken. I let out a yelp. "Why didn't he tell me that the first time?" A half hour later the cook returned. "He says that you never asked him," she reported.

For a time I was troubled by hunters. They swarmed into our wooded valley and peppered away with their shotguns at the swarms of birds that took sanctuary there. At first, when I ordered them off I was obeyed, but they always sneaked back. Later on they didn't even bother going through the motions of leaving. Insolently, they told me to drop dead. Not in so many words. One of them thrust out his left arm and placed the open palm of his right hand on his left biceps. It is a vulgar but most expressive response.

As I drove up the driveway at the siesta hour one afternoon I heard the guns going off. I had Gerhardt stop the car and order them off. The response was Roman and vulgar. I climbed out of the car and shouted at them. I drew the same answer. We went up to the house where I took my .45 caliber Browning automatic from my war chest and rammed in a full clip. I jumped into the jeep and drove back to that part of the driveway from which I had a good view of the hunters. "This is private property," I shouted. They ignored me. Raising my gun, I fired into the tops of the umbrella pines, a good fifty feet over their heads. The sound of the gunshot reverberated like a cannon blast in the valley. I could hear the shocked surprise in the voice of one as he shouted out something about a crazy American. I fired another shot. At least twenty hunters came tearing out of the woods and raced in headlong haste in the opposite direction. As they ran I fired the rest of the clip in the air. I was never again troubled with hunters.

Although Roman winters are not generally severe, they are far from tropical. To heat the villa, I ordered coke at thirty-five dollars a ton and logs at eighteen dollars a ton. The logs were for the magnificent fireplaces in the library, dining and bedrooms. Surprisingly, despite the mildness of this particular winter, we were using a ton of coal every fourth day and I decided to run a spot check. When a ton of coal was delivered I had it placed in an empty bin. Then I had the servants bring in a scale and weigh the coal by hand. It was exactly half a ton short. I hurried to the coal merchant, whose property adjoined mine, and confronted him with the evidence.

He didn't seem surprised. "Errors can happen," he said mildly. "You shall have the other half-ton before the day is out."

"And what are you going to do about all the other half-tons you've been stealing from me over the years?" I yelled excitedly.

He drew himself up haughtily. "Are you accusing me of theft?"

"I most certainly am."

"In that event I shall not permit you to do business with me any longer."

I most certainly would take my business elsewhere. It would be less convenient, but at least I could start fresh with a new merchant. Again, what looked easy in theory was quite different in practice. If my driver went to supervise the weighing of an order, the new dealer would find excuses to keep him waiting, sometimes for the entire day. Things came to such a pass that when the driver had to sneak time off for his own business, his excuse invariably was that he had been detained at the coal yard. In the end I admitted defeat and returned to my neighboring coal merchant, apologized for my loss of temper and was taken back into his good graces.

I knew that the customs and laws of this country were different from those of my native land, and I wanted to do everything according to the book. I needed a residence permit for myself and my family. I went to the *ufficio straniero* at the *Questura* for my *carta di soggiorno,* as it is called. I had to furnish not only the names of each member of my family, but also my father's name, my mother's maiden name, where and when they were born and whether they were still alive, then all the same information on my wife's parents and my father's grandparents. Even for so simple a request as a telephone, this lengthy pedigree was required.

A policeman friend came to the house for lunch one day and, noticing our license-less cocker spaniel, said, "As a foreigner, nobody will say anything to you about it, but if you wished to be *in regola*. . . ." I insisted, and after the formalities of registering the dog, the license tag arrived along with an annual tax bill of nine thousand lire. A few years later the dog died. When the bill for the tax came, I telephoned the tax office to advise them that I was not paying it since I no longer had the dog. The tax people politely informed me that this would be a fair and logical solution but that they, unfortunately, had no further control over the matter, since it was now in the hands of the tax collector, and that if the bill remained unpaid, the collector would seize enough of my property to satisfy the debt. Since justice always triumphs in the end in Italy, all I needed to do after the seizure had been made, was to file suit against the Italian government and with luck, in some six years and several millions of lire in expense, I would win a nine thousand lire verdict. Since I did not wish to put the Italian government on the losing end of a lawsuit, however small, I told the dog-tax clerk that I would pay, but that he was to take note that I was the bereaved one-time owner of a cocker spaniel named Duke.

The next year, along with various and sundry tax bills, it came again. I called the dog department of the bureau and with a touch of impatience in my voice, pointed out that the situation was as of a year ago.

"That is because you did not make notification," he told me.

"But I did just that, to you, one year ago on the telephone," I said with some heat.

"Telephonic notification is insufficient," he said, quoting the law. "You must make it on *carta bollata* of one hundred lire and add to this the death certificate of the dog."

Still wanting to be completely *in regola,* I paid the bill, then bought a sheet of legal paper, filled in a formal notification of the dog's death, secured a death certificate from the veterinarian who had treated the deceased Duke and filed this with the dog-tax office.

The following year, arriving with the punctuality of the seasons, came the tax bill for the dead dog. I felt trapped. I consulted my attorney, who went down to the tax office to investigate the case and try somehow to put an end to this comedy. An hour later he phoned me, and from his cheerful voice I knew he had solved the problem.

"What happened?" I asked eagerly.

"You merely forgot to give the pedigree," he said.

"Pedigree!" I shouted. "What difference does a pedigree make to a dog that's been dead four years now."

"You're quite right," the lawyer said smoothly. "It's not the dog's pedigree you forgot to give. It's yours."

Just for the record, I still get the same dog-tax bill each year. I don't know the inner workings of this office, but I am willing to bet that they have wrought a modern miracle. Dogs, in their files, must live to be thirty and forty years of age!

Once a year, before Easter, a local *monsignore* would call upon us for permission to erect an altar on the exterior wall of our gardener's cottage, which fronted on Via Trionfale, for the Corpus Christi procession. He would stay for tea, and then go from room to room blessing the house. Every neighborhood in Rome has its own patron saint whose day is duly celebrated. Monte Mario long ago opted for Corpus Christi, and its inhabitants observe it seriously. Two weeks before the holiday, bedsheets dyed blue, green, red, yellow, every color of the rainbow, hang like pennants from windows. On the afternoon of the big day the procession starts out of the parish church. Out in front, dressed in a white robe and hood like a Ku Klux Klanner and carrying a heavy wood sculpture of Christ, was our head gardener. The procession came down Via Trionfale to halt directly in front of the gardener's cottage. I had ordered the huge doors of the driveway opened, and I stood with the servants in the courtyard as they celebrated mass. What a warm feeling it was to be part of the color, the pageantry and life of Rome.

Chapter 11

Hammer + Sickle = Murder

I LIVE in a country in which one out of every three people votes communist. Amongst those countries where the popular will of the electorate can still be freely expressed, it holds the dubious distinction of having the largest Communist Party outside the Iron Curtain. How can this be in a country so predominantly Catholic, where until quite recently more than 90 per cent of the people voted fascist?

There were many reasons for the communists' growth in power. As mentioned earlier, the policies laid down by our military occupation brought them a land office rush. This had nothing to do with politics or religion. Key jobs were open only to those who could prove that they had been anti-fascist, and a membership card in the CP was accepted as absolute proof. Further, the Reds were the only ones prepared for the fall of fascism. In Moscow Italian organizers were given extensive schooling and the necessary financial help. They came in, as a noted Civil War general might have put it, the firstest with the mostest.

Since these Italians owed total allegiance to the Communist

Party rather than to the land of their birth, it was easier for them to dedicate themselves with rare single-mindedness to building their party. They began by taking control of the partisan movement. Whereas only a handful had fought actively against the Germans, by the time the war was over scores of thousands were inducted into the ranks, most of them joining at war's end. What was insidious about the operation was that they were able to get these partisans integrated into the regular army, holding the grades that were given them by the communist organization.

The errors of the Allied occupation were compounded by the fledgling Italian government. In their new cabinet they appointed communist leader Palmiro Togliatti as minister of justice, an act of sagacity comparable to making Dillinger head of security at a bank. The ministry of defense was offered to another Moscow-trained commissar, Vincenzo Moscatelli, who will reappear later. In this instance he was blocked at the last moment.

Russia had made a heavy investment in the operational phases of the party. She poured in thousands of tons of newsprint when it was difficult and expensive for other newspapers to obtain. They had then and still have the best party press in the country. This build-up was done openly and unashamedly. Should the West have tried to finance a party openly, there would have been an enormous outcry in the so-called liberal and leftist press. The hard truth is that their propaganda apparatus has limited our actions, while ours has had less effect upon them than a gnat on an elephant's rump.

They took early control of the labor unions, again with an unpardonable assist from the Allied occupation forces. At a time when the condition of the Italian worker was little short of disastrous, they began a determined and loud fight for higher pay and shorter hours, and they kept on fighting for these ends even when the results of their actions sometimes threatened to pull the country to ruin. It was a sort of heads-I-win, tails-you-lose operation. If they succeeded in bettering the lot of the worker (and they did), then they got the credit for it. If the country fell apart in the attempt, it would have been even better from their stand-point, for the worse the disaster, the surer it was that the com-munists would take over.

Pushing the voters to the left were the numerous scandals in the early turbulent days of the new republic. Those that found their way into the daily press were like the peaks of icebergs: the public knew that the greater part of the scandal still lay sub-merged. That the leaders of government appeared less than energetic in eliminating the abuses can be noted from the Montesi investigation in a later chapter.

But there were other more glaring instances of corruption: America had sent Italy large quantities of penicillin as a gift. The head of the government agency that was to distribute the anti-biotic medicine to the people put it out for sale at extremely high prices and used the profits to build apartment houses for himself and his associates. Much of the wheat that we sent as a gift in ten-thousand-ton loads found its way into the hands of specu-lators. Food frauds were so widespread that the confidence of housewives was shaken. Much of the pure olive oil was dis-covered to have been made from animal fats, pigs' hooves and caustic chemicals. An expert estimated that out of every ten bottles of wine actually on sale, at least two had not a trace of grape in them and six had dishonest markings on the labels. Land-speculators, builders, movie-makers, money-changers and dope-dealers made illicit fortunes and were rarely called to the bar of justice to account for their misdeeds.

A scandal that shook the very bones of government involved the *Ente Nazionale Imposte e Consumo,* a taxing body that levies duties on merchandise shipped between the various provinces of the country. The actual tax collecting is done by private conces-sionaires. An investigation by judicial authorities revealed that most of these private tax collectors received the concessions by making payments, also known as bribes, to various members of Parliament, communist as well as their democratic brethren. These legislators could not be brought to trial unless Parliament

voted to lift their immunity. This the governing body refused to do
—for once the communists voted with their democratic enemies—
giving as their reason the fact that the legislators were not guilty
of a crime, though they did admit taking the money, because they
turned the funds over to their political parties!

A local journalist, far from being a left-wing follower, wrote
that the political leaders had formed a Mafia, with the insiders
fighting for principles and for power, but always ready to make
common cause against any outsider who tried to interfere with
their operations. Voters checked the hammer and sickle on the
ballots as a protest.

American influence still stumbles about in the maze of Italian
politics. Our embassy has restricted its financial aid to the Christian Democrat Party (a fact that will immediately be denied by
our State Department), although many observers have suggested
time and again that this same aid be extended to *all* democratic
parties that are anti-communist, so that if, for internal reasons,
the electorate switches allegiance, there will be other strong
groups to contest the Communist Party for the protest vote.

Fortunately, the Italian government has some dedicated states-
men, and it is largely due to their efforts that the communists
haven't taken over. One of them is Randolfo Pacciardi, one of the
true anti-communist and anti-fascist personages in the government. He is a robust, keen-eyed, fearless fighter who has been in
the front lines all his life. He proved his love for democracy by
being a leader in the International Brigade during the civil war
in Spain, even though this meant fighting against his own brothers
in the Italian army. When the communists gained control of the
loyalist forces, he loudly denounced them. After two attempts had
been made to kill him, he fled to France and continued his fight
against both the communists and the fascists from there.

As minister of defense in the new Italian cabinet, he inherited
the Red-ridden army. But he was equal to the task that faced him.
He had partisan officers called up for new physicals, and his
medicos retired the Reds from service so fast that it looked as if

such grave ailments as in-grown toenails, enlarged tonsils and overdeveloped muscles were epidemic. This took great courage on his part, because the outraged screams from the communist press and fellow-traveling orators were so threatening that other members of the government ran for cover.

Pacciardi is a friend of many American writers, including the late Ernest Hemingway, who got to know and admire him during the Spanish adventure. He is one who had seen and recognized the enemy for what he truly is long before most of us. He is a friend of mine and I know his views, which are as direct and basic as the man: Russia trains agents from different countries and sends them back to their native lands. These Russian agents are often elected to the parliaments of their home countries, which gives them inside positions from which to practice espionage and sabotage. If another power reversed the procedure, sending trained Russians back to the U.S.S.R., they would be hung immediately. This double set of rules makes the communist task much easier. Pacciardi makes a very simple equation. If the Reds get into power in Italy, they will kill him and destroy all those who stand in their path. Why, then, should he permit them to use the weapons of democracy to destroy democracy?

In the 1948 elections, while the American press and the Italian cabinet trembled about the possible success of the Communist Party, he was the only one who did anything concrete. He moved out his tanks and unashamedly set up a program of force to keep them from assuming power.

Naturally, Pacciardi was a prime target for the communists, and they continued to stalk him. They had failed to kill him in the outlaw days of the Spanish war; they came closer to destroying him in the legal days of democratic Italy. In 1962, the dominant Christian Democrat Party, lacking a clear majority in parliament and having difficulty in keeping their center coalition with the Republicans, Liberals, and Democratic Socialists together, decided to make a deal with the Soviet-oriented Socialist Party. The Republican Party was split over this issue. One wing, headed by

Pacciardi, was against it. So was our embassy in Rome (but not our State Department, which erroneously regarded this opening to the left as a sort of New Frontier, Italian style), understandably, because the cardinal plank in the Red socialist policy is that Italy get out of NATO, get rid of its U.S. bases and become neutral. No one who knows the history of the Red socialists has any faith in their "neutrality."

On the eve of the Republican Party convention at which Pacciardi's wing was favored to win, *Paese Sera*, the communist daily, came out with a scare head announcing that a Senate investigating body had uncovered that Pacciardi, as a cabinet member, had used undue influence in getting a lucrative contract for a friend on the Fiumicino airport project and that he had been paid off with a number of cooperative apartments. Under the weight of this grave accusation, Pacciardi withdrew from the party convention and the opposing side won. This was precisely what the communists wanted.

Pacciardi filed criminal libel charges against the paper, and in the trial it was established that the Senate investigating committee, far from accusing him of wrong-doing, had gone on record as saying that the minister of defense's actions had been correct, both morally and legally, and that his friend had received the contract on his own. In fact, instead of benefiting from the minister's influence, the friend had found his contract voided almost at the outset of his work. As for the apartments, they had been regularly purchased by both the minister and his wife long after the contract in question had been irrevocably broken. The editor and writer of the article were both convicted, but there was little solace in this for Pacciardi. He had already lost control of his party, and it had turned to the left.

My post-graduate course in communist power play came quickly. Shortly after the end of the war I left Rome to cover the first free elections in Hungary, Romania and Czechoslovakia following their liberation. It seemed amazing that these people, with the guns of a Russian army of occupation literally sticking in their backs, dared to give the Communist Party less than 20 per cent of their votes. What was even more amazing to me was that the Russians appeared to take the results in good grace. I had expected them to use their naked power to declare the elections invalid.

Instead they permitted the dominant party of each country to form its own government. The Soviet Army merely made a single request: that the communists be represented with three portfolios in each cabinet. These were to be the minister of interior, the minister of defense and the minister of justice. At the time anything short of outright seizure seemed eminently reasonable. For the Soviets to request only one-fifth of the posts was so surprising that the three countries—not that they had any other choice—readily agreed. Very shortly thereafter, with the power of the police, the army and the machinery of justice in their hands, they threw out the parliament and placed control in the hands of the local Communist Party. The elected representatives of some 80 per cent of the populations were either killed, imprisoned or permitted to join the CP. All this has so endeared this party to the electorate that today 100 per cent of the voters put a cross on the ballot next to the hammer and sickle. What helps make this percentage perfect is the fact that by law no other parties are listed. Merely trying to start one is considered an act of treason punishable by death.

Communism is a fact of life one lives with here, as one might live with a shortage of water in the desert. It is an ever-present menace, a force for evil that can affect the lives of my family and my country. During the post-war advance of communism, I watched with more than passing interest. Though I was making a reputation covering gazelle boys in the east, interviewing bandits in the south, revealing army corruption in the north and testifying before congressional investigations brought on by my articles in the west, I looked forward to an assignment dealing with this issue.

When the opportunity finally came, it was not in Italy, but Greece. General Markos, the legendary leader of the revolutionary army in Greece, had seized control of the northern provinces and was more than holding his own against the loyalist Greek army. My assignment called for a profile that would reveal whether he headed a purely national uprising or one dictated by Moscow in an attempt to extend its colonial possessions.

Basic in my coverage of a story of this sort would be to meet with the subject of the profile and observe him in his natural habitat. Trying to reach Markos posed the same sort of difficulty I had faced in trying to reach Giuliano. Physically, there were only three ways to get to the Greek rebel leader: The first and most direct was to charter a plane, fly over the inaccessible mountains in northern Greece and parachute down. The second was to come down through Albania, Yugoslavia or Bulgaria, all three solidly in the communist camp. The third was to fly to Athens and go overland. This latter method was the most feasible.

The most direct route was the road running westward from Salonika to Durazzo, the Albanian port on the Adriatic Sea, cutting through the triangle formed by the Albanian and Yugoslavian borders between Florina and Grammos, where I believed Markos had his headquarters. The very directness of the route warned me that it was bound to be most heavily covered by the military forces of both sides.

Instead, I decided on the northward road from Athens. I would get a jeep, provision it with food and gasoline and take off on a three-hundred-mile trek, following the main highway for some two hundred miles to Larissa, turn westward to Trikkala and then northward along the bad roads and towering mountains along the Greco-Yugoslavian frontier.

The plan looked reasonably simple and there was little doubt in my mind that I would succeed. One thing was certain—I would let no one, neither loyalist nor guerrilla, in on my plans.

I telephoned Jean Ghikas, Press Attaché for the Greek Embassy in Rome, and told him that I would like a visa as soon as possible. At that time approval had to come from Athens. Somehow word of my mission leaked out, and the Greek foreign office sat on my request. Had they turned it down, I would have fought them. Word of what I planned also reached two colleagues of mine, Homer Bigart of the *Herald Tribune* and George Polk of the Columbia Broadcasting System. Bigart was in Germany, but George Polk happened to be in Athens.

Polk hurried to be first. He sent out feelers that reached the communist underground in Athens and established a contact with Kyriakos Tsakiris, alias Captain Thessalos, an officer in General Markos' forces and a member of the Politbureau of the Greek Communist Party. He told Polk that he would arrange for the interview with the general on the sole condition that absolute secrecy be maintained. On Tuesday, May 4th, 1948, Tsakiris telephoned a well-known journalist at his office in Salonika and told him that at noon the next day he was to be seated at a sidewalk cafe on Halkeon Street, where he would meet a person who would introduce himself as Nikos.

The Greek newspaperman contacted by Tsakiris was Gregorios Stactopoulos, thirty-eight years old, born in Trebisonde in Asia Minor, educated in the American School in Salonika, and a reporter for a Macedonian daily. Until the outbreak of the war he had been a devout monarchist and Anglophile. During the German occupation he had collaborated with them and edited one of their newspapers. At the end of the occupation he had become editor of *Popular Voice*, the official communist daily for Macedonia and Thrace. With the arrival of three British divisions removed from the Italian front by Winston Churchill, Stactopoulos had changed sides again, ostensibly resigning from the Communist Party and going to work for British intelligence. No one gave more than a passing thought to these switches in allegiance, because the journalist was known to be a thorough-going opportunist.

Stactopoulos met Nikos at the appointed time and was told that George Polk, an American correspondent, would arrive in Salonika on Friday, May 7th, and would check into the Hotel Astoria. The journalist was to meet with Polk and then advise Nikos, at which time he would receive new instructions. Polk arrived on schedule and was met by Stactopoulos, who then hurried to report to Nikos. At seven o'clock in the evening Polk again met the Greek journalist and was told that at one minute past midnight he would meet the man who would guide him to Markos' headquarters.

Through the dark, tree-lined streets of the Aegean port city, roughly midway between Athens and the Turkish border, Polk moved like a stealthy conspirator. At the appointed time he stood on the corner of Metropoleos and Haghia Sophias Street and met with Evanghelos Vasvanos, a political commissar with the rank of lieutenant colonel in Markos' army.

The burly Vasvanos, born in 1914 at Tsaritsani, had been Moscow-trained and had been an active organizer of communist youth clubs before the war. With Stactopoulos acting as interpreter, he informed Polk that the departure would take place the following night and that Polk was to hold himself in readiness at the Astoria Hotel, telling absolutely no one of his plans. The exact hour, place and means employed for the departure would be communicated to him at the proper time.

On the following day, Saturday, May 8th, he was told to be ready at nine that evening. He arrived a half-hour early to find Stactopoulos already waiting for him. After their dinner, they walked to the pier. It was now ten-thirty. A rowboat was tied up there. Seated in it were three men, one of whom was Vasvanos. A second man in simple fisherman attire, already leaning over the oars, was Adam Mouzenidis who, under the name of Captain Vassos, had been a heroic fighter in the partisan battle against the Germans. Born in Trebisonde in 1901, he had had several convictions for communist activities before the war. Now he was a member of the central committee of the Greek party. The third man sat in the prow. Mouzenidis helped Polk climb in, then sat down in the rear. Immediately in front of him were Polk and Stactopoulos. Vasvanos, facing the journalist, took over the oars and pulled away from the pier, making good time as he headed into the blackness of the Aegean Sea.

An hour out the silence was broken by Mouzenidis. Stactopoulos, translating, said that for reasons of security it would be necessary to blindfold Polk and tie his hands and legs. Polk resigned himself as Mouzenidis pulled a rough fisherman's handkerchief from his pocket and tied it about his eyes. "Even blindfolded, as long as I get to where I'm going," he said. Then his hands were tied behind his back and his feet bound. As Mouzenidis finished tying his feet, Polk added, "And now let me move toward my destiny." They were the last words he ever spoke.

Vasvanos continued at the oars with a strong, steady rhythm. Mouzenidis returned to his seat, pulled out a pistol and, holding it close to the back of Polk's head, fired a single shot. The American fell forward without a sound, twitched in death agony, and then was still. Mouzenidis went through his pockets, pulled out a wallet, letters, notes, money and a small Pan American Airways notebook. Keeping only the war correspondent identification card and notebook, he replaced the rest in Polk's pockets. The card and notebook were passed to Stactopoulos with orders to mail them to the local commissariat of police. The body was thrown overboard and the durable Vasvanos again leaned on the oars and headed back toward the Salonika shore.

A week later, early on Sunday morning, May 16th, the body was washed ashore by the tide.

I was still in Rome, locked in battle with the Greek government, when I heard the news and faced the grim fact that there but for the grace of God went I. My educated guess was that Polk had made contact with a lower echelon group of communists and that somewhere along the line they had become concerned for their own safety and had jettisoned him to save themselves.

(Under Greek law communist activity was regarded as espionage and was punishable by death.) I had foreseen this danger when I had interviewed Giuliano in Sicily, and it was the chief reason I had avoided gangster intermediaries.

The politbureau of Markos' forces issued a "blue book" to explain that "this most diabolical murder was committed by the monarchist-fascists in order to keep the press in bondage and not allow them to learn the truth about the great patriot Markos." At least the part of the accusation about the Greek government's sensitivity to the American press getting to the general was true. I was proof of it. The entire cominform press trumpeted the charges and said that the Greek government, having tried to put the blame for the crime on the communists, now found that the charge had boomeranged.

Homer Bigart moved into Greece by hiding himself in a freight car in Yugoslavia that was headed southward into Markos' territory. His arrival did not come as a surprise to the Greek rebel leader. It seems that the loyalist government also knew about it, for that same day they advised me that my visa had been approved. That evening, at a reception given by Ambassador James Dunn at Villa Taverna, a member of the New York *Herald Tribune* staff tipped me off that Bigart had already gotten through.

The Greek government didn't quite know what to do with Bigart after he had finished interviewing Markos, filed his stories and arrived in Athens. Arrest him for illegal entry? Or illegal communication with the enemy? Or any one of a dozen offenses that were committed in gaining the interview? It was a delicate situation. The nation was locked in a death struggle, and the outcome depended on the amount of aid they would receive from the United States. It was therefore dangerous to upset American public opinion. They decided to do nothing, if only Bigart would get out of Greece quickly. He did, with the satisfaction of having beaten me to the big story.

I had already left for Greece when Bigart arrived in Rome.

He telephoned my villa, asked for me and got my wife. She explained that I was out of town and asked who was calling.

"This is Homer Bigart," he said.

"I didn't get the name," she said.

"Never mind the name," he replied airily. "Just tell him that it's the man who saved his life."

On the morning of May 11th, the police of the Third Commissariat in Salonika received the envelope containing Polk's war correspondent card and the Pan American notebook, which had been mailed to them anonymously. Since the names of all strangers who check into hotels are registered with them, they found Polk's residence to have been the Hotel Astoria. The *concierge* informed them that Polk had left on the night of the 8th and had not returned since. On the desk in his room was an unfinished letter that he had written to Edward R. Murrow, then head of the CBS newsroom. In it Polk announced that he was already in Salonika and that he felt it would be a great triumph for him to reach Markos' headquarters. He said that he would do it even if he had to go blindfolded.

The police, upon questioning the personnel at the hotel, learned that Polk had had only one visitor. They knew him to be Gregorios Stactopoulos. When the latter was brought in, he readily admitted that he had gone to visit Polk at the latter's request. It was the most natural thing in the world, since he, Stactopoulos, was one of the best known of the local journalists and one who spoke English fluently. The American had asked him if there was any way in which an interview could be arranged with Markos, and he told him that this was an impossible task and advised him not to try. No, Polk had never told him whether he had uncovered any other road to Markos.

When Polk's body floated into the harbor a week later, Stactopoulos was again brought in for questioning. This time a sample of his handwriting was tested against a sample of the handwriting on the envelope sent to the commissariat of police. They did not match.

Three months later the police department's big guns from Athens came to Salonika. Again they started with the Greek journalist. After a thorough questioning, his house was searched and all papers were carted off to police headquarters. Although there was nothing incriminating in them, some of the writing bore a surprising resemblance to that on the envelope addressed to the police. These had been written by the journalist's widowed mother, Anna. A bottle of ink found in the Stactopoulos apartment was checked with the ink on the envelope. Chemical analysis revealed them to be exactly the same. Faced with this, the mother broke down and admitted that she had addressed the envelope at the request of her son. Confronted with this evidence he, too, confessed.

He was, he said, a secret member of the Communist Party, even though he had publicly broken with them and had been constantly under attack in their press. This had been arranged in order that he might operate freely on the outside of the party apparatus. He said that he had contacted Polk as a result of the orders given to him by Nikos, and that following these orders, he had brought Polk to his appointment with death. Before embarking in the rowboat, the two had had dinner at a small waterfront restaurant. Polk had eaten shrimp, he said. This was an important detail, because the autopsy showed that shrimp was the last thing the dead man had eaten.

Why had Polk been killed? Because it had been ordered by the Greek Communist Party. At the time their entire hope of a successful revolt hinged on the United States withdrawing its military aid from the Greek government. The communists believed that by putting the blame for the murder on the loyalists, they could create a scandal big enough to make America pull back, much as was done in China when, disgusted with the corruption and double-dealing of the Nationalist forces during World

War II, we abruptly withdrew our aid and let the country fall by
default to the Reds.

Although the plan was crude and cruel, and although it didn't
have much of a chance of success, the life of a "capitalist tool"
was a cheap enough price to pay for the attempt.

Markos, a Greek, threw his country into bloody civil war, but
the ensuing struggle was not Greek in character, although the
blood spilled was Greek. It was basically a war between the
U.S. and the U.S.S.R. It was an aggressive, bold attempt on the
part of Russia to secure an outlet on the Mediterranean Sea.
Through the centuries the czars had tried diplomacy and war to
accomplish it, but without success. Now the Russians were using
communism, and this would have succeeded except for determined American opposition.

To the everlasting credit of Harry Truman, he gave the
U.S.S.R. to understand in unequivocal terms that any Russian aid
would be counterbalanced by massive American aid, including
direct intervention if necessary. These bare words are not meant
to belittle the heroic efforts of the Greek soldiers who fought and
died to keep their land free. But if American aid, and the promise
of unlimited aid, had been withdrawn, Russia most assuredly
would have poured into the breach and even the most heroic army
would have been swept away.

This letter written by Markos, who never intended it to fall into
Western hands, tells the story.

E.D. 1053 December 3, 1948.
To Comrade Zachariadis,
Secretary General, Greek Communist Party

Comrade,

   As the chief of the democratic army, I am obliged to tell
you once more, and in writing, what I told you before your

trip to Moscow, about my criticism of the military tactics being followed by the government of Moscow. You know well
the historic message of Comrade Stalin in December 1944
that ordered the popular revolution and its tragic aftermath.
The tragedy was brought on by the fact that, when we asked
aid of Moscow, Comrade Stalin forgot what he had promised
and pointed instead to his diplomatic obligations.

. . . when we said that we wanted a big army, well-armed,
so as to be able to face victoriously that of the monarchist-
fascist one, which has, in addition to its exceptional resistance and courage—we must not forget that they, too, are
Greeks—the help of the Anglo-Americans. Comrade Stalin
through his agents advised us to have patience, because international politics did not leave a large enough margin of
gain for Russia if they were to work in the open now. . . .
Advised by Comrade Molotov, we created the "government
of the mountains." I accepted the nomination as prime minister and I gave orders for the assault on Konitza, so that
we could seat the new government there officially. I did this
depending on the promises that General Popovich would at
the same time unleash an offensive with his foreign legion
against Florina.

But once again, in spite of all the promises, Moscow has
decided to put off the offensive so they could be guided by
the seriousness of the Anglo-American reaction to the proc-
lamation of the "government of the mountains." Thus we
lost the battle and we have reached the point where we are
following orders without any initiative, where we are taken
advantage of and, in general, where we don't even know
what Soviet diplomacy thinks of our battle that is costing us
so much blood.

After all I have pointed out, and it is no more than the
crude reality of things as they are, I have decided, Comrade
Zachariadis, that if Tirana, Belgrade, and Moscow will not
come through with what they have promised, that I will de-

nounce all our agreements and follow the destiny of a soldier
who has fought and lost his battle.

You may communicate by letter with the political office
of the Greek Communist Party so that they may take note of
what I have said and so that they can come to a decision.

(signed) *General Markos*

The answer was given on the rebel radio three months later.

The Fifth Pleniary Assembly of the Central Committee
of the Greek Communist Party met in the Grammos mountains. The assembly discussed the following arguments:
Greece on the road to victory, the decisive turn—Speaker:
Comrade Zachariadis. The opportunistic deviation toward
the right of the Greek Communist Party—Speaker: Comrade Mitsos Vlandas. The Fifth Pleniary Assembly, con-
sidering that for several months Comrades Chryssa Hadjivas-
siliou and Markos Vafiadis have been gravely ill and have not
been able to attend the important duties that were assigned
to them, the Central Committee has decided unanimously
to exonerate them from all work in the party.

(signed) *The Central Committee*
Grammos, 31, January, 1949

The speaker recounted the heroic efforts of the communist
partisans in driving out the nazis from Greece during World
War II. "We most assuredly would have taken over the entire
country but for the perfidious British who moved in with their
guns," he said. He decried the talk of defeatists and opportun-
ists (in later speeches he was to name Markos as one of them,
but now he kept him in blessed anonymity) and finished with
what was the nub of the talk.

"Today, in spite of support of every kind, moral and material,
that has been given to us in the past by the humanitarian

democracies, the defeat of the monarchist-fascist armies and their backers in today's struggle, and the consequent liberation of all Greece, will have to be brought about by the efforts of the democratic Greek Army alone."

This was the answer to the question Markos had raised. Stalin would send no arms. He would not dare affront America in Greece.

Chapter 12

Clare Boothe Luce—Lady with a Plan

Trieste is a jewel-like city that sparkles in a half-shell setting at the northern end of the Adriatic Sea. To the west, curving southward past Venice, Rimini and Bari, is the coast of Italy. To the east, also curving southward, the coast stretches down through Yugoslavia, Albania and Greece. It is an old city, founded by Romans who came here looking for salt during the time of the Caesars, yet the spirit of its architecture is more akin to Nineteenth Century Paris and Vienna than to Rome.

In ancient times the hills dropped sheer down to the sea, but through the centuries the hand of man cut them away to form the saucer in which the modern city now stands. The climate is temperate, with more rain in the autumn than in the spring. During the summer an occasional *sirocco*, the hot wind from the Sahara that picks up humidity as it crosses the sea, makes life briefly uncomfortable. In the winter the *bora*, a cold, dry wind, roars down from the mountains with such force that it has been known to blow people off the streets and into the sea.

The city's two famous landmarks are San Giusto Castle, built by the Venetians as a fortress after they captured the city in 1369, and Miramare Castle, a delicate structure with many small turrets set on a promontory that thrusts out into the sparkling blue-gray-green Adriatic.

Miramare, small by castle standards, was built a century ago by Archduke Maximilian, brother of Franz Joseph of Austria, for his bride, Carlotta of Belgium. The couple sailed from here to ascend the throne of Mexico where, shortly thereafter, they were overthrown in a bloody revolt. Maximilian was taken prisoner, but Carlotta fled to Rome with an entourage that included the palace chef, her wedding gift from England's Queen Victoria.

Carlotta had hoped to persuade the Pope to intercede on her husband's behalf, but when she arrived in Rome she heard that the revolutionaries had already put Maximilian to death. Carlotta became insane. The stranded chef, Ranieri, opened a restaurant on Via Mario dei Fiori. It is still operating today in its original location, and it is one of my favorites.

Trieste's location is in many ways superior to Rome's, since it is on the sea yet only minutes away from vacation paradises in the mountains. It is an easy ride to Vienna and Budapest (which I prefer to Paris), and to Belgrade, Milan, Switzerland and the Alps. Its men are cosmopolitan and cultured and its women combine the best features of the Austrians, Slavs and Italians, a magic blend that makes them among the loveliest in the world.

From the first moment I laid eyes on Trieste, I felt that it was to be more than just another town I had passed through. If I hadn't loved Rome more, and if Trieste hadn't been handcuffed by politics over which its people had no control, this book might well have been called *An American in Trieste*. Each mention of the city still evokes tingling memories: of a hair-raising escape from death during my first journey there, of spy-thriller adventures in its treacherous political back alleys, and of a harrowing, eleventh-hour battle to save the life of a beautiful woman. It also reminds me of my first memorable and dramatic encounter

in Rome with Clare Boothe Luce, who was then the American ambassador to Italy. But this was much later, and it will have to
wait its turn.

A few days after the end of the war I set out for Trieste in a
captured German artillery-observer plane, a light Storch two-
seater. My pilot was an American press wireless operator who
held an amateur pilot's license. We took off from the Bad Aibling
airport on a clear, sunny morning. I was the navigator; on my
knees I had an air force map showing the topographical features
of the Alps on our route. We cruised at ninety-five miles an hour
eastward to Rosenheim, banking south to follow the valley of the
Inn River. Visibility was good, and I ticked off landmarks as we
flew over them.

At Kufstein we nosed upwards. When we had gained altitude,
we swung left around the Kaisergeberg in the heart of the Tyrolean Alps and followed the transverse valley over St. Johann
to Rofer, about thirty-five miles away. Here we took another
southward turn to follow the Saalach River. Now the mountains
closed in with frightening rapidity. Again we nosed upwards until
the altimeter registered eighty-five hundred feet, our limit, as we
headed for the Edelweis pass. The peaks on either side of us were
lost in the clouds that came down to within five hundred feet of
the pass. We squeezed through the opening and quickly descended again on the other side, picking up the valley of the ever-
widening Moll River. Behind and just to the right was the perpetual glacier of the eleven-thousand-foot Gros Glockner.

We heaved sighs of relief; the toughest part of the trip had been
handled with no more discomfort than one might expect in a light
tourist plane left to the mercy of strong mountain drafts. It was
about an hour since we had left Bad Aibling, and we were over
Lienz on the broad and fertile valley of the Drau River. A few
minutes later, at Oberdrauberg, we banked south into the mountains again. It was the last range, one that could be negotiated
easily at five thousand feet, before reaching the north Italian

plain. The pass was covered by a low-lying cloud. We flew into it and groped around for a few minutes, but without a radio or other means of flying blind it would have been suicide to move on, so the pilot banked tightly and flew back into the sunshine. We made the attempt to break through twice again, and each time we were forced back. There was nothing to do but put down somewhere and wait for the cloud to lift.

We flew back to Lienz, where my map showed a landing strip. Swooping low we saw that it was nothing more than a pasture with a bumpy five-yard-wide path running through it diagonally. We came around again and started our landing run in a cross wind. It is not quite clear to me whether we misjudged our altitude or whether the wind flipped us over. Whatever the cause, the landing wheels hit a log fence and we crashed nose-down on the strip. A wing snapped off and we skidded in the dirt to a halt. Somehow the fuselage remained upright and the webbed safety belt kept me from crashing through the windshield. The instant we stopped I flipped open the catch of the belt, dived headlong to the ground and scrambled away from the plane just as it burst into flame. The craft was reduced to a charred skeleton in the space of minutes.

It had happened so fast I didn't have time to be frightened. The pilot, who had thrown himself out of the plane the same instant I had, limped up to me. "You better get a bulletin out on it," he said flippantly. "The Luftwaffe just lost another plane."

A British army truck gave us a lift to a guard unit about a mile down the road. I dropped off at a Quonset hut that served as the officers' mess. It was at the edge of a rectangular prison camp with guard towers in each corner and far more barbed-wire barriers than a simple prisoner-of-war camp required. There were a few lines of ramshackle wood and tarpaper shacks that looked too small for the crowd of German-uniformed soldiers I could see milling about in the enclosure. The executive officer of the unit was most hospitable, asking us to stay for lunch and offering us a ride in a courier jeep leaving for Trieste the next day. During lunch I asked him about the barbed-wire encampment.

"It was built by the nazis to house the slave laborers who worked these fields for the surrounding farmers," he replied.

"Who's in it now?" I asked.

"Jerry prisoners."

"I never saw them guarded that closely."

"These are very special. If they thought they had one chance in a hundred of breaking out alive, they'd take it like a shot. And there are five thousand of them who think alike."

"What makes them so special?"

"This is a brigade of Ukrainian Russians who enlisted in the German army. Not that they had anything against us, poor devils. It's just that they hate Stalin and communism more than anything else in the world. If Hitler had come into Russia with a carrot instead of a gas chamber, he'd have picked up half a million troops in the Ukraine alone."

"How come they're here?"

"We were fighting them in the Balkans. With the end near they fell back in an awful hurry to keep from being captured by the Russians. They surrendered to us without a fuss. In fact, they were looking for us in order to give up. Only now are they beginning to realize that we might have to ship them back to Russia, and that's a death sentence from which there is no appeal."

"Are they going back?"

The captain nodded his head. "The orders came through to-day. I imagine it must have gone all the way up to Churchill for a decision. Can't think that the military would have wanted to handle this hot potato. It's going to be a devilish job to get them packed into boxcars. I've tried lying to them, saying that we were only moving them to other camps. But they know better. We've been getting six and seven suicides a day."

These men were returned to Russia, where they were swallowed up in silence. The fate of five thousand men was so unimportant an item that the press—not just the controlled press of Russia, but the free Western press—didn't devote a single line to it.

Yugoslav partisans were in evidence from the moment I reached the plains on the Italian side of the Alps. The walls were scrawled with slogans, *Zivel Tito* (long live Tito) being the most prominent. Only a few of the soldiers were dressed in a semblance of a uniform, and this was a baggy khaki topped by an almost round overseas cap that appeared to be held up by the ears. Others wore only armbands and red scarves and parts of a uniform. They had just come through the most terrible kind of war, a clandestine hit-run-and-hide affair in which their chances for survival, since they were completely surrounded by the Germans, were not very good. Capture had meant torture and certain death. It was a new experience for them to be able to walk openly through a town, and they swaggered about in a cocky attitude that they wore as uncomfortably as their overseas caps. Having no food supplies of their own, these soldiers had to live off the countryside, and it became an immediate source of friction with the Italian peasants.

Actually the Yugoslav Army had no reason to be in this area. A military accord between the Allies and Russia had fixed the boundaries at which each army should halt. Russia was to stop at the line of the Elbe. Tito was to stop at the Italian border below Trieste. Instead he had overrun the province of Venezia-Giulia, and the British, who were supposed to occupy it, had tried to force him out. This led to such unpleasantness that it threatened to erupt in open warfare, at which point it was considered wiser to withdraw the British forces and substitute Americans.

The courier jeep dropped me off at the headquarters of the 91st Infantry Division, the American unit that had just replaced them. It was commanded by General Bill Livesay, a field commander who had made a good record during the difficult warfare in the Apennine mountains. The general, a good friend of mine, gave me quarters with his division. I had last seen him during the jump-off for the final offensive against Bologna. Although the war was now over for the rest of the troops in Europe, it might just be beginning again for his, for he had inherited the British impasse.

The Yugoslavians had set up roadblocks in the hinterlands just outside of Trieste, cutting off all traffic eastward. Their guns were aimed directly at our soldiers, and it would take little to set them off. Tito's strategy was simple. He would take physical possession of the city so that he would have a stronger arguing point when it came time to write the peace. Of course, the Italian partisans, who had fought on our side and who were loyal to their own country, knew what he was up to and were very unhappy about it. Just how much they had suffered in the war against the nazis and the fascists could be gathered from a visit to Soldiers' House, a building with a central staircase that spiraled to the sixth floor. As a reprisal against their activities fifty-five Italian partisans had been hanged by the neck from the railings, and their bodies had been left dangling for days. The cold war over Trieste had already begun, and there seemed to be something symbolic in the pattern in which the respective forces were deployed; the British held City Hall, the Americans grabbed the best hotels and the Yugoslavs controlled the jail.

With the aid of an interpreter I covered the city, speaking to literally hundreds of people. The Italians, whether ex-fascists, partisans or neutrals—and they represented three-quarters of the population of the city—were unanimous in their desire not to be annexed by Tito. Overwhelmingly they desired to remain united with Italy.

Some dissenting voices spoke in favor of a free city-state and open port. Among the Slavs a heavy majority opposed being annexed to Italy, but a large percentage of them did not want to belong to a communist Yugoslavia, either. They, too, favored a free city.

Mayor Michele Miani showed me a large painting hanging over the desk in his office. Commissioned by the Hapsburg emperor to celebrate the opening of the free port, the canvas shows fifty people, all readily identifiable by their costumes. Only one, a Bosnian peasant, is Yugoslavian; the rest are Italian, French, Austrian, Greek and German. Further proof, said the mayor, that the Slavs had no ethnic claim to the area.

My interpreter was an attractive brunette of twenty-four who had been recommended to me by the British military government. She had greenish-blue eyes that seemed to take their color from the Adriatic: when the sun shone they were a sparkling blue; on a cloudy day they were a deep green. Her figure was divinely Triestine, with French ankles and an Italian bosom, and it would have been abnormal to remain indifferent to her physical charms. She was a Slav who had been born in Gregolice, a Slav village in the mountainous hinterlands that had been part of Italy until a week ago. She had attended Italian schools and had worked in an Italian office. The language she spoke at home was Slav, but she felt that she had two mother tongues. While her sympathies were with Yugoslavia—two of her brothers were Tito partisans—she hoped that her home village would remain Italian.

"The Slavs are a very close-mouthed and distrusting people," she told me. "Especially these days. I don't want you to have a bad opinion of them, because they can be very friendly and hospitable. It's just that they don't take to a stranger. And if he's a foreigner, too, it's even worse. But if you want to visit my village, they would be honored to talk to you. You would get a better idea of how the Slavs feel."

After arranging to meet the girl there, I got a jeep from the motor pool officer of the 91st Division and set out for Gregolischie, as the Austro-Hungarian Empire spelled it, or Gregolice, as the Yugoslavians had already rewritten it. I wound through the hills paralleling the sea for a few miles, then turned into the Comeno road at Contovello. I had just come through the village of Gabrovizza—now Gobrovice—seven miles from my destination, when I ran into a roadblock. A group of Yugoslav soldiers, better uniformed than any I had seen thus far and wearing machine pistols

slung from their shoulders, ordered me to halt. Without leaving
the jeep I identified myself as a U.S. war correspondent.

"You cannot pass," one of them informed me.

Thinking that they had misunderstood me, I said that I was
a journalist performing a most important function for the Allied
armies.

"Nyet," said the guard.

I pointed to my identification card, which had "captain" typed
on it, meaning that I held that grade if I happened to be captured. I figured it would impress him.

"Nyet," said the guard.

"But we are Allies. Roosevelt, Churchill, all of us are friends of
Tito."

"Nyet."

I drove back toward Gabrovice. When I was out of sight, I
threw the jeep into four-wheel drive, headed into the fields and
made a wide swing around the roadblock. On the road once
more, it took but a few minutes to reach Goriano and turn right
into the dirt track that dead-ended in Gregolice.

The village contained about fifty houses lining both sides of a
muddy, deeply rutted dirt path. In these houses lived both man
and beast, and the stamp of poverty was evident. On the walls
were scribbled the slogans that had been dear to the heart of the
Italian dictator. *"Combattere—vincere—morire"* and *"Se le culle
sono vuote, la nazione invecchia e cade."* ("Fight—win—die" and
"If the cradle is empty, the nation grows old and falls.") These had
been smeared over with a paint brush, but the words were still
visible.

I parked the jeep flush along the wall of my interpreter's house
and entered the courtyard. The poor farm implements scattered
about were already ancient at the turn of the century. Collected
there were the girl, her father, her mother, an aunt and a friend.
The greeting was warm and sincere. A bottle of white wine and
heavy gray bread was brought out, and we sat in the sunny
yard gossiping.

The father had been born in this house under the Austro-Hungarian Empire, but neither he nor his parents had ever felt any particular sentiment for that far-off colossus. He was a Slav, and the Hapsburgs were outlanders. For the fascists he harbored a feeling of deep resentment. They had taken his money for taxes, drafted his sons for army service and forced him to sell his produce through government cooperatives. He managed to make a fine distinction between the fascists and the nation they governed. He was an out-and-out anti-communist, not only because communism, in his deeply religious mind, represented the anti-Christ, but because Soviet collectivization was even worse than the fascist cooperative. Even so, if his only choice were between a democratic Italy and a communist Yugoslavia, he, as well as an overwhelming majority of the Slav peasantry, would choose Yugoslavia.

While we spoke there was a growing hubbub beyond the wall, and soon a Yugoslavian patrol of four soldiers marched into the courtyard. They seemed to be in an ugly mood. Two of them leveled rifles and jabbered.

"Americanski," I said, reaching for my identification card. Again they jabbered, and my interpreter said, "They want you to leave immediately."

"Tell them that I am a friend and ally and that I will leave as soon as I have finished here."

She started to speak, but their angry rejoinder cut her off. I saw one of them take a hand grenade from his belt, while his men began to back off. "For the love of God!" she cried, fear making her voice tremble. "You must leave now. I heard them. They are going to blow up the house!"

"Tell your father I shall return tomorrow," I said with as much dignity as I could gather.

The patrol watched me as I climbed into the vehicle. I noted that the five-gallon gas can that had been strapped to the rear was now missing, but at this late date I am making no accusations.

Back in Trieste I went directly to the headquarters of the Yugoslav 2nd Army and spoke to a major who seemed sympathetic to my story. He gave me a pass that was valid for the next day. I returned to Gregolice and to the interpreter's house, which I found immersed in an atmosphere of tragedy. The girl had been arrested, charged with being a spy. The family had no doubts about what would happen to her, for they had seen the SS, the fascists and the Slavs operate quickly, illegally and cruelly. Proof that she was a spy was the fact that she was helping me gather information. And to nail down the charge, they had found in her possession a card that I had secured for her permitting her to eat in an American soldiers' mess.

Her parents had no idea of the soldiers' unit, where they had come from or where they had gone. I assured them that I would be able to secure her liberation and that they were not to lose faith, but my words had no effect on them. I left with their weeping loud in my ears.

My blood was boiling as I sped back to Yugoslav headquarters in Trieste. It was not uncommon for a girl to be shaved bald and paraded naked through a town on her way to execution. Nor was it uncommon for the partisans to bury a prisoner alive with honey smeared across the eyes to attract carnivorous sweet ants. I calmed somewhat when I saw that the friendly Yugoslav major seemed to be as upset as I was. A former attorney in Belgrade, he was young, personable and more nationalist than communist. Together we returned to Gregolice and began an investigation that lasted long past dark. We found no trace of the girl or the soldiers.

"Don't worry," he said sympathetically. "It was all a mistake and we will correct it. The trouble is that we have no table of organization. Mainly we are self-sufficing units who had to fight a clandestine war, so all marks of identification were carefully eliminated for the sake of self-survival. That's what makes our job so difficult, but I assure you that by tomorrow we will find and free her."

On the third day there was still no report. Only more apologies.

He took me to his superior, General Dopsovic, commanding officer of the 2nd Army, later to become minister of defense. My complaint was couched in bitter language. I told him that what was happening was something to be expected from Hitler's SS, not from friendly allies. I said that I was giving him twenty-four hours before I broke the story of Tito's injustice. Once more I had a promise that within twenty-four hours she would be found and liberated.

At the end of the fourth day the general apologized for his failure to find her. By this time I was certain that she had already been executed and that I had been the unwitting cause of her death. At 91st Division headquarters where I was staying, General Livesay, seeing that I was depressed, asked what had happened. I told him the story.

"This is not an unusual occurrence," he said. "Let me call in my CIC."

I repeated the story to the Counter Intelligence Corps. Several agents drove to the city, grabbed ten Yugoslavs off the streets and brought them to a place of detention. General Dopsovic was informed of the arrest and also told that they would not be freed until the girl was returned, alive. Within an hour the exchange was made.

The girl had been in a cell in the local Trieste prison across the street from 2nd Army Headquarters, where I had spent futile hours in argument with General Dopsovic. A guard opened the cell door and told her that she was free. Since this was a common method of taking a condemned person to the place of execution without having them create a fuss, she was sure that it was the end. She begged for one minute to say her prayers, got down on her knees, clasped her hands and prayed. Then she arose, head held high, and said bravely, "Take me, I am ready."

Bloodshed, political tension, divided loyalties—these are not novelties in the troubled history of Trieste. Over the centuries the city has been invaded by Romans, Goths, Lombards and Greeks.

Charlemagne captured it in 787 and his heirs lost it to the Venetians. Not until 1719, when Emperor Charles VI made it a free
port, did the city know a period of relative tranquility. For over
a century it fulfilled its natural function, serving as a port for inland Austria, Hungary, Yugoslavia and southern Germany. Then,
after a period of growing wealth and importance, Trieste was
struck by what the Triestini still call the *bufera Napoleonica.*
After Waterloo the Congress of Vienna took the city from the
French and restored it to the Hapsburgs.

Although there had once been great unanimity of feeling that
Trieste should remain a free city-state, nationalist factions arose.
In the latter part of the nineteenth century there was a marked
upsurge of pro-Italian sentiment, and with the defeat of the
Austro-Hungarian Empire in World War I, this sentiment grew so
strong that Italy was able to annex the port and a good part of
the adjoining Istrian Peninsula.

When Clare Boothe Luce was appointed ambassador to Italy,
Trieste was suffering from a chronic overdose of that insidious
ailment called "international politics," for it was again in the
hands of foreign invaders. The city and its immediate environs,
Zone A, was being ruled by an Anglo-American military force,
while the hinterlands to the north and east, Zone B, was being administered by the Yugoslav army. This was a temporary arrangement, an aftermath of wartime confusion, and it made no one
happy.

The dynamic Mrs. Luce felt she could resolve the situation, and
she devoted much of her considerable energy and intelligence
toward that end. The belief that a single broad stroke of diplomacy could wipe out centuries of political error might have
seemed unduly optimistic to some, but Mrs. Luce, who had had a
long and more-or-less successful career as journalist, war correspondent, congresswoman and playwright, was not to be
daunted by history.

Her view was that a permanent settlement would help restore
Trieste to her former glory and affluence and would remove a

continuing source of friction between the Western powers and the communists. In addition to these admirable goals, she felt she would be a powerful influence in properly guiding Italy's leading political party. The left and right wings of the Christian Democrat Party were locked in an internecine battle, with neither side gaining the upper hand. While the behind-the-scenes battle for control went on, the warring factions agreed to name Giuseppe Pella as prime minister because he was too weak politically to use the office to build up either side, let alone himself.

Pella, a right-wing friend of the West, made so favorable an impression on Mrs. Luce that she believed that by letting him get credit for solving the Trieste question in favor of Italy, she would make him a grassroots hero. The acclaim from the common people would put his job on a less precarious footing. At the same time, our ambassador's own popularity with the Italian people would soar, for the people have as deep an emotional attachment to this part of their country as Americans do for California. Naturally, as the chief architect of the settlement, some of the glory would reflect on her. In this diplomatic *tour de force* she was assisted by her husband, Henry Luce, head of the *Time-Life-Fortune* magazine chain, who was now staying in Rome and participating actively in his wife's work. He would start his regular briefings with the embassy section chiefs in no-nonsense fashion. "Well, gentlemen," he would ask, "how are we batting against communism today?"

The curtain opened in the Trieste drama with the *Time* issue of September 14, 1953. It was a lengthy article that sounded the alarm about Yugoslavia's aggressive intentions. "Italy is completely disqualified as a partner to whom it is worth making concession," it quoted from *Borba*, official Yugoslavian newspaper. Against this implied threat Giuseppe Pella stood firm, *Time* said. He alerted troops and sent gunboats to the area. "Having won support that even the renowned Alcide de Gasperi failed to win before him, the new Premier felt he could consolidate his regime with a favorable Trieste settlement." In 1948, the U.S.-

British-French announcement favored a return of Trieste to Italy, but now Dulles had issued a statement in Washington that the U.S. might consider some other solution. It was a "stab in the back," cried the Italian press. "Unless Western powers replaced lassitude and ineptitude about Trieste with diplomacy . . ." they were clearly in trouble. So reported *Time*.

There it was, neatly spelled out for those who like their news neat and readable. There was the menace of communist Yugoslavia, the American-British-French promise, the American stab in the back that threatened our friendship with Italy and, finally, the crying need for diplomacy. Not the bumbling of Dulles, only the true understanding of Luce could save the day. In any language it was a good first act, cleverly constructed by a competent playwright.

The next week's issue of *Time* raised the curtain on the second act. It gave the extreme positions of each side. Yugoslavia wanted to annex all of Zones A and B except for the city of Trieste, which was to be internationalized. Pella favored a plebiscite, with Zones A and B voting as a unit. Since there were 286,000 Italians, living mainly in the city, to 93,000 Slovenes, living for the most part on farms, there could be little doubt of the outcome. "To the surprise of all, Pella has blossomed almost overnight into Italy's leading statesman," *Time* said.

Mrs. Luce had the solution, and her husband's news magazine correctly guessed it. Turn over Zone A, predominantly Italian, to the Italians, leaving Zone B to the Slavs. Simple and clean, like the problem itself. Converting John Foster Dulles, a man sensitive to press comment, was comparatively simple. Much to Mrs. Luce's surprise, it was the Allies who gave her trouble. The British were cool, the French were cold, and some of Trieste's political leaders were actively against her. The Mayor of Trieste hurried to Rome to present his argument. Such a solution would mean that Zone B would be lost forever, he said. His own family, in common with thousands of Triestini, had left property and homes in Zone B. This plan would give juridical approval to their seizure. As long as the status quo existed, there was at least hope for a future settlement that might safeguard both their private interests and national aspirations. Zone A, under the present benign occupation, was practically Italian anyway, and the withdrawal of the Allied troops would bring little benefit when compared to the permanent damage. The British felt that the timing was wrong. Tito had just broken with Stalin, and we were trying to wean him toward the West. To impose a unilateral solution in a matter that he regarded as so important might even drive him back into the arms of Russia.

The French Foreign Office, which has shown a surprising and irritating independence, merely turned its back on Mrs. Luce's diplomacy. They felt it to be a grave error not to consult Tito and work out an accord first. Besides, even to think that Pella would become a potent figure as a result of such a move showed an ignorance of Italian politics. State Department pressure could only get them to a point where they would agree to the fiction of not having been consulted. To make sure that their position was understood, the Foreign Office leaked it to the press. The British were easier. It was the pre-Suez Canal era when they, with misgivings, were still following Dulles' lead.

It was, on the whole, a most difficult diplomatic maneuver, and Mrs. Luce was probably the only ambassador with the personal power and prestige to have been able to carry it off.

Thus she could sit back and view her handiwork with pride. It was reported in the October 19th issue of *Time,* which told of the American and British ambassadors in Rome and Belgrade handing identical notes to Pella and Tito stating that as soon as practicable the Allies would remove their occupation troops from Zone A and hand it over to Italy. Zone B was herewith given to Yugoslavia. They trusted that this would provide the basis for a friendly and fruitful cooperation between the two powers. Mrs. Luce believed that this act tended to give Italy more equality when sitting at a conference table with Yugoslavia. As a suggestion, Italy might offer Tito port facilities in Trieste in exchange for the predominantly Italian towns in Zone B.

The Italian press and populace greeted the announcement with "unanimous pleasure" and "thundering cheers," continued *Time*. Naturally, "it was a big boost for Pella." At a press conference, Ambassador Luce "modestly attributed the plan's adoption to concerted Anglo-American efforts." But *Corriere della Sera*, the authoritative Milan daily, knew the truth. *Time* quoted the nub of their article: "What happened has been to a great extent the work of a woman, of Mrs. Clare Boothe Luce, and it is right and necessary that the Italian people know it. . . . Perhaps one day we will know with what patience, intelligence and diplomatic tact Mrs. Luce succeeded in bringing this arduous task to a happy end."

In Belgrade there was quite a different reaction, said *Time*. "We will give our lives, but not one inch of Trieste." The newsweekly, mirroring the thoughts of Ambassador Luce, saw Tito caught between a Russia who hated him as a heretic and an America who distrusted him as a communist. Tito rushed troops and artillery to the border of Zone A and announced that he would regard the entry of Italian troops into Zone A as an act of aggression and that he would invade as soon as the Anglo-American troops pulled out. "We will renounce Western aid— but not Trieste," he said. "There will be no peace in this part of Europe." Although concerned by the violence of his action, *Time* went on, Western diplomats, meaning Ambassador Luce, felt that Tito had climbed out on a limb and that if they held fast he would have to cool himself and his people down. "They do not believe, in other words, that the dictator of Yugoslavia is able and willing to go to war for Trieste."

But playwriting and diplomacy are worlds apart, and what should have been the third act, complete with happy ending, ran out of control. Mrs. Luce began to worry, and the following issue of *Time* noted: "Marshal Tito was expected to boil with anger over the announcement but he was also expected to calm down and resign himself grudgingly to the Allies' *fait accompli*. The disquieting fact last week was that Tito showed little sign of quieting down." His troops were poised along the frontier of Zone A, ready to invade as soon as the Allied Forces withdrew. The cold comfort Americans could draw from this impending conflict was that it would be fought almost wholly with American arms, because we had furnished them to both sides. The anonymous "Western diplomats" still didn't believe that Tito would carry out the threat, but the nagging doubt would not disappear. And Premier Pella had a new worry. What would happen if the Allies indefinitely delayed the withdrawal of their troops?

Pella didn't have long to wait. Two weeks later all hell broke loose at the annual ceremony in Redipuglia. Near an imposing monument under which lie one hundred thousand war dead, inflammatory speakers stirred a crowd of twelve thousand into marching on Trieste. As they moved into Piazza dell'Unitá they were met by members of the local police force who had been recruited and trained by the British provost marshal. These men were of Italian and Yugoslavian nationality, tough and well-paid. The Slav cops were anti-Tito in sentiment; the Italian ones were mainly in favor of an autonomous city under control of local Italian leaders.

The police had orders from Major General Sir Thomas John Willoughby Winterton to meet the crowd firmly and disperse it. They tried ordering the people out of the square and were met with jeers and a hail of paving blocks, whereupon they charged on the crowd swinging riot sticks. Scores fell wounded on both sides, and many were arrested. Some of the rioters, pursued by the police, raced up the steps of the ancient church of San Antonio in a desperate try for sanctuary, but the cops raced into the church after them, still swinging their riot sticks and cracking skulls.

The Bishop of Trieste, horrified at this sacrilege, ordered the church reconsecrated. This ceremony, held the following day, set off waves of new violence. Crowds raced through the city overturning and burning British automobiles. They broke into the offices of the Independent Party and set fire to it. Once again they surged into the Piazza dell'Unità and ran up the Italian

flag on the flagpole of City Hall. The police used tear gas and
water hoses on them—and then real bullets. Six of the rioters were
killed and fifty-six wounded. Among the police there were seventy-
two wounded and no dead. General Winterton then came up with
a fresh idea. He called out the American soldiers and ordered his
local cops withdrawn. The Americans marched through the city
to cheers from the demonstrators.

When I awakened that morning in my villa in Rome, I switched
on the early morning news program on my bedside radio. The
announcer was halfway through his description of the Trieste
battle, but I still caught enough. In a voice that was choked with
emotion, he spoke of British indifference to the true aspirations
of Italy, of the solemn Anglo-American promises that evidently
now were being broken once more, of the number of patriots who
had lost their lives demonstrating for these unfulfilled promises,
of the innocent blood of loyal Italians spilled on the sacred steps
of San Antonio and of the Bishop's horror at the sacrilege. Then
followed an announcement from Premier Pella. In this grave hour
of national tragedy, when the blood of innocent patriots had been
spilled, he asked the nation to remain calm. All schools were being
closed as a sign of mourning for the Trieste dead.

To anyone familiar with the Italian temperament, this was a
danger signal. In America when a university is suddenly closed
down, the students run off to a ball game or pull panty raids or
rustle up dates. In Latin countries they demonstrate. And today's
demonstration was bound to be a rough one, especially on anything British, because General Winterton figured as the villain
of the piece, having ordered the Italian flag hauled down. Even
though my car had American license plates, I decided it was
wiser to leave it at home and taxi downtown. The vision of angry
mobs is generally myopic.

In the center of town some British tourists were beaten up.
Cars with British plates or of British manufacture were overturned
and burned. A German correspondent's vehicle was wrecked because it was foreign and merely looked British. The mob gath-

ered force as it moved up Via del Tritone into Piazza Barberini and up Via Veneto, heading for the U.S. Embassy. A cordon of police and troops was hastily thrown up just twenty yards short of the objective. In the battle that ensued, the demonstrators heaved rocks and bottles while the police fired tear gas and water from high pressure hoses.

Across Via Veneto from my vantage point, a lone woman stood in the courtyard of the American Embassy. She was Clare Boothe Luce. I hurried across the street and joined her. She had just returned from a visit with Premier Pella and, being blocked by the mob, had left her car and arrived here on foot. I remembered her from the war years as a woman of great personal courage who would not take a backward step. Obviously she had not changed. That danger was immediate could be seen by the wounded police officers, blood streaming down their faces, hurrying by us into the inner courtyard of the Embassy where a first aid station had been set up.

She pointed vaguely at the crowds and asked me, "Who is in charge there?"

I looked out over the confused battle. "It looks as if it's every man for himself," I said politely.

"I don't mean there," she said with a trace of annoyance. "I mean the police."

"There he is." I pointed to a husky *vice-questore* in a tight-fitting, double-breasted jacket.

"I would like to talk with him."

I approached the officer and told him that Ambassador Luce wished to speak with him. He straightened his tie, smoothed down his jacket and followed me to the courtyard. There in the heat of battle, with rioters screaming, tear gas shells exploding and the bloody wounded streaming by, Mrs. Luce extended her hand and the official leaned over and kissed it.

She turned to me. "Ask him who the leaders are." I did.

"He says they are communist agitators," I translated.

"I'm not afraid of them. Tell him I will meet a committee of their leaders in my office now." I did.

The officer's reply was, "Tell the Ambassador that it will serve no useful purpose." I did.

"I don't care. I am ready to listen to anything they have to say." I translated.

The police officer argued with me that to do so would lend importance, give a sort of official sanction, to what was only an unruly mob. Mrs. Luce insisted, but the police officer remained firm.

TV newscaster Ned Calmer joined us. "It's dangerous for you to remain here," he said anxiously.

Mrs. Luce looked up at him with untroubled eyes, a beatific smile creasing her delicate features. "Remember, I, too, was a war correspondent," she said.

By one o'clock the demonstrators had drifted off. It was the hour of the large midday meal and siesta, and this, too, was sacred.

Time covered this minor incident by reporting that Mrs. Luce had offered to talk to any qualified representatives of the demonstrators, but that the crowd had dispersed without anyone taking up the offer. The blame for the riots was laid squarely on "the West's continuing failure to make good on its promise to Italy," and Premier Pella was quoted as saying ominously, "Time works neither for Italy nor the Allies. The dead of Trieste have furnished the evident proof of this warning with their blood."

Quite obviously Mrs. Luce was carping about Dulles' lack of courage because he had not ordered our troops out of Trieste at once, and thus she put the blame for the riot squarely on him. But the Secretary of State had already decided that he would attack the problem without Mrs. Luce. He borrowed Llewelyn Thompson from his post as U.S. Minister to Austria and sent him to London to start behind-the-scenes negotiations with a Yugoslavian mission. The job took a year, during which the Trieste problem suddenly ceased being a grave one, at least as far as *Time* Magazine was concerned, for mention of it faded from its columns. Even when Mr. Thompson (later our ambassador to Russia) successfully concluded the negotiations, the event did not hold much interest for *Time*. The magazine announced, briefly, and flippantly, that Trieste had been taken over peaceably by Italy and Zone B by Yugoslavia, and that this had so eased relations between them that Tito would probably pay a courtesy visit to Rome, which would be repaid by a visit to Belgrade by Gina Lollabrigida. There was no mention of Premier Pella, who had bloomed overnight in *Time* as Italy's leading statesman. He was now ex-Premier Pella. The article also omitted the price we paid Tito for the settlement. Part of it was a modern jet air force. The balance, in modern arms and in loans, is believed to have been enormous, but Dulles never felt that the American people were entitled to know the mere details.

A few years later President Eisenhower nominated Mrs. Luce as ambassador to Brazil and passed the nomination on to the Senate Foreign Relations Committee. Although this august body voted sixteen to one for confirmation, the single dissenter, Senator Wayne Morse, was vitriolic in his opposition. "There is nothing in her record to indicate to me that Mrs. Luce is qualified to be an ambassador, and her appointment would be an horrendous mistake," the senator said.

There were many, including myself, who wondered whether President Eisenhower was fully aware of what was happening in international affairs. His answer to Senator Morse allayed none of these doubts. "In Italy Mrs. Luce operated very successfully," he said. "Her work on the Trieste question was particularly brilliant."

Chapter 13

La Dolce Vita

La *dolce vita far niente*, literally translated, means "the sweet life of doing nothing." It is not an Italian phenomenon, though on these sun-kissed shores I find many of its most devoted disciples, people who practice idleness with a fervor that would do credit to a saint. This *dolce vita*, which has been depicted with such success on the screen, is both a set of people and a way of life. It draws most heavily from the landed gentry, who inherited the wealth, but not the ambition and intelligence, of their forebears. Surrounding them are some of the loveliest and most acquiescent women of the world. Their generosity in social intercourse is regarded by the uninitiated as orgiastic, but it would be difficult to convince these women that their conduct is excessively loose. They will go to bed with a man without much urging, but they won't kiss him, because a kiss bespeaks a deeper sentiment. For that the man must wait a while.

A single girl in any branch of show business is rarely able to support herself. She manages to draw from this *ambiente* enough supplementary funds to live rather well. It is a genteel prostitution, at best, but she would be the first to express horror at the appellation.

The *dolce vita* set, while inactive in a constructive sense, does have diverse hobbies, generally expensive and usually futile. In only one activity are the habitués united, and that is in the pursuit of sex; sometimes feminine, sometimes masculine, often mixed. It is personified by a young prince I know who recently married and honeymooned on Capri with his bride and his male lover, the sort of marital triangle that is still virgin territory for script writers of the *nouvelle vague*.

A friend of mine, a landed baron from the instep of the Italian boot, did nothing but race automobiles, a sport at which he was one of the world's best, and he owned a stable of costly Maseratis and Ferraris. With the passage of the land reform bill, the sport became too expensive a plaything and he gave it up. Now he does nothing, aside from romancing an attractive girl or two. His current girl friend has needled him to the point where he considered doing something about it. "I'm fifty now," he confessed to me. "What is there that I could possibly do? I'm not trained for anything, and if I tried to start a new business with my lack of experience and the little income I have left after the government got through stealing my best vineyards, I'd wind up a pauper." So he does nothing.

In ancient Rome the *invertiti* were already so commonplace a phenomenon that it didn't cause so much as a raised eyebrow. These ancients collected in Rome from all points of the globe. They still do. And they still don't cause an eyebrow to rise. Most of them find the *dolce vita* a natural setting for their social life.

What is regarded as sexual aberration on one side of the Atlantic is viewed differently on the other. Thus a famous movie director who has a complete wardrobe of nun's habits in which to dress his occasional *amiche* and an equally famous one who dresses in a child's sailor suit and is whipped by his lover are not regarded as abnormal.

The use of narcotics is also regarded with tolerance. Although easy to come by and reasonably cheap in price, dope is not the problem that it is in the States. In the main the boys and girls take the stuff just for added kicks, but rarely stay with it.

The Italian attitude is illustrated in an incident involving Prince Dado Ruspoli. The young nobleman was arrested trying to smuggle five pounds of pure heroin from France into Italy. When hauled into a local court, he defended himself by saying, "Your Honor, I wasn't smuggling. I was bringing it in for my own personal use."

"But five pounds!" his Honor cried.

"I'm a heavy smoker," Prince Ruspoli explained.

The judge acquitted him.

The *dolce vita* is much in evidence along Via Veneto. The set eschews Caffè Doney, which has in recent years been monopolized largely by American tourists. Caffè Rosati is favored by the Italian political and journalistic community, not to mention the *invertiti*. But the real mecca is the Caffè de Paris, across the street from the Hotel Excelsior, where the movie, *La Dolce Vita*, was filmed (at least it was faithfully reproduced on a movie lot). After a dinner in one of the best restaurants—George's, Sans Souci, Capriccio and Osteria del Orso—the set is back for midnight coffee and cognac at the Caffè de Paris.

The distaff side of the *dolce vita* got an unexpected boost from the Italian government. For years a woman member of the Senate had been trying to get a bill passed outlawing prostitution, which had been, through the centuries, a legal, government-controlled light industry. The senator's campaign attracted the same sort of amused attention amongst her constituents as did Carrie Nation's fight for prohibition or Emmeline Pankhurst's fight for women's suffrage. Like her forerunners, she had to bear the brunt of cruel jests. In America they said that prohibition could never come; in England they said that woman could never get the vote; and in Italy they regarded Senator Merlin as a good-hearted but impractical woman who didn't understand the realities of life—and wasn't it a good thing that all her fellow legislators did?

As ladies will, this one surprised them all. She ran the bill through both houses of the legislature and had it signed into law. I remember writing at the time, tongue in cheek, that it was a measure designed to further the public works program, because it would cost untold millions of dollars to enlarge the sidewalks in all of Italy's cities. I noted, too, that in a country with socialistic tendencies, the government wanted to give proof of its belief in private initiative.

To this day the girls still monopolize the streets. I see long lines of them each evening under the trees of Viale Tiziano as I drive home. They solicit along the west embankment of the Tiber, on Via Capo le Case, in the side streets of Via Veneto, in Villa Borghese, on Passeggiata Archeologica and along Via Due Macelli and Via del Tritone; in fact, on every street whose sidewalk is sufficiently wide to accommodate them and the passing throng.

Before Fellini gave currency to the name *dolce vita* through his film, the set had already received an enormous amount of publicity in Italy through its involvement in a murder case. This affair occupied more space in the Italian press than any single event since the end of the war, and provided a valuable part of my education as a latter-day Roman.

Like many *causes célèbres,* this one had an extremely modest beginning: On a chilly morning in April, Wilma Montesi, twenty-one, a moderately attractive brunette with an exceptionally beautiful bosom (if size is a criteria) was found dead on a lonely stretch of beach at Tor Vaianica, outside of Rome. The police investigated the matter, learned that the girl had been missing from home for two days, that she had suffered from athlete's foot and that she had believed that bathing her feet in sea water was a cure. The official view was that she had taken a fifteen-mile bus ride to the sea, and that while bathing her afflicted feet, she had fainted and drowned. The finding was fortified by the fact that the girl's shoes, stockings and garter belt were missing.

The verdict read: "Death due to accident." Evidently as an afterthought, a cop added the word "exclusively." Since it was an accident, all the evidence collected on the scene was destroyed and the girl was decently buried. If there were any doubts in the minds of local newspapermen about the propriety of the verdict (and there were), they were voiced over espresso cups rather than in the columns of their papers, because the stringent fascist libel laws are still on the books and are interpreted with severity by the judiciary.

But it didn't stop the gossipers. Surely nobody in this enlightened day believes the old wives' tale about sea water being a cure for athlete's foot, they said. And even if Wilma did, why lie to her mother by saying that she was going to the movies? And why, on a cold, blustery evening, did she walk seven miles from the bus stop to the place where her body was found? The curative power of the sea was no different at Ostia, where she would have left the bus, than at Tor Vaianica, where the body was found.

And what about the missing garter belt? It wasn't necessary for her to remove that in order to bathe her feet. But the cops were ready for this one: "The rough sea had carried it away." This explanation was less than satisfactory, because the garter belt had been held in place by six buttons, while a light sweater, found still draped over the girl's shoulders, was held in place by only a single small button. Besides, the girl had been missing from home for forty-eight hours. If she had bathed her feet the night she disappeared, then why hadn't her body been seen in the preceding twenty-four hours by the scores of people who had walked along the shore?

And that's how the rumor spread that the cops were covering up for some big-shot. Weeks went by and these rumors flew thick and fast, but not a single newspaper printed a word about the affair. The closest thing to a comment appeared in the

weekly humor magazine *Merlo Giallo,* which carried a cartoon
showing a girl stretched out on the sand and a pigeon flying off
with a garter belt. This had meaning for the *cognoscenti,* because
Piccione (Italian for pigeon) was the playboy son of Italy's
secretary of state. Young Pigeon, a bachelor jazz musician well
and favorably known by the *dolce vita,* threatened the magazine
with criminal libel. A hasty retraction was printed.

However, this served to bring the case into the open, and
the cops, just to show how unbiased they were, started another
investigation into the death of Wilma. This time, though, they
worked under a handicap, because the body was now gone, the
clothing had disappeared and the original notes on the police
blotter had been destroyed. It seems that a careless cop had
spilled a bottle of ink on the page, making it so messy that
it was torn out and thrown away. In spite of all this, the cops
still managed to come up with a solution of the mystery.

According to the new verdict death was still accidental, but
now they said that Wilma had bathed her feet at the beach
where she supposedly had left the bus. When she had fainted,
the tide had carried her body seven miles to the spot where
she was found. This was a far more logical finding, and it should
have ended the matter, except that a reporter happened to look
up the tide charts and found that they ran in the opposite
direction.

It was unfortunate that the cops had not spotted this detail
first, but then none of us is infallible. The sideline spectators,
though, had a grudging admiration for the minions of the law.
It seemed that the latter had succeeded where science had
failed. They had found a new fatal disease—the footbath.

The new flurry of rumors that the police were doing less than
their duty in solving the mystery, or that they were protecting
some highly-placed persons, made the chief of the national police
very angry. But everyone knows how ridiculous it is even to
suggest that upholders of law and order can be fixed, especially
in Italy, so the whole affair might still have been forgotten in

time if a pretty, sometime brunette in her early twenties, Annamaria Caglio, had not decided to speak up. It seems that she
was very angry with a friend of Piccione's named Montagna,
Marquis of San Bartolomeo, a title of most recent vintage.

About Montagna—well, let's admit right here that he is not
too savory a character. If Piccione's father might be called the
Dean Rusk of his country, then Montagna could be called its
Frank Costello. He is a true financial genius. On a taxable
income of nine hundred dollars a year, he owns three town
houses, two country villas, a number of automobiles and several
businesses. In addition to all this he had paid his mistress, who
was now squealing because he had thrown her over, ten thousand
dollars a year. Before the war he had been a spy for the fascists.
During the war he had worked with the Gestapo. After the fall
of Rome, without missing a beat, he worked with the U.S.
forces. After the war, the fascists were careful to point out,
Montagna worked with the Christian Democrats, because he
was an adviser to government organizations on how to spend
U.S. Marshall Plan money. The Christian Democrats countered
by saying that he used to supply girls for the fascists. The
communists topped both these parties with the crack that he
used to do that for the Christian Democrats, too.

In any event, this was the girl's story: Her ex-lover owned a
hunting lodge at Tor Vaianica, where the *dolce vita* set gathered,
just a hundred yards from where the body was found. Sex
orgies were commonplace, and dope was used to give them
added spice. One day a girl passed out from an overdose of
narcotics. After futile attempts to revive her, one of her companions, convinced that she was dead, carried her down to the
beach and left her there. When the tide rolled in she drowned.
The girl was Wilma Montesi. The man who carried her there
was Piccione. A week later Piccione telephoned Montagna, said
that he was worried about the affair, which was now burgeoning
with ugly talk, and begged Montagna, who was a good friend
of the chief of police, to do something about it. Montagna agreed.

Annamaria went along when he drove Piccione to police head-quarters. She waited in the car. When they returned, her boy friend told her that everything had been fixed. She remembered that this had taken place on April 29th.

(To get the full effect of this story, suppose that Dean Rusk's son had killed a girl, that the cops had got on his trail, and that, accompanied by Frank Costello, he had called on J. Edgar Hoover to get the dogs called off.)

It seemed silly to check any story as wild as this one, but it was done. The chief of police was asked if it was true that Piccione and Montagna had paid him a visit on April 29th. "It is a lie," he cried heatedly. "They came to see me on May 5th." So you see how little faith one can have in the vengeful words of a woman scorned.

And that went for many other details she exposed. For instance, she said that cabinet officers were partners in Montagna's businesses. On investigation not a single one of them was found listed on the official records of his building companies. (Of course, some of their sons were, such as the son of the minister of public works.) As for the loose talk about the freshly-minted marquis being a pal of top government officials, only the communist papers unfairly exploited this fact. One of their correspondents asked Premier Mario Scelba, who was the Lyndon Johnson of his country at the time, whether he was friendly with Montagna. The premier replied that he had never even heard of him. The next day the paper printed a half page photograph of Montagna and Scelba, both in cutaway coats, standing up as best men at the wedding of a cabinet member's child.

By now the scandal had gathered a full head of steam, and a tough-minded leader like Scelba could not allow it to grow un-checked. "The government must defend the honor of officials defamed by unjust accusations, and I promise to clear away the suspicious atmosphere," he said with determination. He ordered a Senate investigation. At the same time, to uphold the honor of his party, he appointed a committee whose job it was to "remoralize" it. With a statesmanlike grasp of the situation, he named the cabinet member whose son was associated with Montagna as chairman of the committee.

The Senate investigation stretched out for many months, but in the end the investigators reported that they could find no evidence of wrongdoing. They found some fault with the chief of police, who, they felt, was guilty of not warning government officials that friendship with Montagna was inadvisable because of his extraordinarily prosperous business affairs and his tarnished record. The report struck a positive note, too. It came out four-square for "the need for care in personal relationships" of politicians. When this was read in parliament, one deputy wondered if the chairman, in reaching so sage a conclusion, had bothered to question Montagna or the Caglio girl.

"Of course I didn't," the chairman said. "I would not pander to public curiosity."

"When one is inquiring into crime, one cannot say that he will question only honest persons," the deputy remarked mildly. "You may be a man of good taste, but you are certainly not the stuff of which inquisitors are made."

It was easy to see how far adrift matters had gone by looking at the headlines of the Italian dailies. Mainly they covered the story according to their political leanings. The moderate ones pointed out that it was, after all, only a case in which a poor girl had died mysteriously, and if murder was involved, then someone should be brought to the bar of justice to answer for it. So, with all this new fuss, a new examining magistrate was appointed and the case was re-opened for a third time.

This time, naturally, Piccione was one of the first to be brought in. He was asked where he had been on the day Wilma disappeared. Being a gentleman, the lad was reticent at first, but finally, because of the overwhelming importance of the matter, said that on that day, and on the nine preceding days, he had been quartered with lovely Alida Valli, the film star, in the Amalfi villa of Carlo Ponti, the motion picture producer and husband of Sophia Loren. He claimed that Ingrid Bergman, Roberto Rossellini and Gina Lollabrigida, all of whom were visiting there, could vouch for him. This was a clear-cut alibi that might have carried the day, except that at the very same time a lawyer in Milan was saying flatly that the youth had been in that city with him, and the boy's family, with just as much assurance, was saying that he had been home in Rome, confined to bed because of illness.

Since the three towns bear a New York–Chicago–Los Angeles relationship to each other, it was obviously a physically untenable position. Besides, anyone who can be in three places at the same time can also be in four. The youth was questioned again, and this time he recalled that he had actually been in Rome that day, having driven up from Amalfi that very same morning.

"If you were actually in Rome, why did you tell me you were in Amalfi?" the magistrate asked.

"When I found out that I was wrong I corrected my statement," Piccione said. "I am very frank about my errors."

The magistrate wondered why, if he had been so ill that he was required to stay in bed, he had driven up to Rome over a tough stretch of road that requires several hours of strenuous effort. But Piccione had a logical answer: his illness was only a sore throat. For this he produced overwhelming proof from doctors, nurses, professors, secretaries, police officers and aides of his father, all of whom testified that they were involved in the around-the-clock mobilization of medical science his sore throat appeared to require. As a clincher, a medical professor produced the report of a urine analysis dated April 9, 1953, the day Wilma disappeared. One of the doctors treating young Piccione had asked for the test, because one cannot be too careful in the treatment of a sore throat. It was not until later, when the report was placed under a microscope, that the original date of January 7, 1953, became visible. It appeared that this date had been erased and the later one written over it. The professor had a perfectly reasonable explanation. "I was distracted when

I filled in the date, and seeing that it was wrong, erased it and wrote in the correct one."

The new examining magistrate was something rare in Italian public life. He was no respecter of personages, no matter how important they might be. He was the kind of holy terror, we used to say when I covered the police run in New York, who would wind up walking a beat in Staten Island. It took him a year, but in the end he charged Piccione with manslaughter and Montagna and the police chief with an attempt at heading off the investigation.

The long public trial held in Venice was handled in an impartial and fair manner by the presiding justice. Witness after witness took the stand to change the stories they had previously told. Those who had given damaging evidence against the suspects now altered their testimony. Why had they signed such statements in the first place? Some said they had not bothered to read what they had signed, others that the stenographer was wrong and still others that they had been afraid of the examining magistrate.

In the end not a shred of evidence connected young Piccione with the murder (the word "murder" was now being used, because by this time the cops had changed their opinion and agreed that Wilma's death could not have been accidental), but with the temper of the readers of the scandal sheets at a boiling point, it took real guts for the prosecutor to get up and ask for an acquittal for all three men and for the judge to grant the request.

Not everybody went free, though. There was a crackpot astrologist who testified against Piccione. He must have read his astral signs through the wrong end of the telescope, because he wound up with a stretch for perjury. Then there was Wilma's uncle. During the trial he was asked where he had been on the day his niece disappeared. His reply was that he had been at work. His fellow workers testified that he hadn't been. He called them liars. It developed that he had been parked in a car with a girl on a lovers' lane, and he didn't want his fiancée to find out about it, especially since it turned out that he had been cheating with his fiancée's sister. He wound up in jail, too.

At the same time there was a young man who kissed his sweetheart in a movie theater in Turin. He was arrested and convicted, for it is a crime to kiss in a public place, and a movie house, by any definition of the word, is a public place. After all, the law is the law, and if you don't vigorously uphold it, how is anybody going to have respect for it?

Chapter 14

The Strange Fate of Major Holohan

THE UNEXPECTED was so normal that I never even considered it strange that I should become a publisher of Italian language periodicals, but it was a venture that was surprising in many ways. One was my consternation at the almost total lack of professional knowledge among the practicing journalists. Such elementary items as format and layout were not even dimly comprehended. The reason for this was that fascism had retarded the magazine field and the war had virtually destroyed it. Magazines were now taking their first feeble steps toward becoming what they are today, herculean giants jam-packed with competent practitioners.

My first effort was a monthly publication in the Italian language called *La Scienza Illustrata*. It was a transposition, rather than a translation, of *Mechanix Illustrated*. My associates on the business side—I was the editor—were the nation's largest printer, the most distinguished publishing house and the monopoly distributor. The publication was well done, its contents appealed to the artisan tastes of the middle classes, and the news-stand sales soared beyond our most optimistic expectations.

What is important to the story is that the printing plant was in Novara, in northern Italy roughly midway between Milan and Turin. Because none of my assistants were capable of putting an issue to bed, I had to make the monthly trip to Novara. It was this circumstance that led me into a chilling chase, in which I hunted down the solution of the mysterious disappearance of an American spy named Holohan. It took several years of my life, and when I had the solution fully documented, I was faced with the sobering thought that many lives would be ruined by its publication, my own included, if I were to err in the story I wrote.

I first heard Major William V. Holohan's name mentioned at lunch in the O.S.S. villa in Rome during the closing months of the war. Along with Lieutenant Aldo Icardi, Sergeant-radio-man Carl LoDolce and an Italian partisan guide, he had taken off in a C-47 from Algiers' Maison Blanche airport on September 26, 1944, and had dropped by parachute on Mount Mottarone, more than a hundred miles behind the German lines. The party carried with it a radio-sending set, arms, and an estimated one hundred thousand dollars in gold and other currency. Its purpose was to secure accurate intelligence on the political set-up in partisan units and to deliver arms to those groups that would use them to fight the Germans, not for the building of an organization that might be seeking the eventual control of the area. Stated in simple terms, its main purpose was to limit sharply communist military strength.

The mission, called by the code name "Chrysler," had been dropped into the foothills of the Alps in a region that was supposed to have been held by a partisan chief named Di Dio. An independent operator without party ties, Di Dio had, under the urgings of the Allied command, proclaimed the Republic of Ossola in the valley of that name between Lake Maggiore and the Swiss border. His "republic" had a population of about eighty thousand. He even printed stamps, samples of which, duly canceled, had arrived on letters delivered by couriers through the German lines. But this bold performance had proved fatal, the Chrysler mission reported in one of its first communications after setting up headquarters, for Germans and soldiers of Mussolini's fascist republic had invaded Ossola in force, killed the chief and destroyed most of his forces.

A few months later Holohan himself disappeared, and with him the Chrysler mission's money.

It was a standing joke that the first thing lost in an O.S.S. mission was its money, like a war correspondent, for expense account purposes, always losing his portable typewriter, and I suppose I smiled when I heard it. The story of the disappearance was a simple one. A few weeks before Christmas there had been an enemy raid on the mission's hideaway on the shores of Lake Orta, and the personnel scattered. Major Holohan was never again seen.

After the war I visited Val d'Ossola and Lake Orta. I should explain that at the time I was a rarity, an American who spoke fluent Italian, and it was easy to approach the people because they liked nothing better than engaging in conversation with an American. Each time I met partisans in the area I would ask them if they had any information about Major Holohan, the American who had disappeared. If they had they weren't about to tell me, because at the mere mention of the name they clammed up. Some of them demonstrated actual fear. I had doors slammed in my face. It seemed certain that they all knew who he was, and for a time I had the feeling that he had been done away with by the partisans on a mob basis and his money divided among them. Certainly there should have been no fear if the fascists or the nazis had been responsible for his disappearance.

I spoke to one partisan about other matters over a glass of wine, and after gaining what I thought was enough of his confidence, I asked about Major Holohan. He answered, "This lake is full of bodies that have been dumped in it by both sides. Now, I have lived here all my life, and I've risked it many times fighting for the partisans. I knew Major Holohan, and he was a brave American. I truthfully don't know what happened to him, but I do know this: If I don't want to finish up in the bottom of the lake along with the others, I'd better not get curious."

Several years went by before I found myself in the midst of the publishing venture that brought me back to the scene. The monthly trip to Novara, which was close to Lake Orta, gave me the opportunity to do additional work on the mystery. The O.S.S. had already sent several investigating teams, as had the Criminal Investigation Department of the U.S. Army in Trieste, which had assigned Henry Manfredi, a trained police officer who had worked for the Federal Bureau of Narcotics before the war and who is with that bureau once more. Also working on the mystery was Lieutenant Elio Albieri of the *carabinieri*.

I learned the identity of the partisan guide who had parachuted down with the missing major. His *nom de guerre* was Captain Landi—his real name is Tullio Lussi—and he had served bravely in the non-communist resistance. I found him in the Italian office of the Cellophane Company of America in Milan. He is a slight, sandy-haired man who had taught economics in a secondary school before the war.

Although he had made the drop with the major, he didn't think he could be of much help, because they had parted company that same night and he had never seen Holohan again. "We kept in touch through a girl courier named Marina Duelli. I had messages from him until the very night he disappeared. That was on the night of December 6th, about ten weeks after our parachute jump, when I traveled up from Milan to Orta to see him."

Lussi explained that he had gone primarily to arrange an exchange of prisoners: two Gestapo agents who had been captured, tortured, and sucked dry of information by the partisans for the brother of a partisan leader captured by the Gestapo.

These swaps were not unusual in a war where neither side officially kept prisoners. He intended, incidentally, to pay his respects to Major Holohan who, he thought, might be quite lonely in his hideout. The man arranging for the swap was Holohan's regular liaison with the partisan command, Giorgio Aminta Migliari, a leader in partisan intelligence who, disguised as a priest, had met Holohan on Mount Mottarone and had led him to the hideout on Lake Orta.

"I went directly to the home of Mrs. Rizzoli, which served as a clearing house for guerrilla intelligence," Lussi told me. "Migliari was there, and he said that the Holohan party was planning to move to a new base either that night or the next, because the Gestapo prisoners had been part of a radio detection team assigned to locate the American center. The partisans feared the Gestapo men had reported the American position before being caught."

Lussi said that at about ten-thirty that night he had heard gunfire, but he had thought nothing of it. Shortly after midnight a breathless Lieutenant Icardi appeared at the Rizzoli house to announce that the enemy had raided their hideout, and that after a sharp gunfight, the members of the mission had scattered. Next morning Sergeant LoDolce and a partisan named Manini put in their appearance. Then a partisan named Tozzini showed up with the mission's radio, weapons and supplies, all intact, but no Major Holohan.

"The story of the gunfight surprised me," Lussi explained, "because we had had no reports of enemy movements. Since we were in fairly effective control of Lake Orta, the local fascists and Gestapo didn't risk going out after dark in small groups. Two days later, when Major Holohan still hadn't showed up, I went with Icardi, LoDolce, Migliari and several other partisans to Villa Castelnuovo, from which the Chrysler mission had fled. Naturally, I was positive that the enemy was nowhere around or I would not have gone there. During these two days the local priests, who ran the schools and who were in on the partisan activity, turned their young charges loose to search the entire shore front (in the form of a game) in the hope of finding the missing major.

"I went through the villa very carefully, but could detect no sign of a search having been made. If the nazis had captured the house they would have ransacked it before getting out. On the villa grounds I found only empty cartridges from American guns. Because of this I concluded that Major Holohan and his men had fired out of fear, and that the sound of their own guns had convinced them that the enemy was returning the fire."

In any event Lussi felt that the story was incomplete. He wrote a long report to O.S.S. headquarters in Siena expressing his reservations. Feeling that he lacked the necessary experience, he asked that a trained agent be sent to the scene to carry on a more complete investigation. He gave this document to a courier for delivery to the American consul in Lugano, Switzerland, who happened to be an O.S.S. agent, for transmission. The courier, however, was caught and executed. By the time Lussi learned of the courier's fate, he assumed that the American consul must already have received a full report from Ike Icardi so he did not try to send another man through. Instead he radioed this message:

"One x Germans captured Lieutenant Ike's courier x courier killed and papers in his possession indicating positions and countersigns x Please immediately advise Ike repeat Ike to take necessary measures x Two x Transmit urgent information and very secret our base in Switzerland is advisable for safety transmit to us and we shall transmit Switzerland x Three x Keep us informed measures taken."

"Do you know where Lieutenant Icardi is now?" I asked.

"The last I heard he was in Lima, Peru, studying international law."

"And Sergeant LoDolce?"

"He lived in Rochester, New York, and I would assume that he returned there."

One month later I was in Novara again, putting my magazine to press. The chore accomplished, I drove up to the east shore of Lake Orta, headed along a precarious dirt road which was no more than a footpath to a shabby villa in the poor hamlet of Gozzano, the home of Giorgio Aminta Migliari. Alongside the villa was a one-story building of fairly recent construction which bore the legend over the entrance, "The Italo-American Toy Co.—offices in Gozzano and Pittsburgh."

In Migliari I found a subject of a type far different from the earnest, essentially simple Lussi. He was an architect, slender and neurotic, about thirty-five. His sharp features, thin, hooked nose and quick, hoppy movements gave him a birdlike quality. He was amazingly voluble. His record in the resistance was good, but immediately after the war he had married the daughter of a high fascist official. This kind of inter-party marriage gave both families political insurance. As a leader of partisan intelligence in the area, he had been assigned to meet the parachuting Chrysler mission and furnish protection for it.

Migliari kept boxes of files, and I spent the better part of a day poring over them. His attractive wife served us a meager lunch, but our talk was not interrupted. He said that he and a band of anti-fascist, anti-communist partisans waited on Mount Mottarone for the parachutes of the American mission to float down. Because German intelligence was bound to hear about it, he hustled the group out of the area immediately. Sure enough, the Gestapo made a massive attempt to rout them out by instituting a house-to-house search over a ten-mile front. Migliari hid his group in a church steeple for five days and then, when the Gestapo effort was spent, settled them in Villa Castelnuovo, on the opposite side of the lovely lake from Gozzano. He assigned a pair of beetle-browed, horny-handed peasant partisans from the local region to serve as handy men and gunslingers in the event of trouble.

The first order of business was to rush urgently needed arms, so Operation Pineapple, an air drop of imposing proportions, was set up. Almost before the arms touched the ground, an unholy squabble broke out between the communist and non-communist partisans. Holohan, following Migliari's advice, had meant this first drop for the remnants of the non-communist group, who had lost most of their meager equipment in the battle against the Germans. The communist partisans, led by Vincenzo Moscatelli, placed Migliari and his men under arrest and grabbed the arms. Then Icardi arrived and shouted that Major Holohan would never stand for such conduct and that there would be no further air drops unless Moscatelli released his prisoners and at least divided up the arms with them. Moscatelli agreed to this deal, but later seized the other half on the tenuous grounds that they were stored in communist territory. Once again peace was restored by splitting this half.

At the time Migliari told me this, Moscatelli was a member of the Senate representing the Communist Party. A former worker in an Alessandria hat factory, he had learned his political catechisms at a school in Moscow.

Holohan was furious, Migliari told me. Moscatelli was both alarmed and hopeful. If Holohan persisted in arming the non-communist partisans, they would grow strong enough to shake the Red hold on northern Italy, but if he could be persuaded to deflect the arms to the communist Garibaldi Brigade, these would become the best shock troops of the revolution. Operation Pineapple alone had brought more modern weapons into the region than all the partisans put together had been able to scrounge in a year of war. He sent a messenger to ask Holohan for a meeting, and the American major accepted. The two met the first week in November at the Alzo–San Maurizio–Pogno crossroad.

Moscatelli was a handsome man with dark, dreamy eyes. But

the major was impervious to his charms. They didn't get along at all. Holohan said flatly that his job was not to saddle Italy with communism, but to kill Germans. If Moscatelli wanted arms, he would have to show Holohan a command set-up that was honestly non-political and obey all military orders designed to beat the enemy in combat. Moscatelli refused, and Holohan gave strict orders that no more arms were to go to the communist leader. That decision not only brought about a break in the relations between the Chrysler mission and the communist forces, but it also brought to a head the hard feelings between Major Holohan and his second-in-command.

Icardi considered the major stiff and old-fashioned. Holohan had insisted on maintaining military discipline, posting guards and indulging in no bravado that might draw enemy attention to the mission. Icardi had liked to move around, showing himself in American uniform at village dances and generally cutting a dashing figure. The major had in fact discouraged fraternizing, while Icardi had said it was necessary in order to get information. The major's personal sources of information had been the village priests, many of whom spoke French in addition to Italian. The major spoke French. He had Mass said at Castelnuovo by a different priest every Sunday morning. Also, he had been strict about the mission's money, and Icardi felt that since it was expendable, they might as well have some fun with it. Finally, there was a fundamental difference of opinion on policy. Icardi thought they should play ball with the strongest potential fighting force, which happened to be communist, while the major could not see arming a group that might not fight the right people. And in that, Migliari said wryly, he was a man of vision.

Migliari recalled that during the crossroad conference he had been waiting a short piece up the road, because there was bad blood between himself and Moscatelli. When the discussion was over, Migliari said, he had hurried up to the Americans and asked Icardi in Italian what had happened.

"There will be no more drops for the communists," Icardi reported.

"How about us?"

"There'll be no more drops for anybody unless we get rid of the bastard," Icardi had said angrily. "If we could send him to Switzerland without shoes, there would be enough arms for everybody." (To the Alpine partisans, this expression signified what "take him for a ride" did to a Chicagoan.)

Migliari explained that the American lieutenant's anger stemmed from two sources. He was anxious to get on with the war and not split political hairs, but more important, he realized that the communists surrounded them as completely as did the enemy, and it was not in their nature to sit by idly while the Americans armed the non-communist factions. More than once he said that they were in greater danger from Moscatelli than from the Gestapo.

I asked Migliari to accompany me to Villa Castelnuovo. As we walked toward my car, we passed the new, squat building adjoining his house. I pointed to the sign over the door. "Oh, that," Migliari said with an embarrassed laugh. "It's a toy factory that Icardi and I built after the war. At least, I built it with the money from our company. But you can see for yourself that it went broke."

"Where did the money come from?"

"We made no mystery about that," Migliari said hastily. "Major Holohan, when he needed lire for the mission, would give gold coins to Icardi who would then turn them over to me. I took them to Alessandro Cancellieri, a wealthy industrialist, and sold them to him at the black-market rate. We made a profit of sixteen thousand five hundred dollars on the first deal. Icardi told me that the major was satisfied with receiving the legal rate, so we kept the difference and formed the Italo-American Toy Company."

He went into the house, rummaged through some papers, and returned with a legal document that formalized the partnership agreement. It read: "Between Icardi, Aldo and Migliari, Aminta Giorgio, with legal residence, the first in Pittsburgh, Pa., 287 Lelia Street, U.S., the second in Gozzano, Italy, it is agreed and stipulated as follows: the two aforementioned parties will form a company with a capital contribution of 1,650,000 Italian lire, contributed in equal parts. The partner Migliari is given the duty of acquiring machinery, land, organizing production and retaining management. At the cessation of hostilities, a legal contract will be entered into. In the case of the death of one of the contracting parties, the succession of his interest will be according to the laws of the succession of families."

The contract was duly signed by both parties, witnessed, and dated November 21, 1944, less than three weeks before the disappearance of Major Holohan.

I questioned Migliari closely about the money transaction. Icardi had given him two hundred and fifty gold Marengoes, divided into ten packages of twenty-five each. At the legal rate of exchange these should have brought roughly forty-five hundred dollars. Cancellieri paid the black market price: twenty-one thousand. Icardi gave the major forty-five hundred and kept the rest, which was invested in the now moribund toy factory.

Villa Castelnuovo is an imposing neo-classic summer home of some twenty-two rooms set on the summit of a series of wooded terraces that rise from the lake. The front of the villa is seen through a tall, gracefully-wrought, spiked iron gate. On the shore's edge is a boathouse, and at the rear of the main house, set off by a double row of ancient Roman columns, a footpath winds half a mile to the minuscule village of Pella.

"It happened like this," Migliari explained. "The mission was slated to move either that night or the next one. The men were supposed to flash a light if they were moving on the night of December 6th, but because there was a mist on the lake I was afraid that I might miss the signal, so I sent Bruno Tabozzi, one of my runners, to ask what the plans were. He came back and said that the major had decided to move the following day, meaning on the night of December 7th. A short time later—the exact time was ten-thirty P.M. because we could clearly hear the sound of the shooting—the raid took place. The major had gone to bed; he wasn't feeling well. The others were still downstairs when they said they heard a noise. Icardi said that he grabbed his machine pistol and ran out the front door, shouting, 'Who goes there?' Somebody opened fire with a Sten gun from the direction of the Roman columns and he fired some shots from his .45 in that direction. LoDolce ran out the front door and opened up with his gun. Manini and Tozzini began hauling the mission gear toward the rowboat. The major came downstairs to see what was happening and Icardi yelled to him that they were cut off from the rear. He ran back into the house and re-turned with a bag containing the money."

I returned to Rome with a fairly complete picture of the mystery. The major emerged as a brave, uncompromising, dedi-cated soldier, one who could look after himself in any kind of a scrap. He was calm, unexcitable, concerned first with his men. He was an odd mixture of religionist and adventurer, a devout and observant Catholic, a non-drinker and non-smoker who had worked on cattle ranches and steamships between spells of legal practice. A graduate of Manhattan College and Harvard Law School, he had been a promising lawyer, but had never settled down to an established practice. For a while he had been an able attorney for the Securities and Exchange Commis-sion, and he had carried out a delicate mission in South America for the State Department in 1940. He was also a reserve cavalry officer. He had never married.

Icardi emerged as a brave, headstrong soldier who tempered his patriotism with a love for easy money. The radio-operator, Sergeant LoDolce, was a misfit. How he got into the O.S.S. in the first place was a mystery, since he lived in fear every second he was behind enemy lines. He stayed locked in his radio room hour after hour, day after day, not out of excessive zeal but as a narcotic against panic. Then, on the night of December 6th, there was shooting. It could not have been the enemy, for aside from the external evidence, the fascist commander of the nearest garrison, Captain Ugo Spazzalli, was located in Milan, and he stated positively that he had neither arrested, nor had he been involved in any battle with, the American mission. This he certainly would have remembered, he said, because he had been made uncomfortably aware of Major Holohan's presence in his district by his superiors who seemed to think he, Spazzalli, should capture the American.

But putting these pieces of the puzzle in place only deepened the mystery of what had happened to the American major as he came racing down the garden path of Castelnuovo toward the shore of Lake Orta.

I had no idea, as I worked with the printers at the *Istituto Geografico de Agostini* in Novara the following month, that the solution was at hand. Having put the magazine to bed, I drove to Pettinasco to see Gualtiero Tozzini, one of the partisan handymen. Here I was told by a weeping woman that Tozzini was in the custody of the *carabinieri*. And it was he who spilled the story. Tozzini was a heavy-muscled, heavy-minded peasant, slow, avaricious and more alive to such a tangible possession as a bicycle than to any world issue. In the resistance he had been known as "Pupo." When he was first questioned by Lieutenant Albieri, the local commandant, he repeated the version of the gun fight that he had recounted to the previous O.S.S. investigating teams.

"When the shooting started, what did you do?" Albieri asked him.

"I ran out of the house, down to the boat."

"Carrying your bicycle?"

"No, of course not."

"Then how did the bicycle get into the boat?"

"I went back for it, I suppose."

"You suppose you went back, right into a stream of fire from

Sten guns, machine pistols, maybe even a cannon—just to get a bicycle? How did you know the enemy wasn't in the house by that time? They could have entered by the rear door or the windows."

It was like shooting fish in a barrel, for Albieri knew the answers before he asked the questions. "What's the use?" Tozzini said. "I'll tell you everything. I've been to church already to confess my part in this murder. The priest refused to grant me absolution unless I told the story to the police. I tried to keep it to myself, but perhaps it's better this way."

And this is the story he told: On the night of December 6th, 1944, Major Holohan came down to the kitchen from his room and took his seat at the head of the marble table. His back was to the stove. On his left sat Lieutenant Icardi and Sergeant LoDolce. Manini and Tozzini were on his right. Holohan said grace, as he did at every meal, and Manini went to the stove to ladle out the soup. As he did, Icardi held the major's attention with talk while Manini dropped three-fifths of a gram of potassium cyanide into the major's plate. After tasting the soup, Holohan complained that it was sour, but he finished it anyway for he was not a finicky eater. When the meat and potatoes were served he said he felt ill and left the table. At that moment Migliari's courier, Tabozzi, arrived to ask if the mission was moving that evening. Icardi told him that Major Holohan was under the weather and didn't want to be disturbed, and that he had decided not to move until the following evening. The runner left without suspecting anything unusual.

They cleared the table and began a game of *scopone*, waiting for the major to die. They could hear him groaning upstairs, but that was all, and time was passing. If he recovered it would be dangerous for all of them. And if he didn't recover, Icardi reflected now, it would be no good, either, because the poison would remain in his body and there might just possibly be an inquest. "We'll have to shoot him," he decided.

Manini said that he had already done his part, the poisoning.

So the other three matched coins, odd man out, and LoDolce was the odd man. Tozzini handed him a 9 mm. Beretta automatic. The sergeant climbed the stairs, followed by the other three, who were afraid that he would lose his nerve.

As LoDolce entered the room, Holohan sat up in bed in the dark. "Who is it?" he asked. The sergeant pressed the Beretta against the back of his head and fired twice.

Icardi wrapped a cloth around the major's head to stop the flow of blood while Manini rolled the body into a sleeping bag and strapped it tight. Tozzini had tried to take off the major's gold wrist watch, but Icardi slapped him on the hand. "The C.I.D. looks for little things like that," he said sharply. The watch remained on the major's wrist. Manini and Tozzini carried the body down to the shore front, tied a thick cord around it and looped the other end around a heavy stone. They loaded it into a boat, rowed out about a hundred yards and dumped it over the side.

They had selected a spot in the lake that was supposed to be bottomless, but in the dark they didn't quite hit it. Still, the spot where they did drop the corpse was almost a hundred feet deep. They returned to shore and joined the two Americans in tidying up and loading their gear, including the bicycle, in the boat. Since Migliari's courier had arrived shortly after seven and they had killed the major not long after that, they must have put in a couple of hours making things ship-shape before they put on the fireworks at ten-thirty. "Remember, we were attacked by either the Germans or the fascists. We don't know which," Icardi told them before beginning this part of the performance. "It was too dark for us to see. If anyone says anything about this, even to his mother, I'll sentence him to death." They then opened fire, and people for miles around, cowering in their beds, heard the fusillade that established the time of the "attack."

Immediately after the murder, the cooperation between Icardi and Moscatelli became open. Icardi told Migliari that one had to face up to reality, and that since the communists had the men, they should have the arms. Fifty-one consecutive drops followed, hundred of tons of modern armaments, all delivered to the communist army of Senator Moscatelli.

I read this confession and that of Manini, which confirmed it, without emotion. As in the case of SS Colonels Dollmann and Kappler, the butchers of Rome, I had become personally involved in a story but I was still an objective observer. No emotional filter blurred what I saw and what I recorded. Certainly this was an incredible story, but I had come through a life in which the incredible was commonplace, and I neither believed nor disbelieved a story because of this.

The details in the confession were subject to check. Manini said that he had first tried to buy the potassium cyanide from a pharmacist, whom he named. I went to the pharmacy and spoke to the man. He recalled having refused to sell the poison without a prescription. Manini said that he had finally procured the poison from the owner of a galvanized tin plant where he had once worked; that he had told the owner he needed it to put in the soup of a particularly obnoxious fascist officer. I spoke with the owner of the tin plant and he clearly recalled the incident, admitting that he had given the potassium cyanide to the partisan. Manini said that he had kept the poison in a jacket pocket for a few days, and that the acid had eaten away the cloth. At his home the jacket, with the right hand pocket eaten away, was found hanging from a hook.

Tozzini had not thrown the Beretta automatic into the lake, as he said Icardi had advised him to do. It still hurt him to think of the wasted wrist watch, so he had sold the automatic to a friend named Maulini. *Carabinieri* visited Maulini's home and found the Beretta. It bore serial number 914287.

Several weeks later, when proper grappling equipment had been brought up to Orta, Manini and Tozzini guided a police boat to the area where they had said they dumped the body. Within an hour Major Holohan's body was again in the world of light. He still wore the wrist watch. Two 9 mm. slugs were

removed from his skull and placed under a comparison microscope alongside one fired from the Beretta. The marks matched
perfectly. The bullets, not the poison, had killed the major. And
the bullets were fired from this Beretta.

There was no further doubt in my mind as to what had actually
happened on the night of December 6th. Four men told identical
stories of a gunfight. They repeated this story without any
change in detail to many investigating teams. Each man was
irrevocably tied to it. The story was either wholly true or wholly
false. All four men were either wholly innocent or wholly guilty.
With the finding of the body of the major, the guilt of all four
was established beyond any shadow of doubt.

But if further proof were needed, it came from ex-radioman
Carl LoDolce. From the records of the Veteran's Administration
I learned that he was receiving disability pay and was living at
10 Taft Street in Rochester, New York. I also learned that former
Lieutenant Aldo Icardi was receiving a monthly check under the
GI Bill of Rights education program, and that this check was
mailed to 387 Santa Isabel, Miraflores, Lima, Peru, where he was
studying jurisprudence at the University of Lima. One feature
of Peruvian law he had perhaps noted: it is one of the hardest
countries in the world from which to extradite a man charged
with a crime.

LoDolce was five thousand miles away from Lake Orta, and
he had no way of knowing what was taking place there. Agents
from the army's Criminal Investigation Division, accompanied by
a couple of Rochester detectives, visited his apartment on Taft
Street. Neighbors reported that Mrs. LoDolce was in the hospital
expecting a second child and that they would find Carl at work
as a punch-press operator in a factory. They found him there
and took him to police headquarters. He pretended to be indig-
nant. They informed him that the body of Major Holohan had
been recovered and that he was accused of firing the shots. He
became hysterical, but denied that he had anything to do with
the killing. He was asked to submit to a lie detector test, which,

of course, he was under no legal obligation to do. But he was not a lawyer, like Icardi, nor even a normally shrewd person, and he took the test. It showed him to be extremely agitated. When he was told that he had failed, he broke down and dictated a confession, which he then signed.

LoDolce told the officers of the friction between Major Holohan and his lieutenant, and of the constant air of tension this created. "Major Holohan hardly ever talked to me about what the mission was supposed to do, and Icardi would tell me continuously that things were going wrong and how operations should have been conducted and I began to feel that we were in a situation in which we could not survive. . . . on the 6th of December, 1944, one of our two partisan attendants brought something that looked like sugar and said it was poison and could be used to kill the major. . . . he said that he had tried the poison on a cat and that it had died instantly. Icardi said we would have to use it right away, that night. Manini and Tozzini prepared a meal of soup. The major was called to dinner and we all sat down to eat. When the major had taken a few spoonfuls, he remarked that it burned. Icardi said, 'Yes, it's hot.' . . . Icardi and I sat in front of the fireplace and wondered what was going to happen. Icardi said something like, if he lives through this, he'll send a message to headquarters so we'll have to make sure he doesn't live. He asked Manini and Tozzini if they would shoot him and they absolutely refused. So Icardi said it had to be him or me. I don't remember clearly my movements from then on. Icardi tossed a coin and I think I called and lost. Manini gave me a gun, his Beretta. We walked in the room and the major sat up and said either, 'What is it,' 'Who is it,' or 'What's the matter.' I went to the side of his bed and fired two shots. Icardi, Manini and Tozzini rushed in. Icardi opened the major's haversack and removed some money and bills which were rolled up. I'm not sure exactly what was taken because I stood there dazed and weak and couldn't think very well. Manini, Tozzini and Icardi picked up the major. He was heavy and Manini told me to help, but I couldn't bring myself to do it. They carried him to the boat which Manini had waiting on the lake. I took my radio equipment and followed them and placed it in the boat. Icardi told the partisans to get the rest of our stuff. I don't remember whether they made one or two trips back to the house, or whether Icardi told Manini to fire some rounds into the house then or whether Manini did this in accordance with a prearranged plan. Manini went back and when he started firing, we fired too, so that people would think we were being ambushed. A hand grenade that had belonged to the major was set off, but I don't remember who threw it. Icardi and I, before this happened but after the major had first been brought down, waited on the shore while they rowed him out to deeper water and dropped his weighted body.

"After the firing, Tozzini and I left for Villa Maria while Icardi and Manini started for the town of Pella by water. Icardi had told me not to worry about contacting him, that he would send for me to join him after he got settled somewhere and that I was to sit tight in Villa Maria with Tozzini. After a few days Tozzini got worried and left the villa, to see if he could get some news. When he returned he said I was to go with him to meet Icardi. We left and he led me to a house in the town of Alzo where I rejoined Icardi.

"I have read this statement consisting of eight pages. I have signed and numbered each page and initialed all corrections. I have made this statement freely and voluntarily. No one has promised me anything or threatened me in any way to obtain this statement."

What was surprising, and fortunate for me, was that not a word about what was happening had leaked out to the press. This kept the pressure off me. I flew to Washington to try to get information from the Defense Department, but that was like running into a stone wall. They refused to speak about any phase of the case. They wouldn't even give me the name of the major's next of kin on the ground that it, too, was top secret. The mere mention of the name Holohan had set them trembling.

The Missing Persons Department of the New York City police found the next of kin for me. This was difficult, because the brother spells his name differently. I visited him in his stock brokerage firm on Wall Street. Bill Holohan, judged from his photos, had had a craggy kind of Celtic face with heavy brows, high cheekbones, a vertical nose and jutting chin—the face of a monsignore or a Notre Dame line coach. His brother, Joseph R. Holahan, was a completely different Irish type: a short, black-haired, florid man who has spent all his adult life on the Street and is now an associate member on the Stock Exchange. He married young and is the father of two children. If he ever went in for high adventure at all, it was vicariously. He held a deep admiration for his big, roving brother, and he had refused to believe that the major was dead until the recent grisly revelations.

He hesitated to speak with me, because he had been warned by some military authorities that any publicity would embarrass their investigation. I pointed out that the only investigation that was going anywhere at all was mine; that the military could not try Icardi and LoDolce for murder because they had already been honorably discharged from the service; that the fact that the crime had been committed on foreign soil meant that there would be no court of jurisdiction in the entire U.S.A.; that even a trial before the Italian courts was problematical, because the extradition treaty between the U.S. and Italy was broken by the state of war that existed between the two powers. These men were free, and the only punishment they faced was the article I was now about to write.

Joe Holahan believed me. He told me that at first he had thought that his brother had been sent on another secret mission, so secret that the army wanted even the major's next of kin to think him dead. Then, when the army informed him that Bill "could be considered dead," and that he should take over as executor of Bill's estate, he demanded to know how his brother had died. Even though all information about O.S.S. missions behind the lines was still rated top secret, he managed to learn the identity of the other officer on the Chrysler Mission, and he wrote to that young man.

In February 1946, he received an answer. Icardi, now back at Pittsburgh Law School on a GI scholarship, wrote that he had returned to the United States the previous summer and had tried to obtain Mr. Holahan's address so that he could call on him, "but my efforts to trace you were of no avail." The letter was almost cordial and, toward the missing man, almost tender.

". . . I first met your brother in Siena in late August of 1944. Our mission had already been planned before we met. We feared that the war would end before we had the opportunity to do our part.

"Your brother was a very courageous man, and our two Italian companions marveled at his calm and self command as we prepared to jump into the unknown. Even more, they were puzzled that a man who had no knowledge of the language could be in such a situation and still not appear to be worried."

Then followed an account of the supposed enemy raid on Villa Castelnuovo. "What happened to your brother I will not venture to surmise for we, above all others, who were accustomed to seeing dead bodies lying beside the road and hardly taking the time to see who it might be, can appreciate how cheap life was in the situation we found ourselves. One's life could be taken at any time by friend or foe, or even a disinterested party, perhaps just for the thrill of killing, or for no reason at all.

"I feel this, that perhaps some day something may come to light concerning the disappearance of your brother, and I for one hope that this should happen soon, for until something does come up, even we who were his officers and men are also subject to suspicion, with respect to his fate."

Icardi came to New York on April 12, 1946. Joe Holahan went to his hotel room; they talked and then went to dinner in a seafood restaurant. Icardi seemed anxious to tell Joe as much as he could remember. He even drew a diagram of just how the thing had happened—where the Americans and their friends had been standing when the shooting started, what direction the shots had come from, in what divergent directions they had all, according to prearrangement, run.

Sergeant LoDolce lived in a modest frame dwelling on Taft Avenue in Rochester, New York. I had rented a large, black automobile and parked it across the street from the entrance to his home. I had been waiting an hour when I saw a tall, slender man, his spectacled eyes blinking in the light, walking out of a side entryway. I jumped out of the car, hurried up to him and grabbed him firmly by an arm. "LoDolce?" The word was an accusation.

I could feel his body tremble, and I tightened my grip.

"You know why I'm here?" I asked. He gulped and nodded his head. "I've come all the way from Rome for you."

Abruptly I released my hold, whipped out a wallet from my back pocket and extracted my Defense Department press accreditation. (At a later date LoDolce told a Grand Jury that I had pretended to be a police officer and that that was why he had spoken with me. He might very well have believed this, since my military identification card can easily be confused with that of a member of the C.I.D., and in the haste with which I whipped out my ID card my thumb may well have covered the word correspondent.)

I replaced the card quickly, gripped his arm once more and propelled him toward his dwelling. I told him that I wanted a quiet place for us to have a heart-to-heart talk. In the modest living room of his apartment I said that I had not come to speak about the murder, since he had already made a full confession, but that I was there to give him the opportunity to repay the nation he had betrayed. And it was most fortunate for him that it was I who was here, because of all the people who had

questioned him, only I knew the complete story, only I had
spoken with all the people at Lake Orta who had lived through
that deadly period of war in Italy, only I could understand the
true motives that had propelled him into the awful tragedy.
My experience as a crime reporter had taught me that when you
deal with the occasional criminal, as opposed to the professional,
you can get more through understanding than you could get
with a rubber hose. LoDolce sopped it up. For years he had
lived in terror. Then the police came and he confessed. But
instead of being locked behind bars, he was set free, and a new
fear gripped him. It couldn't be real. Punishment had to come.
As the days passed, the terrible tension increased.

Then I came, making him truly believe that he could be of
help to his country. He reacted eagerly. "What can I do?"

I said that the clandestine communist forces in Italy still
possessed many of the arms that had been dropped to them by
the Chrysler mission. I wanted to know the location of the
hiding places they had used during the war, for I felt certain
that some of them were still being used. LoDolce swore that
he didn't know. This was information that Icardi had, because
he always worked on the outside, while he, LoDolce, never left his
radio. Also, soon after the murder of the major he had suffered a
nervous breakdown and had been repatriated to the U.S. by way
of Switzerland.

"How did you manage to give all the arms to the communists after Major Holohan's murder?" I asked.

"It was done by not telling O.S.S. headquarters in Siena the
truth," he replied. "I only coded and sent the messages. It was
Icardi who wrote them. He would say that the drops were for
the Di Dio group or for some other non-communist outfit. But
they all went to Moscatelli."

During the course of our conversation Mrs. LoDolce came
into the room. There was a touch of hysteria in her voice when
she spoke. "You don't think he had anything to do with the
murder?" she asked.

"Madam," I said, "I am not at liberty to divulge my findings." With that I turned to LoDolce. "Will you please ask your wife to leave the room."

"He risked his life for his country," she cried. "And now his brother has been killed in Korea. Is this the way his country pays him back—by hounding him?"

LoDolce stood up, walked over to her and whispered a few words. She left.

He had not wanted to kill the major, he said, but Icardi had worked on his mind so that he became convinced that the killing was in self defense, for if the major remained alive, Moscatelli and his communist hordes most certainly would have killed them all. And he is still convinced that this is so. "It was either him or us," he said pleadingly.

Except for Icardi, who was still in Peru, I had located and spoken with every person involved in the disappearance and murder of Major Holohan. I was now ready to write the story. I was about to accuse two American war heroes of one of the foulest acts in our military history. Two men, walking free and honored in their respective communities, were about to have their reputations destroyed forever. No court in the United States could touch them, but a single article would enclose them in the prison bars of public opinion. One who deals with printer's ink all his life is often inclined to forget the power of the printed word. This was a reminder.

I held a final conference with my editors and attorneys before returning to Rome. The consensus was that, despite the mathematical proof of guilt, Icardi and LoDolce would file suits for libel. The burden of proof was on us. And in order to win the cases, we would literally have to convict them of murder in a civilian court.

"It might be wiser to hold up publication," one of the libel lawyers said.

"The story runs," Editorial Director Ralph Daigh said flatly.

An attorney asked, "How will the Defense Department feel about our breaking it?"

"Mad."

"Mad enough to refuse us their records if we go to court?"

"I think so. They can always claim that they are still top secret."

Ralph Daigh asked if I could lay my hands on them anyway, and I replied that I would certainly give it a try. It was impossible to do it in Washington, for I had already had the door slammed in my face. But I knew that there was a duplicate file in Trieste in the hands of the Criminal Investigation Division.

The actual article took form with difficulty. Although I had enough material to write a book, I hit frequent information snags which necessitated trips to Orta, Milan and Geneva. Also, General Bill Donovan, wartime head of the O.S.S., walked up the five flights of stairs to my office in the Foreign Press Building to discuss the case with me, and this gave me new avenues to explore. In the midst of my work my son was rushed to the hospital for an emergency appendectomy, and the post-operative complications kept me at his bedside.

All this delay made Joe Holahan nervous. By now he was convinced that the only justice for his brother would come from my pen, and he feared that I had been called off the story. He communicated these fears to his friend Father Patrick G. Branigan, who was stationed in Rome, and asked him to check it out. This was the answer he received:

Dear Mr. Holahan,

I was delighted to hear from you, but awfully shocked to learn of the way in which your brother died. The same day I received your letter I went down to see Mr. Stern but his son was undergoing an operation and Mr. Stern was therefore not in his office so it was only today that I had the opportunity to see him. . . .

Mr. Stern impresses me as being one of those "ruthless correspondents" where a story is concerned. Some of the persons involved in the case have fled Italy in fear of their lives, afraid that the Reds may rub them out. In pursuing this story Mr. Stern at times has taken his own life into his hands. So after all the risks he has taken and all the money spent on the case by his company, it's a safe bet that he's going to get the whole affair in print. Even if you, the Major's brother, wanted to let matters rest, Mr. Stern would still go ahead anyway.

While I was working on the article, a curious letter crossed my desk. It had been written by the husband of a lieutenant in the American nursing corps stationed in Trieste. It was obvious that he, as well as his wife, was angry with the local command. The letter stated that dope addiction was alarmingly high among the troops and that such cases were disguised in hospital records as pneumonia. It went on to say that the suicide rate here was higher than in any other command and that this, too, was hidden. It contained, in addition, an assortment of other accusations.

I carefully obliterated the name of the writer, placed the letter in my pocket and headed for Trieste. Here I checked in with the colonel in charge of public relations, who was also a good friend of mine, and told him that I was in Trieste on two stories, one of them of a rather serious nature. I began outlining the charges in the letter. Before I could finish, he let out an anguished cry. He had never heard such a ridiculous story in his life, and where the hell had I heard it? I told him that I was not at liberty to reveal the name of my informant, but that it had come from a reliable source.

The news swept through the high command like wildfire, and at dinner that night, my public relations friend couldn't control his agitation. The commanding general wanted to answer the charges personally, he told me. Would I please meet with him the next morning. He stood ready to refute the slander.

When I returned to my room at the military-requisitioned hotel, I noted that the letter from my informant, which I had carelessly left lying on the desk, had been moved from its original position. I don't mean to accuse some over-eager military beaver of entering my room while I was out and photostating the letter —but if I had a suspicious sort of mind, it is a conclusion I would jump to.

The next morning I sat in the office of the commanding general, who was surrounded by his staff, all of them prepared with the most convincing figures. I told the general that it was an overpowering demonstration and that certainly it was fortunate that I hadn't rushed into print first and asked questions afterwards, for all denials, even when backed by solid facts, are looked upon skeptically by at least half of the readers. But what was unfortunate was that I was in Trieste to do two stories, and my company took a very dim view of correspondents who ran up expense accounts without producing copy.

"What is this other story?" the general asked.

"It's a very simple one. Your C.I.D. agent, Manfredi, is investigating the wartime death of a brave American major named Holohan. He's done an excellent job, too. If you would tell him to assist me, I could complete my assignment in a day."

The general turned to an aide. "Call Manfredi and tell him to give Stern the fullest cooperation."

I rose to leave. "You may rest assured, General, that I have been fully convinced by your staff's explanation. I shall cable my office at once that there is no truth in these charges." An hour later I was busy photographing each page of the voluminous top secret file on the Holohan case.

Chapter 15

Crime Without Punishment

THE HOLOHAN ARTICLE was printed in the September 1951 issue of *True*. Subscription copies went out five days before the magazine appeared on the newsstand. A reader in Pittsburgh took his copy to an editor of the *Press*. Since it dealt with a local person, they front-paged it, carefully protecting themselves from a libel action by printing that the information was gleaned from my story. This was enough to make the Defense Department lose its head. Fearful of the full impact of the article when it went on general sale, its Office of Public Information copied it, almost word for word, to make it seem to a casual reader that I might have based my article on its release. It was done with such obvious stupidity that it added impetus to the story.

It was interesting to see how the press of the nation played it. The New York *Journal-American,* which gave it the lead headline, called the principals Sergeant X and Lieutenant Y, but the conservative *New York Times,* which carried seventeen columns devoted to the story in three consecutive days, came right out and named the killers. Within twenty-four hours the reserve of all newspaper editors melted, and Sergeant X and Lieutenant Y assumed their true identities.

Between the writing of the article and its publication, Aldo Icardi, evidently certain in his own mind that the Holohan case had become a dead issue, returned to America from Peru. The immediate effect of the publicity was the loss of his job with an international airline carrier. Federal police officials picked up his passport, but he was not arrested, nor was he questioned by any official. The reason for this was obvious. There was no court with adequate jurisdiction to try him for any of the heinous offenses he had committed.

The ex-lieutenant was loud in his protestations of innocence. These protestations would have gained greater currency if they had been filed before a proper tribunal, since our libel laws grant full protection to citizens who are damaged by the printed word. Icardi never sued for libel. To this day he has not even written me a letter complaining about the accuracy of my article. The reason for not hauling both my publisher and myself into the courts, he said, was that he was too poor and that we were too powerful financially. Instead, he wrote a book titled "American Master Spy." The publisher was Stalwart Enterprises Inc.

I telephoned the printer and asked how much was paid by Stalwart Enterprises for the printing. I was told that the bill, paid in full, was eighty-five hundred dollars. I secured a copy of the incorporation papers of the publishing company from the office of the Department of State of Pennsylvania. It listed the sole owners of the stock as Aldo Icardi, Eleanor Icardi, and Agnes Icardi, all of 287 Lelia Street, Pittsburgh. Obviously, the money spent in publishing this book would have been more than sufficient to secure the finest counsel in the United States. In fact, at a subsequent trial for perjury he was able to afford Edward Bennett Williams, one of the country's best-known attorneys.

The Armed Services Committee of the House of Representatives voted an investigation into the Holohan case, and I was called to Washington to appear as the first witness. LoDolce, now represented by attorney, declined the invitation to appear, but Icardi, deciding to brazen it out, did come to Washington. His heated protests of innocence, this time made under oath, resulted in the indictment for perjury.

I read with interest Icardi's statement in his own defense. "Sometime about ten o'clock, we had been awaiting a signal from Migliari who was attending some kind of dinner on the island of San Giulio," he swore. "He had previously invited the major and myself to accompany him, and we had declined. He was to make some kind of a signal that a certain location, which he was to have arranged for, would be ready. It was very foggy. We couldn't be sure whether no signal had been given, or whether it had been flashed and we had missed it, and the major decided that we would make the move anyway. . . . We were to move north, beyond the lake, back of the village of Pella. We made our way to the lake shore. We packed all our equipment in the boat. Then Major Holohan turned to me as the five of us were standing in a group and he said, 'Ike, tell Manini to return to the house to secure the villa.' That meant that he was to go back to see that the door was locked, that the shutters were closed and anything else which might indicate that we had been located there. . . . Manini went up the pathway and the four of us who remained stood in silence waiting for him to return. A few moments later there was machine gun fire. . . . I immediately fired my pistol which was a .45 caliber, four or five rounds, in the direction of the house. I didn't see anybody there. I guess I fired because I wanted to make noise. I can't explain it rationally. I broke to the right of the group and began running, and I ran along a path which skirted the water."

As far as the body fished out of the lake was concerned, "Just whose it was seems destined to be one of those unsolved mysteries," Icardi said. "The Italian government did not establish the identity of the corpse in question, nor show the time of death, nor establish the manner or cause of death."

He also noted in his book that the autopsy report was defective in other respects. The identification of the remains was made by Angela Rizzoli and her brother, Albino, neither of whom had seen the major more than once or twice when he was alive. He admitted that there had been an external examination of the cadaver by an expert medical man, but he pointed out that the eye sockets had been empty, the face completely decomposed, and the right hand missing. Also, the external genital organs were gone, and he claimed that this made even a precise statement as to the sex of the corpse impossible. "What an identification!" he concluded. "A physician is unable to state whether a corpse is male or female, yet two people who saw a man more than five years before, for one hour, indoors, at night, swear categorically that they recognized this corpse as that man. These revelations should throw some terrifying doubts into the consciences of those people who, accepting third and fourth hand reports of others without ever actually seeing the official report or the official records, have been calling honorable and respectable citizens, murderers and robbers."

About his connection with the toy business. Icardi has made many detailed explanations, the final one to the Allegheny Board of Law Examiners, before whom he had appeared when he had applied for a license to practice law in the State of Pennsylvania. (The Board, incidentally, refused to issue him a license and Icardi has not contested the decision in a law court.) He said that Giorgio Migliari had come to him with the story that the work he was doing for the Chrysler mission was extremely dangerous and that he should therefore be rewarded in some material way. Migliari said that the British were willing to pay for these services, and if the Americans didn't match that offer, then, "I am afraid, dear Ike, that I must leave you." Icardi recalled that he took the matter to Holohan, and that the major told him to find out how much Migliari wanted. He learned that the partisan wanted a cut of the black market profit the next time gold coins were exchanged. Furthermore, he was worried about the trouble he might have after the war if he were found in possession of so large a sum of money, so he wanted Icardi to protect him by signing the toy business agreement. Icardi again took this up with Major Holohan, who told him that if this was necessary to make Migliari happy, he should go along and sign the paper. The major added that he was familiar enough with Italian law to know that the agreement would not bind Icardi in any way, but that he should insist on having two priests witness the signing, so that if any question ever came up, they would know about it. The signed instrument was then deposited with a priest, Don Carletto Murzillo. Icardi swore that he was in no way connected with the toy-making establishment, nor did he ever see or touch one penny of the money, nor did he make any attempt to collect it.

Checking out the truth or falsity in these statements meant a return to Lake Orta and a re-questioning of the witnesses, the first of whom had to be Giorgio Migliari. The man I found now was a far more prosperous person than the one I had first met a few years before. He had given up the squalid house next to the defunct "Italo-American Toy Co.—offices in Gozzano and Pittsburgh" and had moved to a beautiful home on the other side of Lake Orta. He was owner of a prosperous road-building company and had enough money to participate in the rich man's sport of auto racing. I repeated Icardi's alibi to him.

"Icardi is mistaken when he says that he was waiting for my signal," he said. "He was supposed to signal me if they were moving that night. I remember distinctly having given a flashlight to my runner, Bruno Tabozzi, and having ordered him to flash the light if the major had decided on the move. You see, I already had new quarters for them at the home of Mrs. Rizzoli, and Icardi knew that. If they were to make the move that night, then my runner was to lead them to the new hideout. During the early evening I was at the home of Mr. and Mrs. Pozzi. With me at the time were Pasquale Ricapito and Don Carletto. I kept watching across the lake, but it was difficult to see in the heavy mist. At one time I thought I saw a light blinking, and I told the people with me that I had better get to the Rizzoli house because it looked like Major Holohan was going to move. When I got there, Bruno Tabozzi was waiting for me. He told me in front of the others that Icardi had told him the major was not moving until the next day."

Tullio Lussi, who had been present, affirmed the story. So did the priest, Don Carletto. So did the Pozzis and Ricapito.

There was one point that Icardi had overlooked when he gave his alibi. He said that the rowboat had been loaded with all the mission's supplies and that they had stood on the shore waiting for Manini to secure the villa. If this was so, how did it happen that Major Holohan's gear was not in the rowboat, but was re-covered with his body from the bottom of the lake? For this Icardi had no answer. Either *all* the witnesses to this episode lied, or Icardi lied. There is no middle ground.

The identification of the corpse was the base on which he hoped to establish his defense. Obviously, if this was not the body of Major Holohan, then no *corpus delicti* existed. Here are the facts I uncovered. The official autopsy report states that: "from the water in front of Villa Castelnuovo in the town of San Maurizio d'Opaglio was raised a person of male sex, about forty years of age, in an advanced state of decomposition. The cadaver is about six feet tall . . . the teeth were well preserved, both uppers and lowers. There was a gold filling in the second left premolar and another gold filling in the pritesi in the right molar. Attached to the abdomen was part of a khaki undershirt. The external genitals were missing. Near the body was recovered part of an attaché case bearing initials W.H."

It was, therefore, somewhat over-enthusiastic of Icardi to seize on the lack of external genitals as an indication that the doctors could not tell the sex of the recovered victim. Also, although it was true that Angela Rizzoli and her brother, both of whom had known Major Holohan only slightly, did identify the corpse, Icardi failed to note that the brother, Joe Holahan, who had known him intimately, also made positive identification. He also failed to note that the Graves Registration department of the U.S. Army, which has raised body-identification to a science, had, through anthropological and dental charts (the latter being regarded by the courts as as exact a means of identification as fingerprints), concluded that the body is beyond all doubt that of Major Holohan. By the time he came to trial for perjury, even Icardi was convinced about the accuracy of the identification.

I told Migliari that Icardi had sworn before the congressional committee that he had been nothing but a dummy in the toy business, and that he had dealt with Migliari in rather harsh terms.

"Icardi may have been a patriot, but he was mostly a businessman," Migliari answered. "I don't suppose he told you about the time right after the war when he collected the cameras the O.S.S. had given to partisans for use in spy work, or that after he had collected them, he went out and sold them at a good price."

I said no, Icardi had not mentioned this.

"Now, as to the toy business. I want you to know that it was a strictly legitimate deal. My conscience is clear on the matter. I confessed to my priest and he granted me absolution. But as for his being a dummy for my protection, that is an out-and-out lie and I'll give you proof of it." He pulled out his correspondence file, ruffled through it and handed me a letter which had been sent to him by Icardi on March 9, 1946, a date that is important because by that time Icardi had already been separated from the service. After a lengthy discussion of the toy business and a request for an urgent shipment of toy samples in order to get the Pittsburgh end of the Italo-American Toy Co. in action, the following appears: "I have written to my cousin, Aldo Icardi, who has a toy store on Via Balbis, 1, Turin, so that he can come to see you and put together a business deal. Also he will pick up a copy of our contract from Don Carletto, to send it to me in America together with my other papers. And now, it is necessary that our agreement concerning our industry should be written up in more legal form. I leave it to you to put it in order and when my cousin comes to see you, you can give him my copy of this instrument. If you feel that our business should be incorporated, then give him my half of the shares; if you feel that the business should be an agreement between associates, then give him the relative papers. O.K.?"

Here, in his own words, was documentary proof that he was a liar and a perjurer.

Migliari went on with his story about his partnership with Icardi. "His father and mother came from Pittsburgh to visit me. Papa Icardi asked me how is business, and I told him that it was very bad; that we had suffered a very large loss because on the night of my honeymoon, somebody broke into the plant and stole all of our electric motors. He asked me how much money was owing to his son, and I said that he had the situation all wrong. Our business had not only lost the $16,500 which we had invested in our partnership, but I had since advanced $10,000 of my own money, so that the actual situation was that his son owed me $5,000. Mr. Icardi became excited and called me a swindler and left. And if you wish to check on this visit you can ask Cornelia Solbiati, because she drove them here."

I spoke with Don Carletto, who had witnessed the signing of the contract and who was the repository for the document. He said that Icardi had never told him that this was a dummy instrument. When Icardi's cousin and namesake from Turin came to him and asked for it, as Icardi had said he would in his letter to Migliari, Don Carletto turned it over to him.

I went to Busto Arsizio, a large industrial town about a half hour's drive from Orta. The Solbiati family lived here. They had risked their lives and a considerable fortune in fighting for the Allied cause. Cornelia, at the time of the war a partisan runner of twenty, had looked on Icardi as a sort of Sir Galahad. Now, at thirty-two, she was still an attractive brunette. Hers was one of the last of the families with whom he had corresponded, and she permitted me to make photographic copies of the letters. She distinctly remembered the visit of Icardi's parents. She had driven them to Giorgio's house, and had heard them discuss the toy business of their son. "I stayed in the car, so I did not hear what conversation took place inside," she said. "At one point I did hear the father's voice raised in anger."

When I repeated this to Migliari later, he said, "That's when I gave the old man the bill."

Cornelia said that the parents were agitated when they came out. They got into her car and she drove them to the railroad station at Novara. During the ride, Aldo's father expressed his anger over what he considered Migliari's crookedness.

To complete the chain of proof on this point, there is a document in the files of the Criminal Investigation Division regarding a session one of the police agents had with Icardi on June 10th, 1947. Perhaps he had forgotten about it, but on that date, long before anyone even suspected what had happened to Major Holohan, Icardi was shown the contract of partnership that he had with Migliari. Icardi explained to Agent Ciarniello that this paper had been drawn up *without* the knowledge of Major Holohan.

The Italian government tried to extradite the Americans responsible for the murder of Major Holohan, but a federal court denied the request. The murderers were placed on trial *in absentia* in the Napoleonic Palace of Justice in Novara. The proof piled up against the pair was so overwhelming that even their court-appointed defense counsel admitted their guilt, but pled extenuating circumstances. A witness whose testimony was of particular interest to me was the ex-partisan leader, and now senator, Moscatelli.

The witness stood before the court and recited his pedigree, giving "senator" as his profession. He stated that during the war he had been the political commissar of the Garibaldi partisans in an area bounded roughly by Milan to the east, Turin to the west and the Alps to the north.

"I do not believe that I met with Major Holohan more than one or two times," he said. "I had more frequent contacts with

Lieutenant Icardi, his assistant, with whom I could communicate through a common language."

"Do you recall a meeting with Major Holohan at the crossroad of Alzo and San Maurizio at which he informed you that your formations would receive no further arms?" he was asked.

"I remember the meeting, but I do not recall the major having said any such thing. It was not within his province to judge which units were to receive arms. This decision was made by the National Committee of Liberation in Milan."

Migliari, now a defendant, shouted from the prisoner's cage, "You're lying!"

"Have you any information bearing on the murder of Major Holohan?" the court asked Moscatelli.

"I did not know that Major Holohan had been murdered until I read about it in the newspapers. It is obvious that Lieutenant Icardi, whom I found to be an upright patriot, was ordered to put him out of the way by the American State Department. Why, even today Lieutenant Icardi and Sergeant LoDolce are members of the O.S.S. Is it any wonder why they will never be tried in the United States and why the State Department will never permit them to be extradited?" the senator said.

What Senator Moscatelli said was plain hogwash and easy to refute, but it received support in a most unexpected quarter. The Italians forwarded a request to our State Department asking whether or not it was true that Icardi and LoDolce were still members of the O.S.S. With a brilliance for which it had become noted under both Democratic and Republican administrations, the department replied, "No comment." Icardi carefully kept the fiction alive. A reporter for an Italian news agency put the question to him. "Any answer, positive or negative, would be detrimental to the interest of the United States," he replied. Giving further currency to what Senator Moscatelli said was the fact that both LoDolce and Icardi had received medals for their work in the Chrysler mission. To this day Holohan has received none.

I was a witness at the trial. On the day I was to testify I left the press table and waited in the corridor. A *carabinieri* called, "Signor Stern, the court requires you." Walking through a side door and easing past the prisoner's cage, I entered the judicial semi-circle. I was told to state my name and pedigree. The president of the court, Francesco Sicher, asked me if what I was about to state was, before God, the truth, and I replied yes.

"Before testifying about this crime," I began, "I should like to clear up some points at issue. When Senator Moscatelli said earlier that it was the U.S. State Department that denied the extradition of the two Americans wanted for this murder, he was knowingly in error. The facts are that when the request of the Italian government reached the American State Department, the Italian government was allowed to go before the Federal District Court for a ruling. This court is an independent body, having no connection with the State Department, and it reaches its verdict in strict accordance with the law.

"The other point brought up by Senator Moscatelli is that Icardi and LoDolce are still members of the O.S.S. I can tell you flatly that this is a lie. Not only are they not members of the O.S.S., which, incidentally, does not exist any more, but they are not members of any branch of the U.S. government, military or civil."

From the questions and answers one can see how widely Italian courtroom procedure differs from that in the United States, where, at the very best, what I had to say would be regarded as hearsay. In this court it was of prime importance.

"State your view as to the innocence or guilt of Icardi and LoDolce," the president said.

"Their guilt is a matter of mathematical certainty."

"And Migliari?"

"The evidence I have indicates that he is innocent of the crime of murder."

"Can you tell us what the purpose of the Chrysler mission was?"

"The purpose of the mission," I said, "according to General Donovan, the wartime commander of the O.S.S. who personally set it up and who told me about it in an interview I had with him in my office in Rome, was to gather information as to the political beliefs of the various partisan units and then distribute aid in such a way that no party could, with our arms, impose its will on the country at the end of the war."

Moscatelli had testified that it was not the mission that called for drops of arms, but that these resulted from requests made by the National Committee of Liberation, President Sicher reminded me.

"Icardi, testifying before a congressional committee in Washington, made the same statement," I said. "But the truth is that it was O.S.S. headquarters that made the decision. I need only point out that when I questioned LoDolce in Rochester he admitted that in order to get the arms for Moscatelli it was necessary to falsify the messages sent back to O.S.S. headquarters."

"Was Icardi a communist?"

"I have no evidence on that score. He states now that he is a bitter anti-communist."

"Then why did he help them?"

"There are dozens of possible explanations for it—money, for example."

"What story did he tell to maintain his innocence before the congressional commission?"

"He repeated the story of the enemy attack."

"But that has been proven false by the confessions of his three accomplices and by the finding of the body," the president said.

"He said that he is not convinced that the body taken out of Lake Orta is that of Major Holohan."

President Sicher threw back his head. "Ridiculous," he snorted.

"Could LoDolce have refused to follow the order of Icardi to kill the major without risk to himself?"

"Certainly. LoDolce knew that an order to murder his superior officer was a criminal one. Since he had charge of both the code and the radio, he had only to send a message to O.S.S. headquarters in Siena or, more simply, merely tell Major Holohan about it."

I was the last witness for the state. It was time for the summations. The prosecutor, Alessandro Casalegno, a sour-looking individual of about sixty whose pixyish eyes belie a sneering and bitter manner, enjoys a local reputation for courage and honesty, having risked his life many times in freeing partisans arrested by the fascists.

"I know very well that the man in the street wonders why we are trying Italians for a crime committed by Americans against an American," he summed up. "But you citizen judges are not the man on the street when you sit here. It may be that this trial will not satisfy many people. What is important in this trial is that justice be satisfied. No one has uttered a single word about Major Holohan that wasn't a eulogy. He was a perfect officer, authoritative, stubborn perhaps, but bending every energy to insure the success of the mission."

He characterized Icardi as the perfect figure of a paid assassin, a transatlantic gangster committing crime for profit in partnership with Migliari, whose heart also beat faster at the thought of an illegal profit. Icardi, the leader, wanted easy glory and easier women. The shadow of Holohan interfered with his plans. Obviously, then, Holohan had to be eliminated. He traced the murder in detail. "And then when the deed was done," he cried, shaking his glasses at the judge, "what did our two worthy business partners do? Why, they acted like the tired businessmen they were and each went to a *letto mobiliato* (literally, a furnished bed) and each slept soundly with his bedmate until noon the next day. For Icardi and LoDolce I ask *ergastolo* (life imprisonment—the severest penalty under Italian law). For Manini and Tozzini, twenty-two years imprisonment. For Migliari I ask twenty-four years imprisonment and for Maulini, for illegal possession of the murder gun, I ask ten months imprisonment and a twenty thousand lire (thirty-two dollars) fine."

LoDolce's lawyer summed up for four hours. His plea was that his client was a victim of the times, and that when the judge and jury passed sentence, they were to bear in mind that he believed that he was helping to accomplish the work of the mission, in which event it was a political crime for which he would have to be acquitted.

At the evening recess, Mario Del Fiume, attorney for Tozzini, shared my umbrella as we sought out a caffe away from the places frequented by the court crowd. As we sipped our *espresso*, he told me that it was a shame not to press home the truth of the political implications of the murder. "Few men have suffered at the hands of the communists as I have," he said. "Their hands are dripping with blood in this case, yet tomorrow, when I step up to defend Tozzini, I must go along with the prosecutor and call it a crime for money. I do it because it is the best way to defend my client."

The following day Del Fiume made an impassioned address. His client had been a mere dupe, forced to follow the orders of a money-hungry, miserable pig. "And one has to apologize to the pig when he calls Icardi by that name." Icardi was not a patriot who wanted to serve his country, but a vulgar thief who wanted to steal the mission's funds. Icardi planned the crime and persuaded LoDolce and the Italians to help him. LoDolce could have refused, but the Italians could not. They would have been killed if they hadn't obeyed. "Why," he asked dramatically, throwing his arms wide, "should we prosecute these Italians?"

The packed courtroom burst into wild applause. "He is right," they shouted. "Let the Italians go free!"

The sentence in the case of the Italian Republic versus Icardi and LoDolce *in absentia* and Migliari, Manini, Tozzini and Maulini before the bar of justice, was handed down on November 6th, 1953. The standing-room spectator section was jammed almost to the point of suffocation. There was a tense silence as President Sicher and the citizen jury filed to their places. The President raised a document and read: "Aldo Icardi is found guilty on all counts charged and is sentenced to life imprisonment. Carl LoDolce is found guilty on all counts and is sentenced to seventeen years imprisonment. Giorgio Aminta Migliari is acquitted because he did not commit the crimes with which he was charged. Tozzini and Manini are acquitted because they were forced to participate in the criminal plan on pain of death. Maulini is convicted of illegally possessing a weapon of war and is hereby sentenced to four months imprisonment, execution of which is suspended, and a ten thousand lire fine."

I carefully made my way out of the milling mob celebrating the verdict. In the United States Icardi and LoDolce, who had perpetrated the crime, went freely about their daily tasks with nothing to fear except a visit to Italy.

I followed the crowd into the street. A dreary, steady rain was falling. In front of the courthouse stands the statue of King Vittorio Emanuele II, a ruler with a strong sense of justice. His back was resolutely turned on the Palace of Justice.

A recent book by Attorney Edward Bennett Williams dealt with the latter's defense of Icardi at his trial in Federal Court. In his opening statement to the jury, Williams said, "We expect to show you that Lieutenant Aldo Icardi is not a murderer or a thief or a liar—the evidence will show that he was one of the real heroes of World War II."

In the book he goes on to say that he expected to prove this by showing that the Communist Party, fearful as the investigations grew warmer that guilt would point at Moscatelli and his brigands, got Manini and Tozzini, at least one of whom was once a communist, to confess to the murder, shifting the responsibility to Aldo Icardi, the American. Mr. Williams had lunch in Rome with Senator Moscatelli, he said in his book, and the communist senator readily conceded that the partisans under his command had eliminated Holohan.

When Williams argued this arrant nonsense before a jury, nobody could blame him. He was, after all, a defense lawyer engaged in pleading a case, and he had the right and duty to fire what he considered his best shots on his client's behalf. But when he presumes to tell the general public, as he does in the book, that this is the gospel truth, and that by inference my story transforms an innocent war hero "into a desperate and despondent man . . . whose years of living under the accusation of murder had obviously taken a heavy toll on him," then he must be judged not as an attorney but as a fellow reporter, and a particularly inept one, since his error-ridden account airily disregards the body of fact already collected.

The day the perjury trial opened, my article, "The Case Against Aldo Icardi—Murderer," appeared on the nation's newsstands. It blazoned forth from posters on delivery trucks passing frequently before the Washington, D.C. courthouse. Williams and his client could have made a truly valid protest of innocence in an American court by suing for libel. They didn't.

The perjury case against Icardi was dismissed by the presiding judge on the sole ground that: "what congress may not do is to conduct an investigation for a purpose totally unrelated to its constitutional duties. It may not, for example, conduct investigations to punish crimes." The case was lost, also, because pitting the government attorney, a person named Woerheide, against Williams, must have seemed to many like matching a wet firecracker against an atom bomb.

Chapter 16

Death of an Idol

I sprawled on a chair in the warm spring sun at Doney's, the sidewalk caffè in front of the Hotel Excelsior. It was my custom to lunch there on bread, cheese and a bottle of wine. I had the same feeling of pity for my countrymen that a northerner, tanning himself on the sands at Miami Beach, has when he reads that New York and Chicago are having a blizzard. It was all so pleasant, now that military vehicles no longer climbed the sidewalks, army uniforms were a rarity, flowerbeds again bloomed on both sides of the street, and Italian women were once more careful of their appearance. It was nice, too, that the lovely ones chose this side of the street to parade on.

But of late this easy-going existence was being disturbed by visitors from America, nearly all of whom seemed to be connected in some way with the motion picture industry. They were attracted by Hollywood's discovery of gold on the banks of the Tiber. This was the new breed of pioneer, dressed in Homburgs and pin-stripe suits, pouring in on Skymasters and reconverted troop ships. (And they are still coming in today, in crew cuts and Hawaiian sport shirts, on jets and sleek ocean liners.) There were actors, writers, producers, agents, agents' agents, second generation Italians and just plain camp followers.

The first strike, and it was as important to Italy as was Sutter's to California, was made by a private in the American Army of Occupation who picked up a film called *Open City* for the proverbial song, stuffed it into a barracks bag and headed westward for separation from the service. Its success, both artistic and financial, was unexpected. Most surprised of all was Roberto Rossellini, who had directed and produced it. With it he fathered the neo-realistic movement that has brought Italy to a position at least equal to that of Hollywood in the production of films in both quality and quantity.

Actually the only message Rossellini was trying to get across in the film was that he wanted to eat regularly. So did the two men who wrote the script. They, too, were barely one step ahead of hunger. One sold wine on the black market and the other was an itinerant sidewalk cartoonist. They are better known today as Sergio Amidei, a truly great script writer, and Federico Fellini, a great director. Amidei had the basic idea for the film. The opening scene was to be based on an incident in his own life, when he had fled from the SS across the rooftops of Piazza di Spagna. The final scene, the death of Don Giuseppe Morosini, also was factual. The young priest, who had been betrayed to the Gestapo by a tortured partisan, was sentenced to be shot. On the morning of the execution he celebrated Mass and, before being blindfolded, kissed the crucifix, blessed the platoon of soldiers that was about to shoot him and openly forgave the man who had betrayed him. Overcome by his heroism, the firing squad aimed badly and the young priest fell wounded to the ground. He asked for and received the sacrament of extreme unction, after which the commanding officer shot him through the skull with a revolver.

There were a few minor inconveniences that Rossellini had to overcome in order to complete the film. He needed a story to fit between the opening and the closing scenes, a studio, because the

Roman ones had been destroyed in Allied bombings; cameras and studio equipment, all of which had been stolen by the retreating Germans; film, which was nonexistent; and a minor item known as money. Naturally, he was called a madman even by his own production staff. But Rossellini, an eternal optimist, had an answer for every problem.

A camera? "We'll pick up enough broken ones to make one workable one."

A studio? "We'll convert the bookie joint in Via Avignonese."

Lack of electric current? "We'll work out the script so that most of the action takes place in exteriors."

Film? "We'll buy it from the American troops. They're selling everything, including their underdrawers."

Money? "We'll worry about it as we go along. It's either that or we get jobs as waiters at GI mess halls if we want to eat regularly."

Neo-realism became a trend with a film produced by my friend Paolo Tamburella. I had met Tamburella my first day in Rome. As I walked toward the office of the Allied Military government in Piazza Venezia he came up to me and introduced himself in perfect English. To hear an Italian speak English as an American speaks it was most unusual, and I took the time to become acquainted with him. He had been born some thirty years before in Cleveland, Ohio, of Italian immigrant parents, had come to Rome to study law and, at the outbreak of the war, being liable under fascist law to the draft, had found himself a lieutenant in the Italian army.

He was doing a film about the shoeshine boys who were supporting their families by keeping a sparkle on military boots. It was called *Sciuscià*, which is the way the boys pronounced shoeshine, and was directed by Vittorio DeSica, still Italy's most talented director. No professional actors were used; he took the boys off the streets, families out of their homes. It was the ultimate in realism.

Tamburella came to me with some of his problems. One in-

volved American uniforms. He had asked a provost marshal for
permission to use these and had been turned down. More than
that, his actors had been threatened with arrest for impersonating
American soldiers if they were caught in manufactured ones.
This was catastrophic, since his thirty-six thousand dollar budget
for the entire film wouldn't stand the strain of costumes. I had the
stupid order lifted and Tamburella was able to borrow the uniforms from GI's who played bits in the film.

The first publicized forty-niner to arrive on these sunny shores
was Orson Welles. The importance of the visit called for two
press conferences, both of them held at the Hotel Excelsior. The
first was for the American press. I sat in the bar of the hotel with
a dozen of my colleagues, cooling my heels while the great one
failed to appear. At last, three-quarters of an hour late, the famous boy wonder came sweeping in for a dramatic entrance. As
he did, we stood up in unison and swept out.

His conference with the local press the next day, though better
attended, was not any more successful. Welles related his various
triumphs in the field of radio, stage and screen. Then, with a
bright smile, he asked, "And for what am I best known in Italy?"

"For Rita Hayworth," came the quick reply.

In the course of the years I have written several times about
Welles, rarely in complimentary fashion. I finally met him by
accident in the apartment of director Willie Wyler at the Grand
Hotel. At a hot point in the conversation Welles snapped at me,
"You're nothing but a professional bastard."

"I take that as a compliment," I said. "What I can't tolerate are
you amateur bastards."

In the early spring days of 1947 I noticed, among the many
lovely ladies who were habitués of the sidewalk caffès of Via
Veneto, an American girl of striking beauty. She was a tall blonde
with well-turned ankles who wore her clothes with distinction.
From a distance she appeared to be in her early twenties. I was
struck not only by her loveliness but by the sadness and distrust

that were mixed in her large, gray eyes. Let me call her Mary Roberts, and in the easy camaraderie of the street it was not difficult to make her acquaintance.

Close up I could see the lines about her mouth and eyes that were not evident from a distance, and I changed my estimate of her age to somewhere between twenty-eight and thirty-two. Little by little I learned her story, partly from what she told me and partly from others who either had known her or had heard about her in the States. She had graduated from a midwestern university and had tried the movies in Hollywood and modeling in New York, both with small success. She had tided herself over bad financial moments by going out on occasional paid dates, but the inner conflicts this produced always pulled her back to the struggle for an "honest" living. Sometimes she had seen salvation in a man or in a job and had dedicated herself to the one or the other. When they turned sour, she drifted back to hustling, becoming, finally, an out-and-out call girl.

Hers was a tragedy of modern civilization: a person who put in a full day's work at a steady job she despised. What was worse, she could see no way of escape. Then she heard about Italy, the new frontier of the film industry. She collected her meager funds and flew to Rome for a desperate last try.

I liked Mary. She was a person of good basic character whose misfortune it was to earn only twenty dollars for each slip from rectitude. I sent her to my good friends, Gregor Rabinovich and Willie Szekely, a pair of early-day leaders in movie-making, and both gave her jobs. But in the main it was tough going until she met a wealthy Argentinian named Rico Gonzales. He was the very picture of a dashing knight, about forty-five, handsome and ruggedly built. His family was reputed to be the richest in Argentina. Rico's sole interests in life, up to the moment he met Mary, were fast cars and beautiful women. It was love at first sight. Rico showered her with Fontana gowns, Bulgari jewels and an Alfa Romeo. Best of all, he gave her an engagement ring and a marriage date.

Mary's joy knew no bounds. For her, true love had come at the eleventh hour. After a six-week engagement, the wedding was set for a Saturday. On Friday afternoon, in his suite at the Hotel Excelsior, Rico ordered a gourmet luncheon for himself, ate it in front of a large mirror, finished the meal with a rare cognac. Then took a .38 caliber revolver and blew his brains out. In an hour the truth was known. Rico was not worth a quarter. He was a distant and very black-sheep relative of the famous Argentinian family that had long since turned its back on him. When he had learned that he was suffering from an inoperable cancer, he had come to Rome to exit in a final blaze of glory.

The police picked up Mary and held her until they were satisfied that she had not been involved in the swindle of the hotel and the local merchants; had been, instead, the most vulnerable victim. When they let her go, the creditors were waiting to strip her clean. She left town very quietly. I have not seen nor heard of her since.

My favorite caffè seat on Via Veneto was under a small plane tree. We dubbed this spot the Palm Room, and it became a favorite meeting place for visiting friends. One mild September night in 1957 I sat there with Betty and Mario Lanza and Lester and Anita Welch. Lester, the son-in-law of Gregor Rabinovich, a giant in the European film industry between the two world wars, was producing *The Seven Hills of Rome* with Lanza in the starring role. Mario was in rare form, speaking with bitter humor about his past. "I only made one mistake in my life," he said. "I became a singer instead of a fighter." He rose to his feet and took a deep breath. His chest expansion was enormous. "Go on, Mike, hit me in the gut with all you've got. I had the same trainer as Rocky Marciano. He told me that I could take Rocky on, and maybe even beat him, if I devoted myself to fighting."

I asked Lester, "How did you get him so slim?"

"It was easy," Lester said. "A doctor and two keepers."

"Aw, cut the crap. The keepers didn't mean a thing. It's the injections the doctor's giving me that does it. Twice every day."

"What kind of injections?"

Betty Lanza giggled. "Nobody will believe it."

Mario said, "I get the urine of pregnant women."

Whether this unusual treatment was actually responsible for the loss of weight or not, Mario swore by it. He had come from the States a few months before fat and broke but with a contract calling for a hundred and fifty thousand dollars for *The Seven Hills of Rome*, which now was almost completed. He had just about run through most of this money and was in need of another job fast.

In the course of the evening a British press agent stopped to say hello to me. He drew me aside to tell me that he was putting on a royal command performance at the Palladium in London next month. If Mario Lanza would appear he would receive top billing. Did I think that he would accept? I suggested he ask Mario himself, but the agent felt that was a sure way to get a turn-down. Wouldn't I, for friendship's sake, do it for him? I returned to the Palm Room.

"Mario, how would you like to sing for the Queen?" I asked.

"Not particularly," he said. "What's it all about?"

"A Sunday night show at the Palladium for Prince Philip's favorite charity. Top billing for you."

"Do you want me to do it?"

"What's that got to do with it?"

" 'Cause if you do, I'll do it."

"I couldn't care less. All I'm doing is passing on the invitation."

"Well then, what do you think?"

"I think it would be a good thing."

"All right. Then I'll do it."

"I don't care whether you say yes or no," I said, "but I do care if you say yes and then back out."

Mario got mad. "I never backed out on a show in my life," he shouted. There was no arguing with him on this point, because in his own mind he was convinced that it was true.

Lanza sang at the Palladium and brought down the house. He

made a single TV appearance that broke all British records. An agent quickly booked him into a series of Albert Hall concerts and the tickets were sold out immediately. Scalpers were asking and getting thirty-five pounds. Experts in spotting a quick dollar, the agents extended the tour to seventeen shows, booking him into a cow palace in Belfast at seven thousand dollars a performance, into Scotland, France, Holland, Belgium and Germany.

Lanza was on his eleventh show in Brighton when a tooth began to ache. A local dentist gave him penicillin shots and he came down with phlebitis in the legs, a painful and dangerous disease of the veins. He suspended the tour and returned to Rome for treatment.

Here he found a houseful of trouble. His wife, Betty, was a little more unbalanced than usual and was running through his liquid assets as fast as he could collect them. Her trouble had begun soon after their marriage when she developed ovarian cysts that rendered her menstrual periods sheer torture. At first she had resorted to drugs to kill the pain; then drugs, always in increasing amounts, to ease the fear of the cycle. By the time she came to Rome she was already a dope addict.

For a while Mario was able to persuade her to enter a hospital each month, but then she balked, preferring to remain at home with her own special medication. Trying to outwit him in procuring the stuff became a daily game for her. Much of the time Mario was able to locate the narcotics (he showed me a chest loaded with it), but she always seemed to have new supplies.

Her condition was such that she would black out frequently. So that she wouldn't kill herself when she fell, the marble floors of Field Marshal Badoglio's apartment, which the Lanzas rented, were covered with thick carpets, and furniture edges were padded with strips of foam rubber.

"It's for the kids," Mario would explain to visitors. "I don't want them hurting themselves when they ride their bicycles around the house."

One day Betty locked herself in the bathroom, took an accidental overdose of pills and lay in the tub. She grew so weak she didn't have the strength to climb out, and it finally occurred to her that she could easily drown. I happened to be walking on the terrace with Mario, who still limped badly, when she cried weakly for help. We tried to guide her with advice, offered through the drawn *persiane,* but to no avail. Kicking in the bottom of the window pane, I was able to force the blind and climb into the bathroom. Grabbing her under the armpits, I pulled her out of the tub. This was the kind of domestic drama Mario had to live with daily.

Then there was the problem of the four children, all of whom had to have their tonsils and adenoids removed. And added to the worries about his wife, his children and his own painful condition, he had run out of money once more. His way of facing up to problems was to gorge on food and drink. Within a short time he resembled a barrel, and injections of urine from pregnant women no longer helped. Nor were Lester Welch's bodyguards there to keep him from burying his face in heaping platters of spaghetti washed down with cases of Lambrusco, the sparkling red Emilian wine he loved. He ate like a glutton when his mind was disturbed, yet lived in mortal fear of gaining weight. The fear and the gluttony fed on each other, and Mario, trapped in the middle, blew up like a captive balloon. In his own mind his entire career depended on his remaining slim, and he was conscious of it every waking minute of his life.

Of the torrent of words that flowed over him in the press, what he remembered most bitterly was one line written about him when he walked out of the cast of Warner Brothers' *The Student Prince.* Columnist Hy Gardner had called him the "Student Blintz." This cut him more than any adverse criticism of his voice or his acting. Now each time he saw himself in the mirror, he became so depressed that he downed a few bottles of wine, followed by a half dozen bottles of beer and a half bottle of scotch. When he was good and plastered, Betty would administer a shot of sodium pentathol and put him to bed. In the morning, when he was sober, he would give her one.

I was on my way to keep a golf date one Saturday morning at the Acqua Santa Club when I was called to the phone. Mario, without preliminaries, announced that he was in trouble and had to see me right away. Since these calls were rather frequent, I told him that I would see him as soon as I had finished my golf game.

"Please come right away, Mike," he urged. "It's a matter of life and death. You're the only friend I have that I can turn to."

I raced to Villa Badoglio, determined not to let Mario's troubles ruin the day for me. I found him seated dejectedly in an easy chair, his phlebitic leg propped on a marble coffee table, surrounded by half a dozen doctors, lawyers and advisers. On the table was a sheaf of telegrams.

"What's the matter?"

"All I said was that I was too sick to sing," he told me bitterly. "You'd think I crucified Jesus Christ."

A lawyer explained that the resumption of Mario's tour had been announced and that in three days he was due in London for an Albert Hall recital. Yesterday Mario had announced that he would not appear and the heavens were falling in. The impresario screamed that Mario would never be able to get another singing engagement in the British Empire. Metro-Goldwyn-Mayer called from the coast to say they would never use his services again. His business manager threatened to drop him.

"It's all the fault of my booking agent," Mario said. "He did it on his own. Just go ahead and ask him and you'll see. He doesn't have a single thing signed by me telling him to start the tour again. Betty's in the hospital. The kids are being operated on tomorrow. And look at me." He pointed to his vast waistline.

"How can they expect me to go on? Please, Mike, it's the only favor I'll ever ask of you again. Get me out of this jam. I swear I'll never get into trouble again."

The solution suggested itself. "If you tell the public you're sick, they'll never believe you. So at 3 A.M. you go into a coma.

The doctor says you're dying. As you're carried out of the house on a stretcher, a photographer will just happen to grab the shot. That picture will be your explanation." (It happened that my son was working for a news agency, so naturally it was going to be his scoop.) "Until then stay under cover and allow only the doctor to speak to the press."

An ambulance was ordered. A night nurse was engaged for ten o'clock. I looked at my watch. If I hurried I would still make my golf game. As I made my way toward the door, an afterthought made me ask, "You mean to tell me your agent did this without your consent?"

"He certainly did."

"He didn't talk with you on the phone?"

"Sure, he talked to me a few times."

"And he never once mentioned the resumption of the tour?"

Mario hesitated. "Well, he said he wanted to start it up again."

"And you said it was all right."

"Yes, but I never signed anything."

"How's your voice?"

Mario was surprised by the question. "It's fine. Why?"

"Because if you're half a man you'll stop trying to weasel out and you'll sing."

He pointed to his leg and said he would have to use crutches. I said sharply that I didn't care if he went out on the stage and fell on his face; in fact, if he did, perhaps he could win back some sympathy.

Mario didn't try to argue. Now he had a new worry. He had just announced that he was too sick to give the concert. How could he now announce that he would, without appearing to be a liar or a fool?

I said I would handle it. I told the doctors to draw up a single-page statement on phlebitis, dwelling on its dangerous nature, then another page on their patient's actual condition, adding that it was the unanimous opinion of the three doctors that the strain of the concert would endanger his life. I instructed the lawyer to draw up a statement to the effect that in spite of the doctor's prohibition, Lanza insisted on singing for his British audience. Mario was to check into the hospital at once and stay there until after the tour manager had called in the press and issued the releases.

Mario accompanied me to the door. "I am dedicating these concerts to you," he said gratefully.

"I'd be happier if you dedicated an Alfa Romeo to me," I said, but he didn't take the hint.

I arrived at my club too late for the golf game, but the British Sunday press gave the Lanza story top billing. "Lanza Sings Despite Doctor's Orders," said the Sunday *Mirror* in its lead headline.

His concerts at Dundee, Dublin and Albert Hall were loudly acclaimed. The audience went wild as he limped onto the stage. In Paris, drunk, he stumbled onto the stage of the Olympia Theater, sang only two numbers, was hissed and quit. He went on to score tremendous successes at Ostend, Hanover and Rotterdam. For his show at the Festival Hall in Hamburg he checked into the royal suite of the Hotel Vier Jarheszeiten. Having a three-day recess before his appearance, he became bored and amused himself at The Reeperbahn, the city's Barbary Coast. He got drunk, picked up a prostitute who was also drunk and took her to the hotel. In the early hours of the morning they got into a fight and Mario slapped her. The blow knocked her cold and she lay on the floor, blood running down the side of her face from where her earring had cut into the flesh. He tossed a bucket of water on her, put a fifty dollar bill in her purse and dragged her into the corridor.

When she came to, the girl screamed bloody murder and headed for the local police station. Later in the day the police came, questioned him about the complaint and, satisfied with the story he told them, left. At noon his tour manager found him completely drunk. In the early evening the girl's pimp came to collect damages and was thrown out. The following morning, the day of the concert, Lanza wakened with a sore throat and sent for the hotel doctor. The diagnosis was simple. He had a cold.

At noon the impresario was informed of this fact. He stormed into the hotel suite with fire in his eye. Every seat in the theater had been sold out at advanced prices and there is nothing an impresario hates more than to turn back money he already feels in his pocket. What was worse, he had been unable to hedge his investment, because no insurance company would write a policy on the singer.

Lanza, his fat, pasty face covered with black stubble, sprawled on a couch in his dirty, rumpled bathrobe and blinked bloodshot eyes at the angry tirade.

"I will not accept your withdrawal from the concert," the impresario shouted. "You look fine to me."

"It's only a cold—" Mario began apologetically, but the impresario cut him off. "My doctor will fix you up. I've never lost an artist after he's treated him." He marched out.

The doctor was a cheerful optimist who recounted stories of famous singers he had treated for the same complaint. All were able to sing after his ministrations. As he spoke he prepared a hypodermic needle.

"What's that?" Mario asked.

"Nothing to be alarmed about. It's only penicillin."

"Only penicillin! That's what gave me my phlebitis."

"Ridiculous. There's no connection between the two."

The impresario's anger once again mounted. "I was warned about you. Even the insurance companies wouldn't give me a policy on the concert. But in spite of this, I had faith in you. I went along with you, but I'm telling you now, if you persist in this uncooperative attitude, you'll never sing in another house."

Mario bowed before the inevitable. He uncovered his ample rump and the doctor stabbed him with the needle. Then he was wrapped warmly and put to bed. The blinds were drawn, and he was told to sleep until he was called. By evening he would

be fine, the cheerful doctor said. When Lanza was awakened at
6 P.M. and told to get ready, the cold had already traveled from
his throat to his chest, and his voice sounded like an operatic
Andy Devine.

The good doctor was perplexed. The impresario was suspicious. An hour went by before the latter bowed before the inevitable. The concert would have to be called off. But by this
time the opera house was crowded with an elegant audience
dressed in evening gowns and white ties, for this was a gala event.

"Someone will have to make the announcement," the impresario mused.

"You," Mario said.

"You stay out of it," was the angry retort. "You've caused me
enough trouble."

Since Mario's agent had already disappeared, his Greek-Ameri-
can accompanist was selected for the deed. The restive audience
had already waited an hour when he walked out onto the stage.
The announcement filled them with fury. Many ran to the stage
intent on punishing the unhappy accompanist, who was saved by
the police. Others tore up seats as a sign of their discontent.
Hundreds of them marched on the singer's hotel chanting,
"Lanza, go home." The management of the hotel became uneasy
and requested that Lanza take his patronage elsewhere immediately.

Time Magazine's coverage of the event was approximate and
brief. It noted that Lanza, slipping in popularity because of a
fading voice, had used illness as an excuse to cancel an unprofita-
ble tour.

He returned to Rome to find his wife, Betty, acting more
peculiarly than ever. In accord with his mother-in-law, he had
her taken to the hospital by force. He called in three psychiatrists
to have her declared incompetent, so that the ovarian cysts could
be removed against her will. In the hospital she tried to bribe her
nurses to carry a message to a news agency that Mario was trying
to kill her.

Worry had its usual effect on Lanza, and again he gained so much weight he was ashamed to leave the house. One day I brought William Wyler, the director, for a visit. As we entered the music room Mario rose, walked behind his chair so that the winged back hid his great girth and extended his hand. He had rehearsed the greeting so that he could do it naturally.

He was running out of money again, and only a small-time German film producer was willing to take a chance on him, and even that depended on whether an insurance company would write a policy on Lanza's health. The title of the movie was *For the First Time,* and Mario raved about it.

"It's different from anything I've ever done before," he said with enthusiasm. "I play an opera singer. In the first scene I come late to the theater. It's raining and the crowd is stalled in the rain, trying to get in. These are poor people, see, that have to pay out money to get into the gallery. The white tie and tails extras are already in the orchestra. So what do I do? I get up on my taxi and sing in the street in the rain. It makes the impresario mad because I'm singing for free and get a sore throat, besides. But that's the real Mario Lanza. Get it?

"Now I go to Capri to recover and I'm mobbed by my fans, so I sing to them in the square. The dames have orgasms all over the place but I fight them off. All except one, a cute blonde who couldn't care less, so I sing my heart out to her and she still doesn't care, so naturally I fall in love with her. But do you know why my singing doesn't move her? Because she's deaf. So I pay for an operation and in the final clinch I sing only for her because now she can hear and she's in love with the guy who is singing. There won't be a dry eye in the house. What do you think?"

I said it sounded like the same boy meets girl story that had been done several thousand times, generally with fresher ideas. He was annoyed.

"You don't get it. The switch. She's deaf!"

I said that I got it, but that the audience might not. When the film was released, they didn't.

Since it was impossible for him to play this romantic lead behind the backs of wing chairs, he checked into the Walchensee Sanatorium on the outskirts of Munich. By now he was convinced that the injections of urine of pregnant women had no connection with the loss of weight. At the sanatorium they kept him suspended in twilight sleep for twenty days and he lost twenty-five pounds. The insurance doctors examined him, and a policy was written at extraordinarily high premiums. The doctors warned him that such treatment could be fatal and that it was a calculated risk to have had him undergo it.

His next film, *Granada,* was to have been directed by Norman Taurog. When the script was ready in October 1958, Lanza had again put on fifty pounds, and again he had to lose it in order to pass the inspection of the insurance doctors. I was in Naples, in the process of organizing a charity show for NATO, and Lanza was to have been one of my entertainers. But the night before the show he checked into the *Clinica Valle Giulia* to start the same treatment he had undergone in the Munich sanatorium. I had enough talent on hand so his absence was not a calamity, but even so I was angry, because he had promised faithfully to appear.

Betty Lanza called, as did Mario's doctor and his producer, who was in Munich. All assured me that the insurance doctors had fixed the day on which they would examine the singer, and that there hadn't been a moment to lose in getting him into shape. It was, Betty said, a crash program. Just before he entered the hospital, Mario had autographed fifty of his LP albums for me to distribute to the crowd and had begged me to let Betty substitute for him.

She came and conquered. She was the belle of the ball that was held after the show in the Royal Palace. Mario died the day after she returned to Rome.

I called at the Lanza home the next day with my friend Frank

Folsom, the Radio Corporation of America executive, whom the singer had held in great esteem. The blinds in the salon were tightly drawn, and the gloom was pierced by the flickering candles at the head of the open coffin. I stood transfixed at the sight of the corpse. Lanza's face was puffed and unshaven and had bruises on it. Cotton stuck out of his nostrils and ears, and a strip of adhesive tape was plastered across his mouth. His belly was so bloated that it stuck high above the coffin, making it impossible to close the lid. This was the indestructible, strong-as-an-ox ex-longshoreman from the Philadelphia docks. Ten years of success had reduced him to this. Tears came to Folsom's eyes, and he fell to his knees and prayed silently.

The housekeeper informed me that Betty wanted to see me. She had locked herself in her room and for thirty-six hours had refused to see anyone. The doctor had been administering strong doses of tranquilizers to keep her hysteria under control. She was in bed, her face puffed and red, her eyes so vague as to be almost unseeing. As I leaned over to comfort her, she threw her arms about me with the desperation of a drowning woman.

"They hated Mario," she sobbed, "and they hounded him to death. They weren't happy with anything else. They wanted his blood." Her voice grew quieter, and a hard gleam came into her eyes. "But I'm not going to give them the satisfaction of seeing him like this. I'm going to bury him in Italy. We both love Italy. I want Mario buried in Naples next to Caruso's grave. He learned how to sing by listening to Caruso's records and imitating him. Please—please—do this for me. Get the mayor of Naples to give us a plot next to Caruso's and build us a monument just like his—not bigger, but not smaller."

It was pitiful to see and hear her. I knew that any hope of eventual recovery was now a thing of the past. Mario's death had destroyed her.

The funeral was held on the morning of October 10th, 1959, at the Church of the Sacred Heart of Mary in Piazza Euclide. Robert Alda, Rossano Brazzi, Frank Folsom and I were the honorary pallbearers. As we left for the church, Betty, incongruous in a white fur coat amidst a sea of black, begged me to return to the house after the services. It was a matter of such urgency that I had to promise to come back, despite the fact that she was now in the midst of parents and relatives.

Four horses in rich trappings with long black plumes on their heads pulled the ornate, glass-sided hearse to the church. As we passed through Piazza Ungheria, pedestrians crossed themselves and the more devout dropped to a knee. The square in front of the church was filled with a crowd of curious, eager to see the widow and the four orphaned children. I could see no mourners. The widow, the relatives and the pallbearers had to fight their way through the unruly crowd in the church. The burial service was read by Father Paul Maloney of the Paulist Fathers. He was an old friend of the Lanzas, having baptized the children when he was the parish priest at Saint Paul the Apostle in Westwood, Los Angeles.

Photographers ducked under the coffin to get better angle shots of the family. The crowd pressed forward and pushed at the people in front of them in order to get a better view. A dwarf broke from the crowd and ran between the pulpit and the coffin for a vantage spot on the side. My wife, dressed in respectful black, cried copiously. Most of her tears were for the orphaned children sitting in bewilderment between their mother and grandmother, though a small part may have been caused by the sharp jabs she was suffering from the women at her back, who swarmed over her as they fought to get a better view. At the conclusion of the services Folsom took her by one arm and I by the other as we pushed our way to the jammed center aisle. From the fringe of the crowd came the question, "Who is it?" and from the aisle, as the mass melted before us, came the answer: "It's the widow."

The coffin had a rougher passage. As we drove toward the Lanza home, my wife said, "I don't want to go there."

"I don't want to either, but I gave Betty my word."

Without ringing the bell I pushed open the front door and we walked toward the study. Betty and her relatives were in the midst of an argument. I heard her scream, ". . . you dirty son-of-a-bitch, I told you that. . . ." I took my wife's arm as I about-faced, and we quickly walked back out the door, closing it behind us.

A few days later the widow flew to the United States, taking the body of her husband with her. After another burial service in Philadelphia, she went on to California. She got into a court fight there with her mother, who tried to take the children on the grounds that her daughter was insane. A few months later, while living in a house rented from Mr. and Mrs. Fred Clark (Benay Venuta) she went to bed with a paraplegic. Each swallowed a large dose of sleeping pills. When they were found, Betty was already dead. The paraplegic was carried into another room, medicated and sent quietly on his way.

Chapter 17

Rome Today: A City on Wheels

TRAFFIC tells the story of change in Rome. At the end of the war people walked. Traffic consisted mainly of military vehicles, with a few dilapidated trucks and buses powered by evil-smelling methane gas. In the first months the Italian who owned a bicycle was fortunate, but within two years the streets became crowded with them. Bicycles became the subject of topical humor. A classic was the story of the peasant learning his communist catechism.

"Antonio, you have just inherited two castles," the party leader says. "What would you do with them?"

"I would give one to the party and share the other with my less fortunate comrades," Antonio responds.

"You have just inherited two Cadillacs. What would you do with them?"

"I would donate one to the party and share the other with my less fortunate comrades," the dutiful Antonio replies.

"You have just inherited two bicycles. What would you do with them?"

"I would keep them."

"What!" cries the amazed party leader. "Why would you not give one to the party and share the other with your less fortunate comrades?"

"Because I *have* two bicycles," Antonio answers.

Being an inventive people, the Italians built bicycles in every shape and dimension, including enormous bicycle trucks. The more affluent Romans had motors attached to theirs. Even my son whipped through the streets of Rome on his *motorino*. The streets, as well as the laws, were geared to this kind of traffic. Many streets in the center of the city were still without sidewalks. As far as the antiquated laws were concerned, anything on wheels still had to pull over to the right curb to make a left turn. If a vehicle was involved in a fatal accident, the driver was carted off to jail to await a trial that might take as long as two years to come up. Since there is no bail in Italy, he would stay in jail until the conclusion of the trial and then, if found innocent, would receive a profuse apology with his freedom. The only way to protect himself from this indefinite term behind bars was to flee from the scene of the accident. If the police didn't find him within forty-eight hours, he could then report to the local *commissariato*. He would still face the same manslaughter charge, but he would remain at liberty until the trial. Only recently has this curious (at least to the American mind) article in the criminal law been changed.

A short time ago a friend of mine attached to our embassy was involved in a brush with the curious Roman code. He had just climbed into his parked car when a wild-riding descendant of a chariot-racer rammed into him, bounced off and sped away into the night. My friend, after a first startled outburst of anger, took out after the hit-and-run driver, caught him near a police station and hauled the miscreant before the minions of the law. To his utter amazement the policeman on duty informed him that the one who had committed a criminal act was not the hit-and-run driver, who had merely committed a civil offense, but he, the diplomat, who had forcibly hauled the hit-and-runner into the police station. This was abduction, a most serious offense, and it was fortunate that he was covered by diplomatic immunity or the policeman would be forced to lock him up forthwith.

The enormous damage wrought by the war was, in itself, enough to make times rough. The means of commerce and industry had either been destroyed or dislocated. Those who had managed to maintain their wealth had little confidence in the new country. Capital fled to Switzerland, South America, and the United States. But suddenly in 1950 there was a reawakening of confidence. This was due in a large measure to American faith and dollars, but to an even greater extent it was due to the money policy of the ruling Christian Democrat Party. If for no other reason, the Italian people must be grateful to them because they made the lira one of the most solid currencies in Europe and prepared the ground for an economic boom that is unmatched in Italy's long history. They conducted massive operations on the black-market money exchange. When dollars were too expensive, driving down the value of lire, they dumped dollars into the bourse. When dollars cheapened they dumped lire. There was a reawakening of confidence on the part of Italian financiers, and slowly the money that had fled abroad began trickling back.

The effect of all this could be seen on the streets. New buses and trucks, running on gasoline, made their appearance. Bicycle owners moved up to Vespas and Lambrettas, the two-wheeled motor scooters which, at two hundred and fifty dollars, were suddenly within reach of the masses. I remember the opening night at the Royal Opera in Rome, every bit as chic as the opening at the Metropolitan in New York, with Vespas driving up to the entrance and the ladies, in long evening gowns and covered with pearls and diamonds, stepping down from their side-saddle perches on the back fenders.

There was literally a hunger for everything on wheels, and the streets in the ten years after 1947 grew violent with the cacaphony of horn-blowing vehicles of every size, shape and description, from hand carts to enormous double-trailer trucks. Through it

all breezed my son on a Gilera, a snappy red motorcycle to which
he had graduated on his fourteenth birthday.

Almost overnight there was another shift in the kind of traffic
that clogged the streets. Bicycles, scooters and motorcycles
seemed to disappear, and in their place appeared autos of every
size, shape and description, a certain sign of economic boom and
the installment plan. Women, heretofore almost totally absent in
the motorized field, blossomed out as drivers, and today there are
almost as many of them behind wheels as there are men. Rome
has finally achieved the ultimate in American culture—the traffic
jam.

Italians are the best mannered people in Europe, at least in
outward form. At first I was ill at ease in its flowery manifesta-
tion, what with its bowing, curtseying (for girls up to fourteen),
hand-kissing, hat-raising and elaborate titles for each individual.
For example, anyone with a college degree is automatically
addressed as "Doctor." A lawyer is called *avvocato* so-and-so,
an engineer is *ingegneri* so-and-so, a bookkeeper, *ragioniere*.
There are counts, barons, marqueses, dukes and princes. There
are *cavalieri, commendatori, grand ufficiali* and *cavalieri di lavoro*,
not to mention *onorevoli* and *eccelenze*. And it would be considered extremely bad form not to address them by their titles.
I am called *Dottore* and am so accustomed to it that I am surprised only when I am addressed as Mister. As I became used to
the courtly formality, I began to regard it more favorably.

I felt that my children were not sufficiently exposed to this part
of Italian culture at the Overseas School of Rome, now prosper-
ing, thanks to our governmental financial legerdemain. For this
and other reasons, we withdrew them. The girl, protesting, was
placed in Chateaubriand, a school subsidized by the French
government. The basic language was French, both because it was
enforced by the faculty and because it was the only language the
students had in common. They came from all over the world, and
I'm sure they quickly decided it was easier to gossip in French

than in Chinese, Russian or Slavic. Most of them had not yet been in Rome long enough to speak Italian.

"But daddy, my French is awful," my daughter protested. "And I'll have to take two foreign languages besides. Don't you think that's too much for the eighth grade?"

"I'll make it easy for you," I said. "You can take English as one foreign language."

She finished the year with more ease than she had thought possible and then enrolled in Marymount. From this school she carried away a diploma, grace, poise and good manners.

Mike Jr.'s difficulty was arithmetic. His variations on 2 plus 2 were most interesting and original, but rarely four. Notre Dame International, run by the Brothers of the Holy Cross, gave him a diploma, a familiarity with numbers, poise and the manners of a gentleman.

Radio is a fumbling thing, as well it might be, since it is controlled by the government. It is supported by a listeners' tax. Despite its inferior quality, I still tune it in for the same reason a betting man goes to a crooked crap game—it's the only one in town. Sometimes my patience in listening through insipid broadcasts is rewarded.

It was my invariable custom, after lunching at home, to stretch out on my bed for siesta, switching on the radio before dozing off. On one particular occasion, I tuned in just in time to catch the announcer saying, with a note of pride in his voice, "And now I take pleasure in introducing the king of the American press." This captured my immediate attention. I had not known that the American press was a monarchy, but if the person about to be introduced was its king, then it was only logical that I was his subject. I learned that the king's name was Guido Orlando, that he had come from a town in Calabria near the one in which Rudolf Valentino was born, and that it was only my ignorance that kept me from identifying Orlando and the great deeds he had performed.

"And tell me, Signor Orlando, what did you consider your most difficult task?" the moderator asked.

"That is very simple," Signor Orlando replied modestly. "That was when I made Aimee Semple MacPherson the goddess of religion in America, a veritable queen of faith who was able to erect skyscraper temples to Jesus in her native California."

"And what, Signor Orlando, did you regard as the job you did that had most meaning?"

"That is very easy. It was when I made Franklin Delano Roosevelt president of the United States. Not just once, but I took him by the hand and led him through four victories. This was something never before achieved by any president of the country, nor, I can say in due modesty, will it ever happen again."

"And what was your most heart-warming triumph, Signor Orlando?"

"Oh, that was easy, also," the ever-modest Signor Orlando replied. "That was when I made my *paesano*, Rudolf Valentino, the greatest star in Hollywood. I took him from an eight-dollar-a-month job as dish-washer and raised him to a thirty-five-thousand-a-week movie star—and remember, that was when thirty-five thousand dollars a week was a lot of money."

Though television came late, it has become the most popular means of entertainment. The National station offers seven hours of programing, three of them devoted to education. And here the word "education" is taken literally. They break out Duffy's reader and an elementary arithmetic book. Of the three educational hours, two and a half consist of courses of instruction for children up to the third grade, and the other half-hour is devoted to teaching illiterates how to read and write. The most frequent spot show is a reminder to listeners to pay their radio-TV tax. Paying it automatically includes the listener's name in the weekly lottery, where he can win anything from a Fiat 500 to an Alfa Romeo, which is not bad for only a twenty-dollar fee. Of course, if he doesn't pay on the date due he is liable to a heavy fine.

"Now which would you rather have," the announcer says with charm, "a new automobile or trouble with your government?"

Competing in interest with this is a show called "Intervallo." This word flashes on between programs and remains there, with a musical background, for anywhere from one to twenty-five minutes. It means "intermission," and it is in heavy use because Italian TV time is fluid, and producers charmingly ignore schedules.

Filmed drama is a great favorite with the majority of the viewers. I recall a four-hour dramatization of "The Petrified Forest." It didn't bother me too much that the lunch counter–filling station in the American Southwest looked like a Roman caffè, nor that the cowboys were dressed like Tuscan peasants, but I must confess that I was somewhat startled by the background music that ran through the entire play. It was that old Western folk tune "My Yiddishe Mama."

As long as I have lived in Italy, I never cease to be amazed at its administration of justice. With an average American heritage and better than average knowledge of law, I have come to expect that the legal code, both criminal and civil, have an exact and inflexible meaning. When I tell an Italian friend that there is a strong sense of justice here but a very weak sense of law, he smiles condescendingly and says that I should remember that it was Rome that gave modern law to the world some two thousand years ago.

One of the laws on the books in those ancient times, and even an absolute monarch could not violate it with impunity, was that a virgin could not be sentenced to death. Caligula showed how simple it was to get around even this most difficult provision when "justice" was at stake. He wanted to wipe out a family that he considered his enemy. The hitch was that there was a ten-year-old daughter. His solution was quite simple: he had the executioner rape the child so that she could be beheaded legally. Roman law has had many refinements since then, but some of its provisions still are, at least to the American mind, almost as weird.

Under Italian law if you have two witnesses to anything you are in an impregnable position. They can swear to the greatest absurdities and it doesn't matter; it is enough that you can get two people to say it. I have spent a good deal of time in Italian courts, and I know whereof I speak. One case involved my office in the Stampa Estera. It had been occupied by the Japanese Domei News Agency, and it was understandable that they should vacate the office and beat a hasty retreat as the Allies entered Rome. They had paid a rental of eight hundred lire a month, and the figure has a bearing on the story. The person who held the lease, and who in turn sub-let the office to them and to me, paid five hundred lire a month to the owner, and this contract had been duly registered with the appropriate government office. I contracted to pay ten thousand lire a month, but I had the contract state that, since the rent was so high, it was not to be raised during my tenancy. This was somewhat redundant, because the rent law had already frozen both my rental from the lessee and his from the owner. In the years that followed the government passed mandatory rent increases that brought my rental to eighteen thousand lire and the lessee's to nine hundred lire a month. Now this person, impelled by a European's normal love of lucre, started putting the pressure on me for a raise. I turned it all over to my lawyer and from then on had no further direct contact with him. My *avvocato* advised me that I was legally and morally entitled to the office under the terms clearly set forth in the contract and to have no further worries about it.

I, therefore, promptly put the matter out of my mind. Six months later it was rudely brought to my attention when a court decree was served on me, ordering me to pay six months back rent, with interest, and ordering me evicted for non-payment. Since I had already paid this rental, having both canceled checks and signed receipts to prove it, I ran screaming to my *avvocato*.

"How can they do such a thing?" I yelled.

"Calm yourself," he soothed, after having read the decrees. "The owner swore in court that you didn't pay."

"But that's perjury!"

"Not in Italy. The principal in a trial is expected to lie, so the law doesn't punish him. Only a witness can commit perjury. We'll appeal the verdict and present our canceled checks and receipts. We can't lose."

"But how can they try a case against me without notifying me?"

"It can be done by handing it to one of your maids, or to the gate-keeper of your villa. Maybe they thought it was an unimportant paper and threw it in the basket."

The case went up on appeal. My lawyer presented the receipts and canceled checks, and the verdict was reversed. The person from whom I rented immediately filed another suit. This time I was charged with being an American citizen, and it was claimed that, as such, I had no right to benefit from the Italian provisions of the rental laws. My reply was that Italian citizens in America benefited from the provisions of the laws there, that their rights under the Constitution were equal to those of American citizens, and that the Treaty of Friendship and Commerce between the United States and Italy guaranteed that there should be reciprocal treatment. I won the case in the lower court, won it in the Court of Appeals and won it in the Supreme Court.

During this suit, Sey Korman, my office partner, was called back to the States to take over the Chicago Tribune West Coast office. I let the United Press move into his room, whereupon my landlord filed another action, this time charging me with having rented an office in the press building to a commercial concern. I was well on the way to proving that the U.P. was an honored news-gathering organization when I was hit with the two-witness gimmick. It seems that there is a clause in the rent law providing that if the owner had previously received a rental as high as or higher than the sum presently blocked, then he is entitled by law to far higher automatic increases. Eleven years of litigation had passed before they came up with this one. His claim was that he had received ten thousand lire a month for the office in 1943. The actual value of this sum in 1943 was sixteen hundred dollars, a figure that would have easily bought the entire office, including its furniture. In 1943 half the offices in Rome were vacant, what with business and commerce being practically at a standstill. In the Foreign Press Building itself there were vacancies, and the same space could have been had for closer to one hundred dollars a month. The man who had supposedly rented the office at such a munificent figure was given as Signor Allessandro. An investigation showed that my tormentor did not have a copy of this fabulous lease, nor had he ever filed it with the appropriate government office. None of the personnel still working in the press building had ever seen, heard, or known anything about this Allessandro. The electric company had no record of his name. The *Guida Monaci,* which has a listing for every businessman in Rome, had no listing for the mysterious Allessandro. The Rome telephone directory for 1942, 1943 and 1944 bore no listing for him, nor did the records in the telephone company have him listed as having been a subscriber.

I told my lawyer that this case was even sillier than the others. "I would not be so hasty in my judgment," he told me. "This time I am really worried. You see, they have two witnesses. One claims that in July 1943, as a favor to his cousin who was ill, he collected the rent. And he remembered that he was given ten thousand lire. The second is a friend who claims he collected the rent in August of that year and that he, too, remembers that it was ten thousand."

"But that's ridiculous. Who would ever believe a story like that?"

"We have to find two witnesses who will swear that Allessandro never existed. That could cancel their two witnesses."

Since it is impossible to find anyone who can swear that a phantom does not exist, I found myself on the losing end of the case. Not only was I sentenced to pay back rent for fourteen years, back rent being based on new calculations that our contract never foresaw, but I was sentenced to pay the court costs for all the actions I had won up to this point. Naturally I pursued the matter through the Court of Appeals, which held against me, and up to the Supreme Court, which ruled that the lower court had decided it on the basis of facts and that they could enter only if I had a point of law to argue.

Whatever it was that made the judge decide the way he did, it couldn't have been collusion. In American courts, yes; there have been judges who have been caught red-handed. But in Italy even to hint at such a thing is *oltraggio,* and it is enough to send you to jail. Here police do not take bribes or do anything else that is not consistent with the highest code of honor. To suggest otherwise is *oltraggio,* and insures the slanderer a jail sentence by *direttissima.* An Italian army may retreat, but be sure that they retreat with honor, for otherwise it is *oltraggio alle Forze Armate,* another crime that sends you to jail without bail to await a trial *direttissima.* You can call an ordinary citizen an imbecile and risk nothing more than a punch in the nose. But if you call the man who paints the white stripes at road crossings an imbecile, you go to jail for *oltraggio,* because he, too, is considered a public official under the law. These laws were passed under Mussolini, and the present government, nineteen years after the end of the war, has not gotten around to modifying them.

The two-witness routine could also work in my favor, and in one case it did. When *L'Unitá,* the daily communist mouthpiece, attacked me as an "American spy" and "vicious anti-communist," I sued for libel. I won the action in criminal court (libel in Italy is a criminal matter), and with it won the right to ask for damages civilly. Two editors in America gave testimony in letters rogatory that, because I had been accused of being an anti-communist, my objectivity as a political reporter had been questioned and therefore I had suffered several million lire worth of damages. Now if anyone went into an American court with a claim that he had been damaged because he had been called an anti-communist, he would be received with mirth. Here, armed with the power of two witnesses, I swept to victory and a 7,000,000 lire verdict.

My articles were widely reprinted in Italy, and they brought me a measure of local notice. They also brought me face-to-face with Italian libel laws, which would make every member of a freedom-of-the-press committee in America squirm with professional discomfort.

Suppose I write (as I had written) that a Milanese pharmaceutical house was manufacturing heroin and that one *ton*, more than double the total legal needs of the entire country, had been sold to a number of individuals, all of whom presented forged health department certificates, all of whom had paid in cash, and none of whom the drug firm could identify. Suppose, too, that the owner of this pharmaceutical firm had previously been involved in narcotics violations but had not had to answer these charges because of an amnesty. (Every five years, with the election of a new president of the republic, an amnesty law is passed that wipes out all misdemeanors and a variety of felonies. Libel is always included in this open-handed forgiveness.) Suppose, too, that Lucky Luciano, in the company of a notorious American drug smuggler, had paid a three-day visit to this pharmaceutical factory, and that all three had been arrested during the course of this visit. In America it would not be regarded as libelous for me to speculate that the encounter had nothing to do with the flotation of a bond issue. This would be regarded as fair comment.

This is exactly what I did, and I immediately found myself charged with the crime of libel and brought before the criminal courts like a common felon.

Since all libel is criminal, the complainant need only file a *querela*, or information, and the prosecutor does the rest. Suppose the writer is acquitted. The prosecutor can, and almost always does, appeal the case, and it is tried again. If the writer wins this one, too, the prosecutor has another chance to appeal. The writer-defendant must win this, too, if he wants to go free. Should this happy state be reached, after having suffered triple jeopardy, the innocent writer has no recourse against the complainant or the state for false arrest.

In my own case, I got off lightly—an amnesty law was passed and the case was wiped out.

Some of the niceties in libel law I learned in a brush I had with Jaime Ortiz-Patiño of the Bolivian tin family. The series of articles I had written about his madcap marriage to Joanne Connelly Sweeney, reprinted in the Italian papers, brought on a *querela,* this one *senza faccoltá di prova,* which means that the complainant charged that I had defamed him but that he would not permit me to produce proof as to the veracity of what I had written. Such an action, of course, is inconceivable to an American journalist. I went through this trial with difficulty. How, I asked the court, could they judge whether I had been malicious as well as false in my writing if they didn't permit me to furnish proof of what I had written? This, I discovered, was not necessary, because the judge and the prosecutor take it for granted that you have written the truth, already a moral victory, when the complainant resorts to such a formula.

I was acquitted, and this case, before it could be taken up on appeal, was wiped out by the passage of another amnesty bill.

Chapter 18

The Law and Mr. Olian

MICHEL OLIAN was a man of mystery. He had gone to some lengths to remain out of the public eye, and he might have succeeded in preserving his anonymity indefinitely if he had ignored a brief mention I made of him in an article that was reprinted in *L'Europeo,* a leading Italian news weekly. He had been involved in a transaction dealing with a large number of American tanks, an action I felt was to the detriment of my country; hence, the comment in my article, which resulted in a *querela* for libel. Since I had the *faccoltá di prova* in this action, I set out on an intensive investigation of Mr. Olian's affairs— and uncovered a Twentieth Century success story as modern and as frightening as the hydrogen bomb.

Olian lived in the *dependence* of Villa Madama on the slope of Monte Mario, just down the road from my villa. One of the most beautiful in Rome, it was originally designed by Raphael, who died before its completion. In its lovely gardens is a marble statue of an elephant whose trunk throws a jet of water into a green marble urn. The model for the fountain was Annone, a

gentle and intelligent Indian pachyderm given to Pope Leon X
by the Portuguese ambassador.

The villa itself has an interesting history. It passed through the
hands of the daughter of King Charles V, Madame Margaret of
Austria, who was married to Allessandro de Medici and from
whom the villa acquired its name; it passed through the princely
hands of the Farnese, the Bourbons of Naples; and finally it
became the property of Countess Dorothy DeFrasso. Many
aristocratic guests have found hospitality within its secular
walls, and the last among such notables have been Olian, Orson
Welles and the late Benjamin Siegel, better known as "Buggsy."

Welles, the one-time boy genius, had once paid a visit to
Villa Madama and explained to his host that he was just finishing
a film, *Othello,* in which he was both star and director. Five
shooting days were left but, unfortunately, no funds were available. If Olian would put up the thirty-five thousand dollars
necessary to finish the picture, Welles would gladly grant him
first recoup rights in England and the United States plus a 50
per cent general ownership. The dinner brought Orson not
only a backer but a home as well, because he moved into Villa
Madama and stayed for a year.

They made a merry pair in Rome's gay night life. But one
year and two hundred thousand dollars after Olian had made his
agreement with Welles, *Othello* still was not completed. (When
it finally was shown, it was a record-breaking financial disaster.)
The parting of these amiable companions was inevitable, because
a chief facet in Welles' genius lies in his ability to run through
a bankroll, his own included.

While walking through the lobby of the Hotel Excelsior one
night, I saw the pair in a heated though thoroughly one-sided
discussion. What the Russian millionaire was angrily shouting,
while not clearly audible in the street, could be overheard by
anyone in the lobby. He made a point of calling the actor-
director-producer a fool, dwelling on the reasons, while the
embarrassed Welles tried desperately to mollify him with *"Tu as*

raison, Michel." Much later, after they had gone their separate ways, Welles produced, directed and starred in a film called *Mr. Arkadin,* a character who bore a striking resemblance to Mr. Olian.

My investigation produced an interesting life history. At one time an almost penniless Russian, today Olian possesses hundreds of thousands of acres of timberland in the Cameroons, factories in Argentina, utility companies in Switzerland, and (at one time) one of Europe's largest film studios in Rome. He was known to carry a fabulous emerald collection in one pocket and an even more fabulous diamond collection in the other, to have safety deposit boxes stuffed with cash in Paris and gilt-edge securities in such concerns as Standard Oil of New Jersey, Westinghouse Electric and Chase National Bank (now Chase Manhattan). How much all this amounts to is known only to himself, and he has intimated that it totals a modest one hundred million dollars.

There is nothing in his appearance that would make him stand out. He is of medium height and has the clean, scrubbed face of a bank clerk with round owlish eyes set in a pink face that turns purplish when he is angry. He was born July 27th, 1897, in Riga when it was still a part of Russia, and he has described himself variously as Lithuanian, Rumanian and Latvian. At one time or another he has held passports from Italy, Russia, Latvia, Venezuela, and the League of Nations, and nationality status resulting from residence in Germany, France, Switzerland and Italy. His attitude toward the law is highly individual. Where a criminal statute restricts his financial operations, he will blithely ignore it, and only occasionally do the *gendarmes* know or care. For example, soon after he reached Paris he hit on a very profitable gimmick in the money business. The value of dollars, marks, francs and pounds fluctuated each day, and the changing values were signaled to the Parisian bourse by telegraph. Because of the early state of this means of transmission and because national boundaries were crossed, messages took anywhere from one to four hours to go through. Being a clear thinker, Olian reasoned that by setting up his own network of radio receivers and transmitters he could get the information through in a matter of minutes. Thus Olian would be in the position of a horse player who knows the results of a race before he lays his bet. Assisted by radio operator Jacques Parent, banker Alfred Goldwasser and two others, he got the scheme rolling and the profits pouring in. There was one minor defect in the plan, however. It was illegal. The sudden prosperity of these gentlemen brought them under suspicion, and pretty soon the *gendarmes* collared the whole crowd. Before the common criminal court of the Seine, Olian was convicted of violating the government radio-telegraph monopoly laws and was sentenced to one month imprisonment and a five-hundred-franc fine.

He began his experiments in shifting nationalities during his Paris residence. Bolshevik passports were not regarded with great favor in France, so Olian renounced his Russian citizenship and in its place secured a police residence permit. But the French authorities were not too happy about their new guest, and on April 26th, 1926, they ordered his expulsion from France as an undesirable. Olian managed to secure a chain of three-month extensions on the expulsion order until February 21st, 1933, when the order was canceled.

His great fortune stemmed directly from World War II. It is entirely likely that he would have achieved wealth in time of peace, also, although not as much or as fast, because he recognized early that the Horatio Alger hero who becomes a success through hard work and honesty is as out of place among international finaglers as a virgin at a Polly Adler soirée.

At the start of the war Olian, a Jew, went to Switzerland and became a nazi agent, and he is listed as such on our wartime blacklist, and it became a criminal act for any citizen of the United States to trade or even communicate with him. His activities were so notorious and profitable that the Swiss government levied a fine of one-and-a-quarter million dollars against him and ordered him expelled from the country. The Panamanian Holding

Corporation, doing business in the United States, was wholly owned by Olian. Its assets, consisting of stock in Dupont, Standard Oil, Shell Oil, Westinghouse, A.T.&T. and Socony were seized by the Treasury Department and turned over to the Alien Property Custodian.

After the war, Olian's lawyer filed an action for the return of the property. In order to insure the success of the claim, he had to prove that his client had had no business transactions with the Axis powers. Olian promptly swore an oath to this effect. Somehow the French government found out about it, and their Embassy in Washington told the Alien Property people that they had a criminal action pending against Olian on a charge—financial dealings with the nazis—that, if proven true, would render this oath false. They asked the Alien Property Custodian to take no action on unblocking Olian's funds until the conclusion of the case. The case was tried in the Douxieme Chambre Correctionelle in Paris, before which Olian was convicted, sentenced to two years imprisonment, stiffly fined and ordered to pay pecuniary damages of forty-three thousand dollars.

This information was passed on to the Alien Property people, but they evidently had preconceived notions about the rectitude of their actions in returning the funds to Olian. They apparently didn't know or didn't care about the veracity of other Olian statements in their file or they would have discovered, as I did, that he was also careless with the truth in such minor matters as swearing that he was a Swiss national, when, as a matter of actual fact, he had already left that country a month earlier because of an expulsion order.

Mr. Olian is a rich and powerful man with friends in many quarters, and it was impossible for me to keep news of my probing from him. I happened to be going over the galley proofs of the Olian article in the Fawcett Building in New York, a place I used on my brief, semi-annual visits to the States, when the latter's lawyer appeared in an unannounced visit. The publisher refused to see him. Being an insistent person, he went to the office of the editorial director, who also refused to see him. He didn't budge from the outer office of the editor until he was told that I would receive him. My instructions were simple: Listen to what he has to say, but say nothing in return.

The attorney seated himself in front of my desk and told me just how important a man his client was. Then he asked, "Do you have anything against him personally?"

"No, I never met the man. I made one attempt to arrange an interview, but it was never held."

"When is the Olian article going to press?"

"The decision on what appears in the magazine, and when it appears, is made by the editors."

"Mr. Olian is a very rich person. He wishes to know if there is anything he can do that will keep you from proceeding with the article."

A remark such as this can be given several interpretations. I said that this, too, was a decision that could come only from my editors. I was merely the instrument they sent out in the world to gather and write articles that would be of interest to the readers. As for Mr. Olian, who at the moment had a libel action pending against me in Rome, if he were to show me anything I wrote about him that was in error, I would be most pleased to print a retraction.

The lawyer came to the nub of the matter. "I am authorized to tell you that if you do not print this article, the libel action will be dropped." He waited for me to make some kind of reply, and when I remained silent, he continued. "I am also authorized to tell you that if you do print the article, you will be sued in every court that can possibly have jurisdiction. You'll be hit with all the force he can bring to bear."

The threat was not an idle one, I knew. Although Fawcett was a courageous publisher and was not frightened by threats, and although I knew that the company would defend me at its expense in an eventual action in the United States, the overseas problems I would have to face by myself. My articles in *True* were reprinted in various countries, such as Holland, England, France and Italy, and they brought me additional income. My publishers received no part of this, so it was only natural that, if Olian sued me in those lands, I, alone, would face the heavy expense of defending myself. Aside from this, there was the risk of losing a suit for which I would be personally responsible. Such a loss could destroy me financially. In Italy, where the libel law is heavily weighted against the writer, it could conceivably happen.

In the attorney's conversation with me there hadn't been a single mention of the accuracy of what I had written or was about to write. It was a blatant attempt to throttle the truth. It was censorship by threat of lawsuit, and censorship is repugnant to any person who earns his livelihood in the reporting business. It made my blood boil, but I said nothing. My answer appeared in the cover story of the August 1953 issue of the magazine. It was known in the trade as a tough story. It pulled no punches.

Olian filed a libel action in the Supreme Court of New York claiming eight million dollars in damages and naming Fawcett Publications and myself as defendants. He filed a second suit in the same court, claiming seventy-five thousand in damages, against Random House and myself for an unfavorable mention of him in my book, *No Innocence Abroad*. Then he proceeded to file suit in Italy against me and my publishers where, as I have explained, libel is a criminal offense.

Now this was a curious turn of events, for the article had not been printed in Italy. He was asking the Italian prosecutor to place the American press under Italian process for articles printed in America. Can you imagine the outcry if, for example, *The New York Times* correspondent in person, and his editor *in absentia*, should be placed on trial in Moscow for the crimes of deviationism, enmity toward the regime, and furnishing information to a capitalist country to the detriment of the Soviet Union—all crimes, incidentally, punishable by death under the Soviet criminal code, and all acts being committed almost daily by all the U.S. correspondents stationed there in the articles they cable. The principle is the same, even though one involves a friendly, allied power and the other an unfriendly one. Such a restraint is bound to influence the quality of the reporting from Italy, and it does. I hoped that the question of the freedom of the American press would be close to the heart of our Ambassador, Clare Boothe Luce, and I tried to interest her in it through her press attaché—but without success.

Part of Olian's claim that I had erred in my articles about him concerned my statement that he was a stateless Russian. To prove that I was wrong in the New York Supreme Court he produced a valid passport issued by the Latvian government in exile, an organization recognized by Italy, the United States and the United Nations. Under Italian law he could not proceed against me if he were a foreign national, but he could if he were stateless. So he produced an Italian certificate of statelessness (*certificato di appolide*), which he also possessed. So I found myself in the curious position of being sued in the U.S. because I had said he was a man without a country and in Italy because he could prove that he *was* a man without a country.

In all some nine separate actions were filed against me, between original complaints and trials. Some became extinct through the passage of amnesty laws, others I won. I lost none of them. Today, ten years after the attempt to silence me by threat of lawsuit, only two remain on the books, those in the New York Supreme Court.

I did come within a hair of losing one of the cases. I had mentioned Olian in the columns of the *Neue Zuricher Zeitung*, Switzerland's leading daily, and for this he used the Roman tribunal to bring me to justice. He did not grant me *faccoltá di prova*. He did not sue in Zurich, nor did he name the newspaper as a co-defendant. I did not even know that a charge had been filed against me. I happened to be in Germany on an assignment while my family was visiting in the States when, twenty-four hours before I was to appear in the tribunal to answer criminal libel charges, a process server handed my maid the official notice. By coincidence a friend of mine, a member of Parliament who looked out for my affairs, called the villa and asked if there was anything to report. The maid said that a legal paper with many stamps had arrived, but being semi-literate, she did not know what it meant.

It so happened that the member of Parliament, ordinarily a very busy person, had a free moment; he also happened to be passing through our section of town, otherwise he would not have known about the impending trial and I would have been automatically convicted *in absentia.* As it was, he hired a lawyer, defended me and got an acquittal.

I have often wondered about the delay in notification. The process server claimed that he didn't know where to find me, though I was listed in the telephone directory, the *Guida Monici* and with the police department, as are all strangers in Rome. I don't know what the difficulty was, but by a strange stroke of fortune he did manage to find me at the very last moment. If he hadn't, the case could not have proceeded. I will say flatly that this minion of the law did nothing wrong, for even to hint at misconduct would bring me before the criminal bar of justice with the certainty that I would come out with far less fortune than in my encounters with Mr. Olian.

While this book was being prepared, his attorney made another offer to the noted law firm of DeWitt, Van Aken & Nast, who represented me in the libel actions in New York. He promised that Olian would drop the two cases in the New York Supreme Court if I promised not to write about him again.

Olian is not very important in the scheme of things today. The menace I foresaw did not materialize, so it mattered little to the world whether the words I had written about him were printed or not. But what did matter was the principle involved. Freedom of the press is a sacred trust, and I did my small part, risking jail and financial ruin, to uphold it.

Chapter 19

A View from My Terrace

THE SUBURBS of Rome have swollen outward like the spokes of a wheel along the seven ancient roads of the Caesars that spread from the center of the city. There are seemingly endless rows of apartment buildings stretching out along the Cassia. The Casilina, where once Caesar's legions trod and I, later, groveled to escape exploding bombs, had then been nothing but rolling fields dotted by the ruins of an occasional Roman watch tower and rude farmhouse, now was a forest of reinforced concrete apartment houses. Garbatella, Centocelle, Ostiense, Primavalle, Monte Mario, Quadrata, Cristoforo Colombo, Monte Sacro, Pietralata, all sprouted block upon block of concrete buildings.

There have been complaints that these are the new slums of Rome, that they are so big that they change the character of the Eternal City. Certainly, Rome was more colorful, more architecturally homogeneous, without the new constructions. If the new buildings had copied the more expensive façades and uneconomic though charming plans of the old, it would have benefited the *bellezza urbana*. But a city whose population has doubled since the end of the war owes a duty to the living present, also.

It was interesting to show my visiting friends from America the caves, carved into the sides of hills for air-raid shelters in the center of Rome, in which families were still living. But it was far more humane to remove these families from the caves and the packing-case huts and place them in apartments with modern plumbing and steam heating. The city of shacks that was leveled to make room for Olympic Village had used the banks of the Tiber for its toilet. Although the character of the new village is more Elmhurst, Long Island, then Rome, Italy, it filled a need that could not be denied. I must confess that I applauded the decision for more hygienic arrangements for the unfortunate residents of the old shack city, even though the city fathers haven't gotten around to cleaning the excrement from the stone embankments of the Tiber. Because they are sometimes more sensitive to the printed word than they are to a deplorable fact, perhaps this evil will soon be corrected.

To a city that has watched the majestic procession of centuries, the two decades of my presence can be no more than a tick of the eternal clock. Yet Rome has changed since first I met her, and illogical as it may seem, to me she is like a beautiful woman I knew in her youth. Having seen her in the prime of her beauty, and having grown older with her, the aging process being so gradual as to be imperceptible, my mind continues to see her in her original charm.

The time came when I had to consider giving up Villa Spiga. It was a real wrench, because it was the only real home I had ever known. But a faulty foundation had rendered one wall dangerous, and vibrations from the Rome–Viterbo railroad, which tunneled directly under the villa grounds, had made conditions worse. To put the house back in habitable condition meant a major rebuilding job, including a new foundation. The owner, quite naturally, was not about to do it on the rental I paid, and I, as a tenant, would not.

There were other reasons, too, why my wife and I finally came to the reluctant conclusion that we must look elsewhere for a home. Our children were now grown and off to college in the U.S. (both went to Syracuse University, which my wife and I had attended), and we rattled around in a house that was now much too large for us. The servant problem had become more difficult, too, and it was the fortunate family that could boast one good one. Salaries had gone up to seventy dollars a month, with some Americans paying eighty dollars a month (we were thorough-going Italians). In the villa a minimum of four were needed, and it was most difficult to find that many good ones at one time at almost any price.

Since we knew that Rome was to be our permanent home, we decided that we wanted to own a little corner of it. For a year we covered every quarter of the city, concentrating on the rooftops in old Rome, on one of which we hoped to build our own home. Religiously we scanned the classified ad columns in the Thursday and Sunday *Tempo* and *Messaggero*. Finally we were rewarded. A classified ad in *Tempo* announced the auction of an *attico-superattico*, meaning a duplex penthouse, just off Piazza Ponte Milvio. We hurried to the address and found it to be exactly what we were looking for. It was in a quiet section, in a well-kept building only five minutes from the center of Rome. It had some five hundred square feet of terraces and balconies overlooking the Tiber, midway between the city's oldest and newest bridges, with St. Peter's in the foreground and the roofs of Rome and the *Castelli Romani* off in the distance. The flat itself, having stood vacant for three years, was in deplorable condition. It was nothing, however, that a score of workers couldn't adjust.

The auction was held in the Palazzo di Giustizia before a magistrate. At least two bidders had to be present. The rule was that 10 per cent of the amount eventually bid had to be on deposit with the clerk of the court. The morning of the auction I deposited three million lire in two names, so that if I turned out to be the only bidder, the auction would still be valid.

This precaution wasn't necessary. There were over one hundred people crowding the chamber. On the magistrate's bench stood a miniature black candelabra containing three tiny wax tapers which took the place of an auctioneer's hammer. Having never been to an auction before, I was worried that there might be some secret art to bidding. My wife was crushed close to me by the crowd, and I could feel her trembling. After hunting for more than a year, she had finally found the ideal place, and now there were over a hundred hostile people here ready to steal it away from her.

The opening bid was ten million lire (sixteen thousand dollars), and eighty of the bidders gave up. The figure quickly rose to fifteen million. A clerk lit the first taper. It flickered for three seconds and sputtered out. He lit the second taper. It flickered and died. "Last candle," he announced, as he lit it. "Sixteen million," I said. This was my first bid. We went up by millions until the clerk finally lit the three wax tapers in turn, and I was the proud possessor of the apartment. I had twenty days to pay the difference between the deposit and the price bid. This could be paid, in cash only, at the post office in the Palazzo di Giustizia. Any person, even if he had not bid before, had the right to re-open the bidding in this twenty-day interim by making an offer 25 per cent higher than the closing bid. We worried through this period and finally, on the twentieth day, with nobody trying to top us, I carried a suitcase bulging with ten-thousand-lire notes to the post office window. It took the clerk the better part of an hour to count them. The receipt sealed the sale.

The twentieth anniversary of the Ardeatina Caves massacre took place Monday, March 23, 1963. I attended the ceremony. Parking my car at a goodly distance, I made my way past push-carts loaded with souvenirs of Rome—toy Swiss guards, brass

statuettes of Romulus and Remus, scarves depicting the Colosseum and all manner of pennants flying in the breeze. Scores of
buses, none of them with German license plates (and this was
most unusual, because the Germans are frequent visitors),
jammed the roadway. I pushed through the crowd, which had
started to gather early. The large bronze gateway was open.
Towering above it was the monument, carved of local Travertine
marble, showing three of the victims, bound together and ever-
lastingly resigned to their fate, walking into the caves. In front
of the gateway stood a double line of *Lancieri di Montebello*
in black berets and khaki uniforms, holding their rifles at attention.

The courtyard in front of the caves was crowded. On a platform
a *monsignore* helped prepare the altar. TV cameramen were
setting up their lights and cameras. There were scores of floral
wreaths bearing large, ribboned emblems sent by the *Provincia
di Roma*, the *Unione Combattente, la Camera dei Deputati, il
Senato, il Presidente della Republica, L'Unione dei Avvocati e
Procuratori*, all remembering the victims. At the entrance to the
caves was a large, gray marble plaque which read:

> Wayfarers thirsting for liberty were raked in by chance
> from the streets and from prison cells and in reprisal were
> slaughtered in mass and buried in these caves.
>
> Italians, do not curse.
>
> Mothers, wives, do not cry.
>
> Sons, carry with pride the memory of the holocaust of your
> fathers. Let the havoc wrought upon us carry us beyond the
> spirit of vendetta; instead let us repay the crimes of the
> assassin by seeking to consecrate the right of human
> existence.

The monument to the Ardeatina Caves is simple and dramatic.
It is the caves themselves, in which the victims were machine-
gunned. They were cleared of bodies and debris, and the sides

were lined with tufa. I walked into the damp, earthen-floored passageway, dimly lit by hidden lights. One hundred feet inside shafts of sunlight sent probing fingers of light from an opening overhead. This hole had been blown out by German mines. I remembered that morning in May, 1944, when I stood on the lip of this very same opening and looked down on the mutilated corpses.

Following the caves around a horseshoe turn, I came to an enormous marble and concrete gallery covered by a cantilevered roof. One reached it so suddenly that its unexpectedness was a shock, for as far as the eye could see in the dimness of the chamber were row on row of rough-hewn marble caskets. On each was a wreath in which was sculpted either a cross or a Star of David. Each casket contained a photo of the victim, his name, age and profession. Today they were covered with cut flowers, wreaths and flickering candles. On one was a glass case displaying the medals earned by a victim in his military career.

Outside in the courtyard the speeches had already begun. Minister Giulio Andreotti was saying, "From this tomb comes the final condemnation of violence. For an instant all clamor and argument is silent. We promise to these dead of the Ardeatina that we will always be conscious of their sacrifice to a great cause, made by many without knowing it. Truthfully we can repeat with the Holy Scriptures, 'Where, O death, is thy victory? It seems to the foolish that we are dead; instead we live in peace.'"

Mayor Pietrucci said that the city of Rome does not exist only as stone and marble, but that it has a spiritual life, and the deaths of these victims has given added strength of character to it.

The military and the communal bands blared forth their music, prayers were intoned by the *monsignore* and the chief rabbi of Rome, and the ceremony was over. The families of the victims wandered through the tombs and then, at the end of this rainy spring morning, made their way home.

The ceremony had brought me full circle. I looked back over the years since my entry into Rome. The intervening time had done nothing to change my feelings about SS Colonels Dollmann and

Kappler, who had then personified all that was evil. When Rome fell in 1944, my mind could not conceive of a punishment heavy enough to expiate their terrible crimes.

Twenty years had now passed, and I looked back to see how a civilized society had treated these men. Colonel Kappler, who was caught at war's end by the British forces and tried for murder, was convicted and sentenced to death. But in the general aura of forgiveness that prevails in democratic countries when they are victorious, the sentence was commuted to life imprisonment. He is currently installed in the military prison of Gaeta. Many attempts have been made to secure his freedom on the grounds that his crimes were political. After all, his supporters argue, it was Hitler who had personally ordered that ten Italians be shot for every SS trooper who had been killed. Kappler had been merely the instrument used by the evil Führer. If he had not obeyed, he would have been punished and some other SS officer would have carried out the distasteful assignment.

These bleeding hearts are weak in their arithmetic as well as in their reasoning. It is true that Hitler had ordered ten for one. But after Kappler had machine-gunned three hundred and twenty innocent men and boys, he found that he still had five prisoners left over. Since it was too much trouble to return them to wherever they had been picked up, he ordered them thrown into the caves, too, and shot to death. At least for these five victims there had been no Hitler order, just a bloodthirsty, murderous nature showing itself in its true colors.

Today he is as arrogant and unrepentant as he was in his jack-booted heyday, when he was a leader in a race of supermen who wrote their own rules of life. It was merely a political accident that he hadn't impressed his way of life on the whole world. And there is nothing in the nature of his confinement that should lead him to change his attitude.

His cell is tastefully furnished with carpeting, curtains, a radio and a TV set. The window looks out over the blue waters of the Bay of Gaeta, which is one of stupendous beauty. He practices his hobby of raising carnivorous fish and tends lovingly to the tanks in which he keeps them. A pair of fresh whores from the mainland visit him twice a week and receive from him the going rate. All of this he can well afford, since his living expenses are taken care of by the Italian government and the pension he receives regularly from the German government is more than ample for his extra needs.

And what of SS Colonel Eugene Dollmann? How did he fare? During the concluding days of the war, when he saw that all was lost, he deserted Himmler, whom he had served in Italy as confidential agent, and contacted Allen Dulles, then an O.S.S. agent in Switzerland. The war ended before anything useful could come from these conversations; useful, that is, to the Allied armed forces. This personal contact, instead, was of the greatest usefulness to Dollmann. From it stemmed a strange protection that has kept him from serving a single day in prison.

After the war was over Dollmann, a free citizen living in Rome, was seen in the La Fenice cinema on Via Salaria by a member of the family of one of his victims. The man hurried to the local *commissariato* of police, and two agents placed the former SS leader under arrest. At first Dollmann denied his identity, pulling out an identity card made out to Giulio Cassani, merchant, but he was soon unmasked.

To the Italians he was a war criminal who had to be placed on trial, as was Caruso. However, the following morning a pair of American counter-espionage agents showed up at police headquarters and ordered the freedom of the SS colonel. *L'Europeo*, a leading Italian weekly, made the mild comment that the liberation resulted from "the indelicacy committed by the Allies in dealing with one of the most noted criminals of war."

Since then Dollmann has become an author, earning a profit on his SS past, much as did Caryl Chessman on his deathhouse residence. He has been able to fool the reading public with as much ease as he did Allen Dulles and the O.S.S., and he has managed to make his journalistic self-defense pay off rather well.

Reading him I learn that Hitler was a man of certain immoral tendencies, and that he, Dollmann, was a "good" SS officer whose worst offense was that he once slapped a prisoner in the face, but that only upon provocation. He remembers that he saved one man from certain death. This was Sancio Curiel, a prisoner in *Regina Coeli* whose name was on the list of hostages to be consigned to the Ardeatina Caves. He says that he telephoned Police Chief Caruso, who was shot for his part in the crime, and ordered that the name Curiel be stricken from the list. Naturally it was done. Dollmann omits the fact that automatically another name had to be selected, so that, indirectly at least, he was guilty of the murder of the substitute. His memory as to those he did not save is not so good.

And why did Dollmann, the "good" SS officer, recognizing that Hitler was an immoral person (the worst that he would bring himself to write about his ex-Führer), still serve him? Because there was historical precedent for doing so. Voltaire adored Frederick the Great, who was so similar in many ways to Hitler, and Carlyle, England's great historian, picked this king as his hero. And didn't Diderot and Grimm, with unconstrained enthusiasm, place culture and science at the feet of Catherine the Great of Russia, the most libertine of queens? And didn't Jean-Jacques Rousseau, who represents for a great many people the social, political and human ideal, brutally describe his own sexual aberrations in his *Confessions?*

Eichmann's defense before his judges in Israel was that he had merely worked on train schedules. Dollmann went him one better. He was, to quote him, "an interpreter and commentator on the political, artistic, and literary currents in Italy." To those familiar with Dollmann's sexual aberrations, his defense that he did not always follow the dictates of Himmler is somewhat ludicrous. He wrote that despite SS orders for racial propagation, "I did not step before a local magistrate and offer my arm to a blonde Gretchen."

I frequently think back to the day I drove through the prison compound at Dachau, when the prisoners grabbed two Deaths-head SS guards out of my jeep and beat them to death, an act which I made no attempt to prevent. I wondered then if the time would come that I would regret it. Now, many years later, with the heat of the moment long past and with the opportunity to view the event from the distance of greater maturity, I can truthfully say that my feelings have not changed.

That Dollmann today lives the quiet life of a country baron outside of Munich does not mean that the machinery of international justice has failed, any more than Al Capone's freedom until an income tax violation tripped him meant that American justice had failed. At least, this is what I keep reassuring myself. But I still can't escape the thought that it would have been more salutary for both Dollmann and Kappler to have been punished in a manner fitting the crimes they committed.

I thought back to the tens of millions of people who had died in the war and to the soul-searching I had done as I moved through the holocaust. Close to it, I could see only the tragedy and feel only the pain. The death and destruction seemed senseless, and only blind faith in the rightness of life and in the existence of God helped keep me sane in a world gone mad. Now, from a perspective of twenty years, I could see that it was the price we paid to eliminate an abominable disease, just as we paid a price in human sacrifice to eliminate yellow fever and bubonic plague.

It would have been more satisfactory if we could have destroyed every germ of the Hitler disease, but it was not essential. The important thing was that we were able to isolate it. That a Dollmann and a Kappler and others of their kind escaped destruction may anger me, but it does not render futile the sacrifices. There are other evils in the world, and only by constant vigilance can we keep from succumbing to them. This has been true in the past and will continue to be true in the future. No generation can do any more than hold the line for its own time. We live in a world that has known the constant conflict between good and evil, and the base on which good is built is so precarious that a single blow, as happened in nazi Germany, can often topple it.

Did we pay too heavily in the wars of the Forties? Was the cost disproportionate to the evil it eradicated? Would one million deaths have been a just price? Or one hundred thousand? Or one hundred million, for this is surely the minimum price we will have to pay in this age of missiles and hydrogen bombs if it becomes necessary to destroy an evil called communism.

I have learned a simple fact: there is no yardstick by which we can measure the price we pay to protect our liberty, our freedom and our dignity.

My housebook, a brown, Florentine leather affair ornamented in gold filagree, sits on a library table close at hand. It is heavy with the autographs of the thousands who have descended on me in a score of years of Roman residence. They have been both a delight and a plague. Abel Green, editor of *Variety*, wrote, "Once around the Colosseum, twice around St. Peter's and three times around Mike Stern and you have Rome." Somehow I became a Mecca for the faithful tourist.

I am filled with nostalgia as I thumb through my book. The first signature in it is that of Richard Mowrer, the foreign correspondent, who gave us the book as a gift and who was our first houseguest. Many years have passed, but I remember vividly racing into Massa on the Italian west coast while partisans and Germans were still shooting it out for control of the town. Dick sat alongside me as I piloted a jeep over a half-destroyed bridge zeroed in by enemy artillery, praying that they wouldn't waste expensive ammunition on so puny a military target.

I also remember sitting at his bedside in the Hadassah Hospital on Mount Scopus outside Jerusalem, where he was being treated for multiple fractures of both legs. Dick had come through the war unscathed, though danger was never far off. Now he was stretched out, miraculously alive, but wondering if he would ever walk normally again. He had been in his rooming-house office in Jerusalem when a bomb exploded nearby in the King David Hotel. Like the able newsman he is, he jumped up and ran toward the scene of the explosion. What he didn't know was that the first blast, set off by the Irgun Zvai Leumi, was a pilot bomb designed to warn people away from that area. Just as he got to the hotel the big blast went off. The force lifted him off his feet, blew him across the street and smashed his body against a stone wall. Ninety-one people were killed. He was one of the forty-five who were wounded.

At my insistence, Dick convalesced at the Villa Spiga. At the end of his stay he wrote, "So, thank you, dear Sterns, for a wonderful and restful reprieve before I hit the hotel existence again in Cairo, Jerusalem and Jericho."

Sinclair Lewis visited with us in the twilight years of his life. He wrote, simply, "Dear Estelle and Mike." He had planned this trip to Rome as a honeymoon, but the girl jilted him at the last moment. As always, he could be depended on to react in a manner that for him was entirely logical, but that would be regarded as bizarre by the uninitiated outsider. He brought the girl's mother instead. The only thing that bothered him about this arrangement was that people might think that the old lady was his girl friend. When he spoke about Dorothy Thompson, from whom he had been divorced, bitterness crept into his voice. "She stepped on my toes, she stepped on my chest, she stepped on my head; and when there was nothing left to step on, she left me." Red Lewis loved Rome, and he died in Rome in Clinica Stuart on Via Trionfale, across the street from Villa Spiga.

A tall, florid politician with a breezy manner wrote flattering, though flowery, prose about the "distinguished gentleman and his talented wife" who were his hosts. He tipped me off confidentially that he was to be appointed the next ambassador to Rome and that he was in town to unofficially look over the terrain. He signed himself T. Lamar Caudle. A deep-freeze-and-mink-coat scandal followed by a prison term ended his dreams of a diplomatic career.

Robert Ruark used the greater part of a page to do a remarkably good pen and ink self portrait. He added a dagger, dripping blood, which is aimed at his chest. He wrote, "For Mike, the only guy who didn't do this to poor old Ruark."

It recalled the Donnybrook in which we were involved many years before. Ruark had written a series of articles about General John C. H. Lee. The columns created such interest that they broke out of their columnar format and spilled onto the front pages to become the leading story of the day. General Lee had an image that was already somewhat tarnished, having been the commanding general under whom the notorious Lichfield Barracks operated, and he was so unpopular with the press that he had been ordered by the War Department not to speak to newsmen without having his statements cleared first in the Pentagon, a lack of confidence rare in military affairs.

The articles pointed out that General Lee lived like a latter-day Caesar and showed instances where some of his troops lived in squalor and were treated like servants. As journalism goes, it was the sort of story that should have been forgotten the next day. Instead, it triggered a wave of indignation. General Lee called Ruark a liar. Ruark's columns gave sharp answer, and they battered the hapless general to a pulp.

At this point there was a curious change of sentiment on the part of the Roman press corps, who now took up the cudgels in defense of General Lee. Although they could find no evidence of the misdeeds of which Ruark had written, they did find, assisted by General Lee's Criminal Investigation Department, Counter Intelligence Corps and Civil Affairs Administration, which had carried on a full-scale investigation of Ruark, the exact number of days he had spent holidaying in Capri and the name of the attractive blonde seen in his company. Even the United Press, which is a Scripps Howard organ and the syndicate for which Ruark still writes, supported General Lee.

It was at this point that I entered the battle. My first reaction to Ruark's stories had been one of envy; the story had been right under my nose and I missed it. But why, if the truth was so obvious, did the rest of the press turn their backs on it? The only reason I could find reflected no credit on my colleagues. What had General Lee done that had changed his image from mustachioed villain to outright hero? At the depth of his unpopularity he had turned over the military larder to the press with such lavishness that many correspondents were able to sell the excess on the black market at profits far exceeding their salaries. He did this in spite of a Pentagon order that had taken correspondents off military subsistence. He returned PX privileges, gave us free gas and car maintenance, free hospitalization, free vacations on Capri, and a private plane to take us to the re-opening of repaired LaScala, with the royal box for our use and free hotel accommodations.

It wasn't easy to reach the decision I did, for I had been somewhat responsible for General Lee's generosity. He had called on me, using as intermediary a general who was my very good friend, and asked for my advice in overcoming his unpopular standing with the press. I remember telling him that if he had personal contact with us, we might regard him less as a martinet. Why not tell us what he was doing in Italy, what the mission of our armed forces was? With understanding we might have more sympathy for his actions. I also pointed out that being thrown so soon on the local economy, where cigarettes were still twenty dollars a carton, coffee from three to five dollars a pound and so on, was a sharp blow to those of us who had already brought our families over. I never expected the flood of goods that came from this encounter, but as head of the governing board of the American Press Association, I administered it and saw that it was apportioned equally amongst all the correspondents, including Doris Duke, who picked up her rations regularly. Though the decision was not easy, I made it quickly. At the time I didn't know Ruark, but I did know the truth.

I said the last word on the subject in a speech before the Overseas Press Club in New York. "I do not know whether this openhanded generosity bought the sentiments of the local correspondents, but I do know that General Lee gave it to us in the fervent hope, and belief, that it would. I know because he told me so."

Another name in the book brings a veritable flood of memories —Tony McAuliffe. General Anthony McAuliffe emerged from World War II as one of the great leaders of troops. He is a man of tremendous heart and courage, the sort that you expect from a paratrooper. As long as histories of wars are written, his gallant stand at Bastogne, the key toward turning a rout into victory, will quicken the pulse of those who are stirred by heroism. I always felt that one of the qualities that made him something special as a general was his high regard for the welfare of his men. It was something that came from deep within him, and not from a volume on the principles of command. The men sensed it and would, and did, go through hell for him.

But the name also brings back other memories, not of his glorious triumphs in battle against his nation's enemies, but of his one defeat at the hands of his own State Department. It took a singular act of diplomatic dishonesty to accomplish it. I was with Tony McAuliffe at the time it happened and well remember his feel of impotent rage.

During the Battle of the Bulge, one hundred and twenty-nine American prisoners of war were shot in cold blood on the snow-covered field of Malmèdy by SS Colonel Joachen Peiper's combat regiment of the First SS Panzer Division. Many of the Americans had their hands wired behind their backs. It was murder most foul, and at the trial of the SS killers before a U.S. military tribunal, Colonel Peiper and forty-two of his troopers were sentenced to death for the crime. Before the sentences could be executed, the late Senator Joseph McCarthy raised a storm of protest because, he claimed, the SS prisoners had been mistreated by the Americans who questioned them. All the sentences were commuted and eventually the prisoners were freed. All except SS Colonel Peiper.

Then the day came when, for some unfathomable reason, our State Department wanted to free him, too, and thus close out the case. Perhaps John Foster Dulles thought that it was a matter of simple justice. Or perhaps he was in need of an act that would be regarded by West Germany as a friendly gesture. I always felt that, if this were so, he would have made a far greater impression by unblocking the dozen or so insurance premiums on the lives of U.S. soldiers who were killed in battle and whose mothers, citizens of Germany, were the beneficiaries.

In any event, the State Department representative in Germany put the matter of freeing Colonel Peiper into operation. This involved getting the agreement of the French and British diplomatic representatives, drawing up a release document and serving it on the commanding officer of the U.S. Forces in Europe, in this case four-star General McAuliffe, whose position in the matter was that of a prison warden.

The State Department representative earlier had asked General McAuliffe for his opinion, and the General had replied flatly that the release of Colonel Peiper would be a grave miscarriage of justice; that it would be damaging to the morale of his troops; that he owed it to the men he had led in the Battle of the Bulge, both living and dead, to oppose such a move vigorously. "I hope," General McAuliffe finished, "that I have made my views in the matter absolutely clear."

General McAuliffe's views were ignored. The release order was served and he was forced to open the prison gates. Then, as the crowning blow, the State Department in Washington issued a simple press release which began, "General McAuliffe today released from prison Colonel Joachen Peiper. . . ." An immediate storm of abuse burst about General McAuliffe. Editorials in leading newspapers took him to task. He felt badly enough that American soldiers everywhere had been let down, and that he had failed in his effort to stop this grave act of injustice. But to be named as the guilty party by the very people who had committed the act was deceit too vile to swallow.

As I look out over the roofs of Rome, a faded orange-brown glow that required centuries of hot sunshine to achieve, I feel small, as small as a child looking up into the infinity of a starlit sky. I feel the smallness of the single individual, but I don't feel lost. For infinitesimal as Rome makes me feel, it also makes me feel that I belong. In this age of machines and automation man has become a slave to his material needs; has become subservient to the machines that should have been serving him. In Italy I found it easier to be an individual, and here I still find it easier to be served by the machine than to serve it.

From my eagle's perch in Rome I have come to see that there is no single method that will cure all evils, no universal vaccine that will prevent all disease. Each one must be treated independently. So with communism. By remaining strong, both in our physical and moral might, we can contain the infection and hope that with the passing years mutations will take place that will render it more benign.

I am sitting in the sun on my terrace, looking down on peaceful Ponte Milvio in the siesta hour. I am at peace with the world around me. It was in this small corner of the world that I found myself, but when one knows the inner peace that Rome has brought me, one is at home anywhere.

About the Author

Born in New York City and educated at Syracuse University, Michael Stern has been a sports writer, crime reporter, foreign correspondent, and author of several books, including *Flight From Terror* (with Otto Strasser) and the best-seller *No Innocence Abroad*. In recent years his stature as a journalist has grown, at home and abroad, to legendary proportions.

During his years as a crime reporter in New York City, Stern broke such headline stories as the armored car robbery in Brooklyn (solving the crime and naming the fourteen participants while some were still walking the streets free men), the Parsons kidnapping, the Ronnie Gedeon murder and the Nancy Titterton bathtub slaying.

As a war correspondent covering the European front during World War II, Stern covered the major stories, including a report on the "Memphis Belle" that became the basis for an Oscar-winning documentary and a first-hand account of the gallant stand of General Tony McAuliffe's 101st Airborne Division at Bastogne that ranks with the finest wartime coverage.

From his base in Rome, Stern has made headlines repeatedly, scooping the press with a personal interview with the famous Giuliano at a time when thousands of police were seeking the bandit, probing the antic exploits of the international set, digging out and reporting on the infamous Holohan murder.

Stern's stubborn insistence on running down stories at the risk of life and limb has brought him many close brushes with death, and his dedication to harsh truth has made him legions of friends as well as a sizable number of enemies. One of the latter, the gangland leader Lucky Luciano, once said, "I hope nothing happens to Mike Stern. People will blame me."